LATIN AMERICAN ISSUES AND CHALLENGES

LATIN AMERICAN ISSUES AND CHALLENGES

LARA NACIAMENTO
AND
GUSTAVO SOUSA
EDITORS

Nova Science Publishers, Inc.
New York

For permission to use material from this book please contact us:
Telephone 631-231-7269; Fax 631-231-8175
Web Site: http://www.novapublishers.com

Library of Congress Cataloging-in-Publication Data

Latin American issues and challenges / editors: Lara Naciamento and Gustavo Sousa.
p. cm.
Includes index.
ISBN 978-1-60692-349-8 (hardcover)
1. Latin America--Economic conditions--21st century. 2. Latin America--Social conditions--21st century. I. Naciamento, Lara. II. Sousa, Gustavo.
HC125.L3494 2009
330.98--dc22 2009001855

Published by Nova Science Publishers, Inc. ✝ New York

CONTENTS

PREFACE

In recent decades, many changes have taken place in Latin America as a result of economic, social and security developments. Increases in inequality and poverty continue to be major problems. As a result of social inequality, there have been increases in crime and violence as well. This book focuses on these recent changes that have taken place in Latin America, as well as the many cultural and linguistic challenges that exist in the bilingual community. The health-care system in the region is also discussed, as well as some of the major health issues that the community is presently facing.

Chapter 1 - In 1989 Cuba began rapidly converting its agriculture from an energy- and chemical-intensive, conventional model, similar to that used in most of the U.S.; to a low energy, organic-based, sustainable model similar to that used by Amish farmers. This wasn't done willingly by most agricultural scientists, policy makers and farmers: but rather was economically forced , due to the collapse of the Communist Common Market in 1989. This collapse plunged Cuba into an economic crisis, which they called the Special Period.

Cuba was successful in making the conversion, as verified, over a three-year period, by five U.S. Scientific Agricultural Delegations. The first delegation found the conversion had, by the end of 1992, reached the point which indicated that it had very good prospects for success. The necessary components of animal traction; organic matter recycling and utilization; biological control of crop pests and diseases; ecologically-based rotations of crops and pastures; etc..; were already in place and working. Many innovations had been developed: effective animal traction implements; cloning of superior crop plants; large-scale vermicompost production; large scale production of biological control agents; etc.... Finally, the last delegation found that, by the end of 1995. Cuba was producing enough high quality food to meet the caloric and nutritional needs of all its people.

However, the conversion had a lot of detractors and reluctant participants. Although the five delegations found the new model to be based on a unique blend of science, innovation and appropriate technology; with promise to be a workable model for practical, sustainable food production in every country; many Cubans, even among the agricultural leadership, were not proud of this. To them the new model was, embarassingly, a step backward, not forward; because it esentially was "peasant" in nature. They were particularly embarassed by their need to replace tractor traction with animal traction.

The speed and success of the conversion were due mainly to three factors; which together form the roots of the nation's agricultural renascence: Fidel Castro, whose leadership, wisdom and untiring efforts, especially since 1964, attempted to convince the agricultural community of the efficacy of appying the principles of Andre Voisin for sustained productivity and good health of the population; a small number of scientists and practicioners, who, for a long time, had been advocating for an ecologically sound, organically-based agriculture; and a small number of so-called "peasant" farmers who had never abandoned wisdom nor the appropriate technologies of animal traction, organic recycling and fertilization, and biological pest and disease control.

Chapter 2 - The U.S. domestic rice market will not likely be able to absorb projected increases in U.S. rice supply. Without export development, rice production would be constrained by limited U.S. domestic consumption. The main objective of the study is to analyze the effect of promotion programs and exchange rates with respect to rice exports to the three major U.S. long grain rough rice importers in Latin America. Ordinary Least Square (OLS) estimation is conducted as the first step. In addition, a Generalized Method of Moments (GMM) fitness test is conducted to correct the efficiency problem in the OLS. The study showed promotion expenditures to be significant only for Mexico and Honduras. The average return of each one dollar investment would result in $5 and $39 in the Mexican and Honduran markets using the Argentine exchange rate, and $3 and $45 in these respective markets using the Uruguayan exchange rate.

Chapter 3 - In the 20th century, Latin American attempts at self-analysis have gotten bogged down in the imaginary invention of the Latin American "being" or have been derailed by scores of foreign blueprints and local revolutionary myths. This chapter focuses on the attitudes of Latin American *intelligentsia* towards modernity and the tasks of modernization of their countries after the Independence. Between the 19th and the 20th centuries, in accord with the changes of the European *intelligentsia* positions, the advocacy for modernization in Latin America has been substituted by the search for the mirage of cultural identity. The postulate of an absolute otherness for the continent has led to the splendors and misery of the *macondismo.* The projects espoused by Domingo Faustino Sarmiento, José Martí, José Enrique Rodó, José Vasconcelos, José Carlos Mariátegui, and Octavio Paz are discussed in some length as a critique of the road to the *macondismo* and of its consequences for the continent.

Chapter 4 - This chapter analyzes the film Madame Satã. It reads the protagonist Madame Satã (João) – a male homosexual – as a femme fatale to challenge the construction of the femme fatale based solely on the biological gender pair: male/female (Stables 1998: 177). It draws on Butler's (1990a) discussion of gender, which asserts that 'there is no gender identity behind the expression of gender; [...] identity is performatively constituted by the very "expressions" that are said to be its results (p.25).' This chapter highlights commonalities that link Satã and the femme fatale to argue that both pose a threat to social gender construction rules and challenge the acceptable gender roles dictated by social order.

Chapter 5 - In 1977, a small group of Argentine mothers formed La Asociación Madres de Plaza de Mayo to collectively seek information on the disappearance of their children during the Dirty War (1976-1983) and to bring the accused perpetrators to justice. Over the years, this organization has expanded its original mission to promote and protect the rights of all of society's oppressed. Members of Las Madres de Plaza de Mayo, Buenos Aires are currently participating in a number of community-based activities to help the "present-day-disappeared", or those individuals society labels as the unemployed, the poor, and the defenseless (children and seniors). For example, Las Madres have established a university with both degree programs and public course offerings to educate citizens against the ignorance that allowed them to fall victims to the Dirty War of the 1970s and 1980s. They also support a local group of workers who became jobless after the owners of the factory where they worked abandoned the establishment. With the support of Las Madres, the workers have re-opened their factory and once again have begun production. These are but two examples of Las Madres' social commitment to improving conditions in the communities of Buenos Aires. In the present project, the authors propose to investigate how the ideology, mission and role of Las Madres de Plaza de Mayo has evolved since its establishment as an organization in 1977. Specifically, they critically examine the types of social activities in which Las Madres currently participate through their humanitarian and civil activism, and to explore the types of support and opposition they routinely experience in Argentine society.

Chapter 6 - This chapter is a revised version of Chapter II of the author's doctoral dissertation at Tulane University.

Chapter 7 - This chapter investigates the relative performance of local, foreign, and expatriate financial analysts on Latin American emerging markets. The authors measure analysts' relative performance with three dimensions: (1) forecast timeliness, (2) forecast accuracy and (3) impact of forecast revisions on security prices. The main findings can be summarized as follows. Firstly, there is a strong evidence that foreign analysts supply timelier forecasts than their peers. Secondly, analyst working for foreign brokerage houses (i.e. expatriate and foreign ones) produce less biased forecasts than local analysts. Finally, after controlling for analysts' timeliness, the authors find that foreign financial analysts' upward revisions have a greater impact on stock returns than both followers and local lead analysts forecast revisions. Overall, the results suggest that investors should better rely on the research produced by analysts working for foreign brokerage houses when they invest in Latin American emerging markets.

Chapter 8 - This chapter presents a comparative overview of income mobility patterns in Latin America. The authors construct a pseudo-panel for 14 Latin American countries between 1992 and 2003, unprecedented in the Region for its length and breadth. Estimates of time-dependence unconditional income mobility show that this is rather limited, as previously found in the scarce existing literature. However, after introducing personal, socioeconomic, demographic and geographical controls, conditional income mobility rises substantively for the Region. Also, unconditional and conditional income mobility show large variations across countries.

Chapter 9 - In the aftermath of the September 2001 terrorist attacks on New York and Washington D.C., U.S. attention to terrorism in Latin America intensified, with an increase in bilateral and regional cooperation. Latin American nations strongly condemned the attacks, and took action through the Organization of American States (OAS) to strengthen hemispheric cooperation. In June 2002, OAS members signed an Inter-American Convention Against Terrorism. President Bush submitted the convention to the Senate in November 2002; on October 7, 2005, the Senate agreed to the resolution of advice and consent on the convention. In its annual report on global terrorism, the State Department highlights threats in Colombia, Peru, and the tri-border area of Argentina, Brazil, and Paraguay. The State Department also has designated four terrorist groups (three in Colombia and one in Peru) as Foreign Terrorist Organizations, and Cuba has been listed as a state sponsor of terrorism since 1982. In the second session of the 1 09th Congress, issues of concern will likely include continued Latin American cooperation on terrorism and oversight related to the release of the State Department's annual report on global terrorism expected in April 2006.

Short Commentary - The United States population is increasing rapidly with high rates of growth among immigrants from Latin America and other Hispanic regions. Latinos are the fastest growing ethnic minority in the U.S. and Spanish is the most common language spoken by non-English speakers. According to projections provided by the Pew Hispanic Center, close to 30 percent of the U.S. population will be of Hispanic descent—both foreign and U.S. born—by mid-century. Linguistic skills among Latin Americans will vary in one or both languages by immigrant status, level of acculturation in the U.S., age and generational status, and educational attainment as well. On the one hand, some of these individuals will have limited English proficiency or none at all (e.g., foreign-born adults). Limited English proficiency and linguistic isolation, particularly of Asian and Latin American communities are major concerns in many social and economic domains including employment, education, and health care which is our current focus. These concerns are warranted because these populations are two of the largest minority groups (with Latinos growing rapidly) in many U.S. cities including New York City, Chicago, Houston, San Antonio, Phoenix, San Diego, and Los Angeles. On the other hand, some Latin Americans will demonstrate some degree of linguistic proficiency in more than one language (e.g., foreign-born youths and second or third generation Latin Americans). Thus, the number of individuals who will consider themselves bilingual, in varying ways, could change over a relatively short period of time within the U.S. This rapid demographic change calls for a concerted effort to better understand shifts in language acquisition and skills, the development of language abilities in bilingual speakers, the ways in which bilinguals store and use their linguistic knowledge, and generally how language influences the degree to which individuals integrate themselves into the larger community.

Cognitively speaking, bilingual speakers possess two sets of lexical entries, some of which are associated across languages and others that are unique within a language. From a developmental perspective, it is thought that an emerging bilingual speaker often translates their word knowledge in a new or second language into their first or better known language in order to understand information at a semantic or conceptual level. Over time, the object of becoming truly proficient calls for the ability to directly access the meaning of words in one's second language without having to rely on translating through the first. In fact, various research studies have supported the notion that the second language in a bilingual develops as a function of this kind of mediation via the first until, ultimately, an individual can think and react as a proficient speaker of their new language.

In: Latin American Issues and Challenges
Editors: L. Naciamento and G. Sousa
ISBN 978-1-60692-349-8

Chapter 1

THE ROOTS OF CUBA'S AGRICULTURAL RENASCENCE

Paul L. Gersper
University of California, Berkeley, USA

ABSTRACT

In 1989 Cuba began rapidly converting its agriculture from an energy- and chemical-intensive, conventional model, similar to that used in most of the U.S.; to a low energy, organic-based, sustainable model similar to that used by Amish farmers. This wasn't done willingly by most agricultural scientists, policy makers and farmers: but rather was economically forced, due to the collapse of the Communist Common Market in 1989. This collapse plunged Cuba into an economic crisis, which they called the Special Period.

Cuba was successful in making the conversion, as verified, over a three-year period, by five U.S. Scientific Agricultural Delegations. The first delegation found the conversion had, by the end of 1992, reached the point which indicated that it had very good prospects for success. The necessary components of animal traction; organic matter recycling and utilization; biological control of crop pests and diseases; ecologically-based rotations of crops and pastures; etc..; were already in place and working. Many innovations had been developed: effective animal traction implements; cloning of superior crop plants; large-scale vermicompost production; large scale production of biological control agents; etc.... Finally, the last delegation found that, by the end of 1995. Cuba was producing enough high quality food to meet the caloric and nutritional needs of all its people.

However, the conversion had a lot of detractors and reluctant participants. Although the five delegations found the new model to be based on a unique blend of science, innovation and appropriate technology; with promise to be a workable model for practical, sustainable food production in every country; many Cubans, even among the agricultural leadership, were not proud of this. To them the new model was, embarassingly, a step backward, not forward; because it esentially was "peasant" in nature. They were particularly embarassed by their need to replace tractor traction with animal traction.

The speed and success of the conversion were due mainly to three factors; which together form the roots of the nation's agricultural renascence: Fidel Castro, whose leadership, wisdom and untiring efforts, especially since 1964, attempted to convince the agricultural community of the efficacy of appying the principles of Andre Voisin for sustained productivity and good health of the population; a small number of scientists and practicioners, who, for a long time, had been advocating for an ecologically sound, organically-based agriculture; and a small number of so-called "peasant" farmers who had never abandoned wisdom nor the appropriate technologies of animal traction, organic recycling and fertilization, and biological pest and disease control.

INTRODUCTION

During the early 1990s there were rumors and trickles of information circulating through the academic and scientific agricultural communities in the U.S., that there were rapid, dramatic changes taking place in Cuba: that Cuba was converting from conventional, petroleum-based, energy-intensive to sustainable, organic, low-energy agriculture. In response a broad-based group of experts was formed and became the first U. S. Scientific Agricultural Delegation to Cuba. In November 1992, this delegation spent two weeks of comprehensive, intensive study of Cuba's agriculture and reported their findings in a published report, The Greening of the Revolution: Cuba's experiment with organic agriculture, as well as in numerous published papers. I was a member of that delegation, and I also led three follow-up U.S. agricultural delegations, during 1994 and 1995. Also, I made two additional trips there, in 1993 and 1998, to participate in Conferences and to continue the gathering of research data.

The U.S. delegations visited many of the agricultural research and educational institutions, mainly in Havana, Pinar del Rio and Matanzas Provinces, as well as many of the state farms and private farm cooperatives in these three provinces. Villa Clara, Sancti Spiritus and Ciego de Avila Provinces also were visited, from time to time, by individuals and small groups from various of the delegations. In addition to gathering comprehensive information and data about the characteristics of agriculture the delegations talked with as many people as they could, throughout the provinces they visited, to get their opinions of what had been taking place in agriculture during their lifetimes, especially since 1989: people from all walks of life and of all ages. What they discovered is astounding.

In 1989 Cuba began rapidly converting its agriculture from an energy- and chemical-intensive, conventional model, similar to that used in most of the U.S.; to a low energy, organic-based, sustainable model similar to that used by Amish farmers. This wasn't done willingly by most agricultural scientists, policy makers and farmers: but rather was economically forced, due to the collapse of the Communist Common Market in 1989. This collapse plunged Cuba into an economic crisis, which was dubbed the Special Period.

The delegations found the new Cuban agriculture to have the potential to be a model for agriculture which is truly sustainable: conserving of the natural resource base; effectively recycling organic matter, nutrients and water; cutting demands for petrochemical energy, fertilizers and biocides to a minimum; using effective biological control of crop damaging insects and disease; developing an effective infrastructure, based on appropriate technology, to produce the necessary inputs for maximizing and sustaining production; shortening the distance between producer and consumer to a minimum; and generally working toward the ideal of making all aspects of their agriculture as ecologically sound as possible. They found the new Cuban agriculture to be characterized by: an exciting blend of state-of-the-art science and technology, practical common-sense, and indigenous knowledge; and by a contagious aura of exciting experimentation, of the exploration of new frontiers, of discovery, of creativity, of contributing to the common good, and of leaving a legacy for future generations.

DISCUSSION

Characteristics of the Agricultural Renascence

Cuba was successful in making the conversion, as verified, over a three-year period, by five U.S. Scientific Agricultural Delegations. The first delegation found the conversion had, by the end of 1992, reached the point which indicated that it had very good prospects for success. The necessary components of animal traction; organic matter recycling and utilization; biological control of crop pests and diseases; ecologically-based rotations of crops and pastures; etc..; were already in place and working. Many innovations had been developed, including: effective animal traction implements; cloning of superior crop plants; large-scale vermicompost production; large scale production of biological control agents; etc.... Finally, the last delegation found that, by the end of 1995. Cuba was producing enough high quality food to meet the caloric and nutritional needs of all its people.

The 1989-90 collapse of trade relations with the common market of the former socialist bloc, together with the ongoing U. S. trade embargo, had plunged Cuba into its deepest economic crisis since the beginning of the revolution. This economic crisis rapidly translated into an agricultural and food crisis because Cuba's Green Revolution-style, highly technified agriculture was heavily dependent on foreign imports, and 57 percent of the food consumed by its population was also being imported. When trade and aid dropped by 85 percent early in the post-1989 period, caloric consumption by the population fell by as much as 30 percent.

In response Cuba immediately launched the most ambitious and far reaching transformation, ever attempted by a country, from modern industrial farming to modern sustainable farming. The reformation that was taking place was truly impressive, and very important to the rest of the world as well as to Cuba, whether or not its motivation was economic necessity. It was a thorough transformation of an agriculture which had been based on an energy and chemical intensive industrial model (a destructive, unsustainable model), in which most inputs had to be purchased from other countries; to an agriculture based on an organic and skill-intensive agroecological model (a constructive, sustainable model), in which most inputs are produced locally; on an unprecedented scale and within an incredibly short period of time. For comparison, pre-1989 agriculture was very similar to that which prevails in California whereas the reformed agriculture is very similar to that which prevails in U.S. Amish communities.

In the new agriculture locally produced bio-pesticides, bio-fertilizers, and beneficial insects, bacteria, and fungi have been substituted for no longer available agrichemical imports; oxen are used in place of, and along with, tractors; intercropping and crop rotations have become commonplace; and many other technological changes abound. Resource reclamation and conservation, and environmental protection have become comprehensive and commonplace. Large state farms have been broken up and converted into smaller private cooperatives. Farmers markets have been opened to partially free the prices that growers receive for what they produce. As a result food production is up quite significantly, and sustainable agriculture has actually become the norm. The transition has occured most rapidly and most successfully in the previously private small farm and cooperative sectors, while the newly privatized former state farms still struggle to overcome their capital intensive history of large scale monoculture, which make their transition all the more difficult.

The delegations discovered that practically all aspects of how we collectively viewed what a truly sustainable agriculture would consist of were included or being addressed by the new Cuban model. Thus, the components of the new model comprised a comprehensive set of requirements for sustainable agriculture: improving agrarian research and development; changing agrarian education to reflect the new model of agriculture; reversing rural migration to cities; extensive urban agriculture and community participation; soil conservation, reclamation, and recuperation; water conservation and protection of watersheds; increasing cooperative use of land; development of animal traction, alternative mechanization, and alternative energy; use of appropriate technology; alternative veterinary medicine; adjusting crops and modes of production to local conditions; mixing crops and animal production; inter-cropping and crop rotation; extensive production of organic fertilizers and biofertilizers; nation-wide application of integrated pest management; comprehensive waste recycling; and focus on food quality as well as quantity.

A year before the first delegation arrived in Cuba, Fidel Castro gave a speech in December 1991 in which he described early developments in the Special Period. In the first part of his speech he talked about the work-study program: explaining that finally the Special Period forced the issue of putting gardens on land adjacent to elementary and secondary schools, throughout the country, to support the agricultural work-study program; a plan that had been advocated by the government, and especially by him, personally, for many years prior to the Special Period.

He went on to describe many of the changes that have already taken place in the country's agriculture: *"Today we have to fertilize with bacteria. Today we have to use biological pesticides, wage the biological fight against pests and diseases. Today we have to rapidly create new plant varieties based on tissue cultures and even cells. We have already succeeded in producing the first sugarcane plants from a single sugarcane cell. . . We are doing many things like this which show a lot of potential. The reason is to solve problems in our agriculture, just as the Voisin rational grazing system, applied in a rigorously scientific way, should solve the problem of the lack of cattle feed. . . We are carrying out an accelerated program of 6,000 rational grazing areas with electrified fences. Researchers and innovators have participated in this, people who have thought up little machines to grind cane and produce sacharina for the cattle there. This sacharina came from our research centers. People are working as teams to produce electricity in the event the electrical system fails, so that they can have electricity for the fences, produced by wind or by hand. In short, they have had to find many solutions."*

He then turned to the importance of animal traction to the country's future: *"This situation, of course, is going to promote the country's scientific development tremendously, because without the special period we could not even dream of the boost many things have received in our country. The same is true of the use of oxen. They had been forgotten. Everything was done with tractors. Now we have discovered that oxen not only save fuel in many activities. Oxen also raise human productivity, because there are times when because of the wetness of the soil or the size of the crops, you cannot send in a tractor. It would destroy everything. It would compact the soil. But a man or woman can enter the fields at any time with oxen."* He added an admonition: *"Now we have discovered that the day we have enough fuel, we cannot simply return to the age of the tractor and that is all."* He went on to explain: *"Sometimes things are clear, obvious, and reasonable, and you can try to convince them, but only when they see the urgent need, and have no alternative, do they look at oxen. Gentlemen, we must domesticate oxen, but as long as there is one drop of fuel, it is a difficult battle to get oxen domesticated. That is what human beings are like. They have those characteristics, and they often need the force, the push from necessity to solve certain problems. That is what is happening to us with the special period."*

He made a final plea for everyone in the country to think in terms of self-sufficiency and of innovations in increasing production: *"I believe that now the importance of the issue of participating in productive activities must be emphasized as much as possible, especially where we can, which is in the fields. The goal of self-sufficiency must be emphasized as much as possible, where it is possible, as a very important task during this special period. Think of it: There are a million students who must be fed. Half of them must be given breakfast, lunch, and dinner every day. Others must be given lunch. This includes the universities, secondary schools, semi-boarding schools, child care centers, etc. Self-sufficiency is very important. Of course, the country is making great efforts to produce food for the national plan, but whoever plants a garden in the tiny plot of land in the courtyard of their building is helping the country in this special period. They are saving transportation of fuel. They are helping: everyone who plants something, everyone who does something."*

Fast forward 12 years, to 2003, when a very large delegation of 90 food and farming specialists from all over the United States, Latin America, and the Caribbean took a two-week study tour of Cuban agriculture. They found that the new Cuban agriculture was still on track, and had made considerable progress since the last of the original five delegations had visited the island nation. Most of the comments which follow come from three newspaper articles written by members of that delegation.

First some random, general comments from members of the delegation. An organic farmer with the delegation declared that Cuba's organic agriculture was quite remarkable and at the "top of the world;" adding that *"the quality of their produce is consistently high, which shows they have the infrastructure in place."* Other delegates remarked: Cuban agriculture challenges *"all conventional assumptions about progress and feeding the world;"* adding that green revolution promoters *"should go get some insights from one of the most fascinating farming experiments in the world;"* and *"Cuba's organic food movement has made the country a world leader in low-input sustainable agriculture."*

The results of Cuba's conversion to organic agriculture was described to be widespread, diversified, well-distributed, and amazing, although not yet complete; consisting of vast *"networks of sustainably run, smaller plots of ground that emphasize cooperative labor, local marketing, farm-based enterprises and a farm's inherent responsibility to the social fabric of its community."*

Very little urban agriculture was evident to the 1992 delegation, but three years later the fourth delegaton discovered a dramatic increase in urban, suburban, and exurban agriculture; especially in the form of organoponicos. Organoponicos are mostly raised bed vegetable plots constructed with deep root zones (usually one-half to one meter), enriched with compost, fertilized with biofertilizer, irrigated, and protected from pests and diseases with biological control agents . They are very productive and produce vegetables year round.

By the time of the 2003 delegation organoponicos had greatly expanded. They reported that there were thousands of organoponico plots (gardens), ranging in size from less than one acre to six acres, and totaling 81,000 acres. They further reported that the gardens were producing 250 pounds of food per year for each of Cuba's 11 million people, and have generated 300,000 high-paying jobs.

They reported further that, *"because of free-market incentives established by the government in response to the crisis, there is now enough organic produce grown within the city limits of Havana to feed each of the city's 2.5 million residents a minimum of 300 grams (about 10 ounces) of fruits and vegetables each day."* Growers buy *"seed, organic crop protection products, natural fertilizers and technical assistance from a 'tienda consultoria,' or consulting store in the neighborhood. "* They *"earn a salary, plus incentives based on production."* Futhermore, after meeting required production quotas, they can *"sell what's left over to the public."* They conclude that, *"the key to the success of urban agriculture in Cuba is that the farms are located in the same neighborhoods as their customers."*

Some of the other highlights reported by the 2003 delegation follows.

"Once food production spontaneously evolved toward decentralized, market oriented, organic production, the government began coordinating and supporting further progress. Virtually all university research in agriculture is oriented to helping solve practical questions. Small manufacturing plants dispersed around the island turn out biological pest control supplies and small-scale agricultural tools. Every square mile in Cuba has someone charged with scouting for pests and diseases."

"This transition of Cuban agriculture is characterized by not only different methods but also different ownership patterns. Most state farms have been broken up into individual and cooperative farms, and a large portion of the daily Cuban diet is grown close to home, on small farms and gardens dispersed through and around the cities."

"Most of the large, state-owned farms have been divided into smaller cooperatives, of Basic Units of Cooperative Production (UBPC), as they are called, with farmers earning approximately four times the national average monthly wage. They achieve this despite the fact that such farms must first provide, as part of their social obligation, food for local schools, hospitals, and nursing homes before selling on the open market."

"The Cuban government still buys a lot of food and guarantees every person a basic diet at very low, subsidized prices. All vegetable farms of significant scale supply schools, daycare centers, and hospitals with low-priced produce."

In addition to these regulated channels, however, many food items are also available on a free market, making food ever more abundant, and returning to farmers among the very highest incomes in Cuba."

"The agricultural curriculum in the universities and vocational high schools in Cuba has been completely revamped to reflect the change from high-input, industrialized agriculture to a low-input, organic system."

"Vocational agricultural high schools are producing biological pesticides that they sell. Income from the sales provides as much as 50 percent of some schools' budgets."

"Another key has been the reinvention and rejuvenation of university extension services. Throughout the country, extensionists, as they are called, adhere strictly to a model of "popular education" that is described as "emancipatory" in nature. By this model, the teacher

is never considered more important than students, but both learn and share in the process together."

"The principle goal of extension services in Cuba is to integrate new technology in support of traditional production systems. Farmers are thought to be the best judge of what to produce and how it should be done."

"The Cuban government eventually hopes to divest itself of all agricultural enterprises except for livestock and crop genetics."

The Reluctant Converts

Out of necessity, things changed. However, the conversion had a lot of detractors and reluctant participants. Although the five delegations found the new model to be based on a unique blend of science, innovation and appropriate technology; with promise to be a workable model for practical, sustainable food production in every country; many Cubans, even among the agricultural leadership, were not proud of this. To them the new model was, embarassingly, a step backward, not forward; because it essentially was "peasant" in nature. They were particularly embarassed by their need to replace tractor traction with animal traction.

Without a doubt Cuba has been successful in rapidly converting its agriculture from an energy- and chemical-intensive, conventional model, similar to that used in most of the U.S.; to a low energy, organic-based, sustainable model similar to that used by Amish farmers. Such a conversion had never before been done on a national scale. This was a very impressive accomplishment. And this, together with the fact that the new Cuban agriculture could serve as a viable model which could be emulated by any other country of the world did not seem to make a difference; because there were still many reluctant converts who could not wait to convert back to their previous "modern" agriculture as soon as the economy allowed it.

There are still detractors and reluctant participants; although the number has considerably decreased over the past 19 years. However, the big question remains: will Cuba scrap the sustainable model and return to the industrial model if and when her economy would allow it? The reason for this uncertainty about the future of the sustainable model of agriculture in Cuba, and elsewhere, has to do with attitudes, perceptions, and perverted logic. Unfortunately, attitudes and perceptions held by farmers, researchers, policy makers, and others in the agricultural community strongly influence, if not dictate the characteristics of agriculture whether or not they are based on reality or common sense (this is examined in detail below in the section about the Amish).

One of many examples which could be used to illustrate this, and which quite obviously pertains to present day Cuba, is tractor versus animal traction. Many of the key people in Cuba, who members of the delegations became acquainted with, were not able to hide their embarrassment over being forced to give up their "modern" agriculture for a "peasant" agriculture. They were particularly embarrassed that they had to revert to oxen to meet most of their traction needs. Moreover, they clearly considered these reversions to be stopgap measures until the economy improves.

The Cubans, of course, are not alone with this attitude, because most people perceive tractor traction as being a necessary component of modern progressive agriculture; to the exclusion of animal traction. However, the perverted logic which underlies this perception ignores the truth about vulnerability to adverse economic conditions, as well as the environmental consequences of dependency on tractor traction-- even when animal traction can be demonstrated to be unquestionably more appropriate, more feasible, and more profitable than tractor traction. Fortunately, the productivity enhancing and environmentally sound characteristics of animal traction are becoming increasingly apparent in Cuba. For example, oxen can enter the fields after rains to prepare the ground when tractors cannot, and, unlike heavy machinery, they do not needlessly compact the soil.

Along the same lines, perverted logic and linear, reductionist thinking also explains the widespread dependency on synthetic pesticides in world-wide agricultural production even though common sense and holistic thinking clearly show that it is not possible to achieve sustainability as long as synthetic pesticides continue to be used as the agents of choice in pest control. Fortunately, Cuba is leading the way in biological control technology which can serve as a model for the establishment of sustainable agricultural systems throughout the world.

The Roots of the Agricultural Renascence

The speed and success of the conversion of Cuba's agriculture were due mainly to three factors; which together form the roots of the nation's agricultural renascence: Fidel Castro, whose leadership, wisdom and untiring efforts, especially since 1964, attempted to convince the agricultural community of the efficacy of applying the principles of Andre Voisin for sustained productivity and good health of the population; a small number of scientists and practicioners, who, for a long time, had been advocating for an ecologically sound, organically-based agriculture; and a small number of so-called "peasant" farmers who had never abandoned wisdom nor the appropriate technologies of animal traction, organic recycling and fertilization, and biological pest and disease control.

The Influence of Andre Voisin

The November 1992 delegation worked around the clock during its two weeks in Cuba: visiting representative facilities of all major government and university agriculutural organizations: including research and development laboratories; experiment stations and experimental farms; state farms and cooperatives; and production facilities for the production of composts, biological control agents (beneficial bacteria, viruses, and insects), cloned plants, etc... We also visited many private farm cooperatives; urban and institutional gardens (school, retirement home, and work-place gardens); and food markets.

Almost immediately we noticed that at the entrance to many of the laboratories and other buildings there usually was a sculptured bust of the famous French agronomist, Andre Voisin. Furthermore, inside the buildings, usually in a meeting room, there often was a large portrait or photograph of Fidel Castro with Andre Voisin. Inquiries resulted in very little information as to who Voisin was or why he was being so celebrated. However, it was very clear that he was considered an important figure to the agricultural establishments in Cuba. The following year, the author read the new book, *Fidel Casto*, by Robert Quirk, and the mystery as to why Voisin was so celebrated was cleared up. The amazing story of the relationship between Fidel Castro and Andre Voisin unfolds in Quirk's book, and clearly indicates the leadership, wisdom and untiring efforts of Fidel Castro, starting in 1964, in his attempts to convince the agricultural community of the efficacy of appying the principles of Andre Voisin for sustained productivity and good health of the population.

Quirk described a conversation between Fidel Castro and Richard Eder, resident correspondent for the New York Times, as they took a tour of agricultural experiment stations near Havana . As Eder was being driven by Castro in a jeep, he noticed on the floor of the vehicle a book on grasses (*The Dynamics of Pastures*) by the French agronomist, Andre Voisin. He told Eder that after reading Voisin he was convinced that grass feeding for cattle was both cheaper and more efficient than dry fodder feeding.

He added that, *"Castro was overflowing with information,"* telling Eder that *"eighty percent of his time was spent 'pushing agriculture'."* He boasted that, *"even your agriculture in the United States will be less scientific than ours. Many of your books are very good on established techniques, but they fail to bring in new ideas,"* adding that, *"American farmers will be visiting us before long to see how we are getting on. We shall hold a prominent place in the world's agriculture."*

Eder's accounts make it abundantly clear that Castro had a very strong personal interest in agriculture, was convinced that Cuba had a tremendous agricultural potential, and was determined that under his leadership she would fulfill that potential.

Furthermore, it is also clear that from the beginning Castro was searching for ways the country could develop a healthy, sustainable agriculture: which explains his attraction to Voisin. Thus, Quirk described Fidel Castro's affair with Voisinism as a *"veritable love match--ardent and star-crossed."* Quirk then described why Castro had extended an invitation to Voisin to visit Cuba. *"Convinced that the French agronomist's theories on pastures and livestock production would give Cuba the finest cattle industry in the world, Casto invited him to conduct a series of lectures in Havana. Voisin accepted. His work was famed throughout Western Europe, and his sixty-acre farm in Normandy was a mecca for the agriculturalists who espoused natural methods of animal husbandry. He was a member of the French Academy of Agriculture, and Bonn University had awarded him an honorary degree. His most important books had appeared in English, German, Russian, Hungarian, and Japanese translations. He proposed a system of rational grazing that would maximize milk production with minimum damage to the soil."*

Casto's great respect for Voisin's writings and the promise they held to rejuvenate the country's agriculture is revealed as Quirk continued: *"In the throes of his initial enthusiasm, Castro determined to make Voisin's works available on every experimental cattle farm in the country. He summoned Heberto Padilla to his office. The prime minister showed him a copy of "Grass Productivity" and a list of volumes. Go to Spain, he said, and get two thousand copies of every one. In Madrid the publishers received Padilla with astonishment. They had never handled such a large order before. At great cost the thousands of sets were packed up and flown to Havana. When they arrived at Jose Marti Airport, Fidel Castro was at the terminal to see them unloaded. For two months Voisin worked assiduously at his farm, preparing the text of his lectures. In September he sent them to Cuba to be translated. At two in the morning on December 3 he arrived in Havana to be greeted by Fidel Castro with an effusive embrace. For the fifty-six-year-old agronomist and his wife it was a difficult, arduous flight."*

Quirk described that after escorting the couple to the house that had been reserved for them, Castro began almost immediately talking about grasses and in his enthusiasm he completely forgot about everything else. *"Words flowed unimpeded by any sense of time or place. He left them at 6:00 A.M., dazed and exhausted. It was noon in Paris. They had been awake and busy all night."*

Quirk then wrote: *"For a week the Voisins visited experimental farms and historic sites and were treated to fiestas, receptions, and state dinners. Castro spared no expense or effort in his attempt to impress the scientist with the accomplishments of his revolution."* He added: *"Delighted by the homage paid to him by important government figures, Voisin ate, drank, and conversed with the vigor of a man twenty years younger."*

Quirk then described a remarkable event which not only demonstrated the great esteem and admiration which Castro held for Voisin and his published works but also clearly revealed Castro's strong personal interest in leading Cuba to agriculutural greatness: *"On the evening of December 8, 1964, the prime minister inaugurated the lecture series by introducing Voisin to the Cuban people. After the French ambassador had said a few words, the agronomist spoke briefly, thanking Castro for his hospitality. The prime minister, he said, had given him a book, beautifully bound, that contained a translation of his lectures--and in a short time. A truly remarkable effort. Castro spoke last, for more than two hours, without notes of any kind, upstaging the French diplomat and the renowned scientist. In an astounding tour de force he presented the gist of Voisin's lifetime of research. Even his closest, longtime associates were dazzled by the effectiveness and completeness of his summary."*

What Quirk next writes about Castro and Voisin is even more remarkable: *"The next day the eminent visitor presented his first lecture at the National Medical College, "The Soil and Fertilizer Produce the Animal," with the prime minister in attendance. He repeated essentially what he had written in his books and Fidel Castro had summerized on December 8. Revolucion declared the Frenchman a "genuine revolutionary" and living proof that the technical revolution was beginning to become a reality in Cuba. Other lectures followed, and Voisin continued his dizzying round of dinners and sightseeing. The strain was too much. On the evening of December 21 Castro appeared at the college auditorium to say that Voisin had died of a heart attack earlier in the day while touring a state farm. His funeral would take place the next day at the university, he said. At the obsequies, the Maximum Leader was once again the center of attention as he gave the funeral oration. He had persuaded the widow, Marthe-Rosine Voisin, that her husband would have wished to be buried in Cuba. Each year thereafter, the agronomist's death was memorialized, and Mme. Voisin was brought back to Havana for the ceremonies."*

On my next trip to Cuba after reading Quirk's book I was determined to verify as much as I could of his account of Andre Voisin. I started by asking one of my Cuban colleagues to help me find the tombstone of Voisin, to verify that he had indeed been buried in Cuba as the account stated. We decided that, given the esteem and honor in which Voisin was held by Castro, according to Quirk, Voisin would likely have been buried in the main cemetery of Havana. My colleague told me that he would be especially happy to take me there because that was the cemetery in which his parents and other relatives were buried. We spent several hours in attempting to locate the Voisin tombstone, and decided to give up. But before leaving my colleague wanted to visit the graves of his parents. While he was doing this I decided to take some photographs of this exceptionally beautiful cemetery. Nearby there was a striking black-marble tombstone, which stood out from the surrounding predominantly white-marble tombstones. I took a picture of it from a distance and decided that its uniqueness merited a close-up. As I positioned myself for a close-up I was shocked to see the name of

Andre Voisin prominently carved in the stone. I was also surprised to see that it was a double tombstone, and carved on the other half was the name Marthe Rosine Voisin - Voisin's widow. I was unable to find out whether his widow was buried there or was still alive; but several inquiries I made indicated that she was not yet buried there. I'm unsure if Quirk was aware of where Voisin was buried, but my discovery verified his account of the event.

After reading Quirk and verifying that Voisin was indeed buried in Havana, I was still somewhat puzzled at the attraction which Castro had for the French agronomist and especially the reasons behind Voisin's burial in Cuba. Eventually I was successful in obtaining copies of the two speeches referred to by Quirk: Castro's 12/8/64 speech inaugurating the Voisin lectures and his 12/22/64 speech at Voisin's funeral; and these provided the answers I was seeking.

In reading the transcript of the 12/8/64 speech, it is easy to conclude that Quirk's description of it as a tour de force is an understatement. The speech indicated that Castro not only had read Voisin's books, but also understood them very well; and the fact that he gave the speech without notes also indicated that he retained the information very well. In the speech Castro describes in some detail the contents, applications and importance of the three Voisin books which he had read: *The Productivity of Grass*; *Soil, Grass, Cancer*; and *The Dynamics of Pasture* (the first book which Castro read, and the one which introduced him to Voisin).

Also in the speech are numerous comments which relate to Castro's admiration and respect for Voisin, and his purposes for applying information from Voisin's books, and especially Voisin's suggestions and recommendations, to the benefit of Cuban agriculture. The following selection of excerpts from the speech are illustrative.

"And here is one of the most interesting aspects which has attracted our attention in the scientific works of Professor Voisin. It is the human aspect of his scientific research and the contribution from a point of view which is entirely new."

"It can be said that Professor Voisin, in addition to being a scientist, is an apostle of man, an apostle of the health of man and above all an apostle of preventive medicine."

"It was through the books of Professor Voisin that we first found, saw, read, and listened to a different point of view. It was the first time in my life that I had heard it said that one tomato might have three times as many vitamins as another of the same variety, depending on the way the tomato was cultivated."

"That was the first time we were able to understand that our future contained the possibility, under the conditions offered by our social system without the interference of commercial interests, of establishing production that would take into account not only quantity, but quality as well."

"It is exactly there where Professor Voisin points out the path for the development of preventive medicine, which consists precisely of giving the organism all the elements which the organism needs to develop its own defense against the attacks of foreign agents: bacteria and viruses."

"Professor Voisin has a book which has not yet been translated into Spanish, called 'The New Scientific Laws for the Application of Fertilizers,' in which he explains the mechanisms through which plants absorb elements, produce vitamins which the human organism later assimilates."

"We will not move toward development of an agricultural technology that seeks quantity alone. We will seek quantity and quality of our food."

"A day must come when each and every one of the products consumed by the population will have a maximum, optimum biological value. This must be the aspiration of our agricultural technology."

"We are also going to carry out an intensive dissemination campaign on the whole problem. We have acquired, so far, nearly 20,000 books on these three subjects: The Productiviity of Grass; Soil, Grass, Cancer; and Dynamics of Pastures."

"Professor Voisin has had the kindness to give our country the rights to publish one of his books, the one that deals, as I said, with the scientific laws governing the application of fertilizers. He told me that the rights he granted us should be used to compensate for the damage caused our country by Hurrican Flora. He has also granted us the rights, for the same reasons, to the 10 lectures he is going to deliver -- lectures, as he has explained here, on which he worked hard for months. These lectures have already been translated and printed in book form in our country."

"We have acquired approximately 1,300 copies of each of his books. We will probably acquire some 15,000 or 20,000 additional copies. However, this will still not be sufficient. If we have newspapers that reach 200,000 or 250,000 copies; if we publish each of these lectures in the newspapers and these issues are read in the fields, many people will be able to gradually compile their own books. Thus our newspapers will have a new function, not simply to publish news and information, but to disseminate technical and scientific matters."

"We not only aspire to develop an advanced technology, but we can aspire to develop it in a new dimension that does not only measure the quantity, but the quality, in a much broader and profound human dimension. It could be said that it is possible for us to become the first country in the world in the development of agriculture according to new concepts."

The speech given by Castro at Voisin's funeral verifies Quirk's account except in one detail. It appears from the speech that the request for Voisin to be buried in Cuba came from Voisin himself, as expressed to Castro by Madam Voisin, instead of, as Quirk wrote, Castro persuading the widow that her husband would have wanted to be buried in Cuba. This is clarified in one of the following four excerpts from Castro's broken-hearted eulogy.

'Madame Voisin, ladies and gentlemen: It is diff icult for us to believe that we have come today to accompany to his tomb one whom we received with hospitality and happiness only a few days ago and who was the esteemed guest of our country. Among the many persons who have read the works of Professor Voisin in various parts of the world and in different languages, I could not imagine that the bitter, very difficult task of uttering these words of farewell would fall to me.'

'He was a scientific man. His concept was a universal one. He did not consider science the patrimony of any one man or the patrimony of a country. He was aware that his research would be of benefit to all men, in any part of the world, without regard to frontiers. That universal characteristic of this thinking was displayed in his conduct, by the many trips he made throughout the world, the interest he showed in the problems of a small country like ours. That universal characteristic was demonstrated in his opinions, in his ideas expressed on repeated occasions to his wife that--according to the way she told it--he said that if he died in any country where he went to do some studying or went to give some lectures, he wanted to be buried in that country.

'He said, or expressed, or wished something perfectly understandable to us when he said that he wished to rest where he died. He knew that he had a right to aspire to that, because as a good and noble man, he knew that those sentiments have universal acceptance. As a man of

science, he knew that science has universal value. As a man aware that he was working for mankind, he knew that whatever nation in the world could shelter his remains--that he had the right to rest respected and in peace in any corner of the earth. Our land, for example, where the remains of Professor Voisin will rest, was therefore also his land. He had a right to our land just as we all have a right to his ideas, to his efforts, to his scientific work."

"He and men like him belong to all countries without distinction as to borders, and countries without distinction as to borders belong to him and to men like him. It can be said that when our university awarded him the title of doctor honoris causa, a degree he accepted with joy, enthusiasm, and pride, it was not an honor bestowed by our university on Professor Voisin; it was a great honor for our university to be able to have Professor Voisin among its doctors honoris causa."

Madam Voisin remained in Cuba for at least 11 more days after the funeral, as indicated from the following excerpt from the speech delivered by Castro in Jose Marti Square on the occasion of the 6th aniversary of the Revolution.

"I have heard that several of you have mentioned Professor Voisin, and I believe that it is a very apt gesture. It shows the capacity of our people to understand, to aspire, and to thank those men who have devoted their lives to research which can be useful to all people. I am certain that your spontaneous sentiments will be an additional source of inspiration and consolation to Voisin's widow, who said that she wanted to remain in Cuba today to be with the Cuban people on this, their day."

Fidel Castro's Attempts to Improve Cuba's Agriculture

After these verifications of Quirk's accounts of the Castro-Voisin relationship, I was highly motivated and determined to find out more about Voisin's visit to Cuba and its impact on Cuban agriculture. I was pleased that as I began to routinely inquire about Voisin and the agricultural practices which he espoused, such as rational pasture rotations and the need to increase the organic matter and nutrient content of soils for improved health of humans and animals, I found people who either recalled or had heard about Voisin's visit, his books, and Castro's promotion of his principles and practices. As my research progressed on this subject, one question kept popping up in my mind: as the head of state, and a supposed dictator at that, why didn't Castro simply force the adoption of Voisin principles and practices by the agricultural establishment? Why didn't the government simply dictate to the agricultural establishment how agriculture should be conducted? As it turned out Castro's advocacy was mostly ignored, until the economic crisis of 1989-90, even though he was persistent over many years and attempted to influence the establishment not only by his words but also by his example of personal experimentation. My inquiries revealed that about the only people following Castro's wishes, that farming in Cuba follow along the lines advocated by Voisin, were: most of the ten percent of farmers in the private sector, who had always farmed organically with oxen; and a small number of agricultural researchers who were experimenting with organic production and biological crop protection. Finally, at the onset of the Special Period, Castro's advocacy of Voisinism quickly came to the fore: to essentially provide the base upon which the nation's agriculture was reformed.

From the beginning of the revolution Castro was very active and visible in urging his countrymen to work toward making Cuba a paragon of agriculuture. Moreover, as early as 1964 it became evident that he was inclined toward promoting a more natural, innovative agricultural system than was taking place in most of the developed world: a system that we now call sustainable. His vision that the nation's prosperity would be built on a strong agricultural economy surely provided the motivation for his actions: including copious personal experimentation and voluminous reading of books on a very wide range of agricultural subjects.

Quirk's book, especially chapter 16, covering mostly 1964, provides abundant evidence of this. Quirk wrote: *"In early August, Castro spoke to a forum on irrigation and drainage. He was making a 'small experiment,' he said , to test the effects of measured amounts of rain on the growth of cane. And he had planted grasses to determine how different varieties grew. He took the country's agronomists to task for the 'backwardness' of their agricultural techniques. Cuba was the largest producer of sugar in the world, he said. Yet the average output was a 'shame.' Growing crops should be simple. It was just a matter of water and fertilizers. Technology was the key to improvement, and Cuba would train fifty thousand technicians by 1970. In September he addressed meetings of medical doctors and sugar producers. To both groups he decried the low level of technology. Open any book on sugar research, he said, and you will find a reference to Java, India, Hawaii, or the Fiji Islands. But never to Cuba. Too many Cubans thought they knew 'something' about everything. 'But when I read a book, I come to the conclusion that people here know practically nothing.'"*

Quirk's next paragraph is even more illuminating: *"He told them he planned to compile a list of all the available works on agriculture, to reproduce thousands of copies and distribute them to experimental farms. He conceded that he was not a sugar specialist. 'That is not my work.' But he read and thought. And he carried out some 'small tests' with cane plants. Everywhere he went he had pointed to the need for more experimentating. 'Naturally, I think that in the main the idea went in one ear and out the other.' So he made his own tests, to establish how far apart cane should be planted, what the best fertilizers were. He checked different cover crops -- cowpeas, velvet grass, canavalia, legumes -- to learn which best replenished the soil. He would test when to plant, when with nitrogen and when without, which strain of cane produced the greatest yields, why plants were diseased. He had 'read a book' about 'all these things.' Some-day, he predicted, medicine and agriculture would be united in biochemistry and the science of soils. When he spoke of advances in agriculture, he talked rarely of the United States and never about the Soviet Union. His books and articles now came almost exclusively from Western Europe."*

The following five random excerpts, in which Quirk gives details of what Castro said in his speech given at the December 8th ceremony to introduce Voisin to the Cuban people (which inaugurated Voisin's lecture series) indicates that Castro was already totally sold on Voisin's methods of production and the rationale for them.

"When he first read 'The Dynamics of Pastures,' said Castro, he had already acquired an interest in the problems of livestock. 'I began to organize a small farm, part of which was devoted to legumes.' He made estimates. 'On one occasion I thought of figuring how much milk would be obtained per pound of maize and how much per pound of soybeans, and what part of that area should be devoted to maize and how much to soybeans. . . . .I looked at the amount of protein contained in a pound of soybeans and the amount in a pound of maize, and the amount of soybeans and maize to be produced in those hectares, assuming that all the crops would grow perfectly well, and the production would be optimum. Moreover, I saw that the maize and the soybeans, which covered approximately one-eighth to one-tenth of the area, should produce approximately one-eighth to one-tenth of the milk. I asked myself where the extra milk was coming from, and I realized that it came largely from the pasturage. I realized

that the areas devoted to grass would, with normal yields, produce more milk than the area devoted to grains, presupposing optimum yields. Not only that. The area of grass would produce milk far more cheaply, because the other crops had to be planted twice a year, every year, and pastures would be sown only once.' Voisin's book, he said, promoted a system of permanent grassland. 'One could see the enormous advantage of the permanent pasture over the temporary pasture.'"

"The condition of the soil, the 'soil poverty,' he explained, was directly related to the amount of microfauna and the number of earthworms. The point was not to cultivate, not to resow, the grasslands. Otherwise, the organic material, the humus that had accumulated over the many years, would be exposed to oxidation. Though grass production in the first years was enhanced, the greater part of the organic material was used up. By the third and fourth years the microfauna and earthworms has practically disappeared. The earth had become compacted. And even without plowing or rotation, he said, there would be a period of soil poverty before fertility was restored. In Cuba, however, superior conditions whould minimize this effect through the introduction of organic fertilizers. His experiments had demonstrated that cattle in Cuba deposited three times as much manure as those in Europe. Suffice it to say, he had never thought of any of these matters, nor had he heard any technicians speak of them, before he saw Voisin's publications."

"The French scientist's most recent book, 'Soil, Grass, and Cancer,' was perhaps even more important. Voisin was an exponent of preventive medicine. He had analyzed the influence of the soil on man's health. A number of human diseases depended on the food consumed and on the condition under which that food had been produced. He had stressed the necessity of close cooperation between farmers and medical doctors, and he had already suggested that Cubans organize a school of human ecology. They could thereby make 'extraordinary progress' in preventive medicine, Castro said, because they could work without interference of commercial factors in matters that concerned health. Revolutionary Cuba could develop a medical system that would avoid the necessity of going to the hospital -- not curing a man in the hospital, but avoiding his ever having to go there in the first place. And suddenly for the first time, like an epiphany, he saw in agriculture and in health maintenance the greatest advantage of the socialist system. 'It was truly a revelation!' People had been abusing their health by the indiscriminate use of antibiotics and fertilizers. The prevailing agricultural methods destroyed important microelements in the soil and created 'hidden hunger.'"

"In the 'natural state' of the soil, explained Castro, there was a balance. But man, to increase production, had upset that balance. He plowed the land. He applied fertilizers high in nitrogen and used plant varieties with a greater ability to metabolize the elements. As a consequence, the soil was robbed of important elements, and only four -- nitrogen, phosphorus, potassium, and calcium -- were returned. Commercial food growers returned only those elements that permitted them to obtain the largest crops, so foods contained less and less of the elements essential to life. For example, Castro said, an excess of potassium made calcium, sodium, magnesium, and boron inassimilable. Too much phosphorus caused a deficiency of zinc and copper. The continual application of nitrogen made soils acid and caused a deficiency in phosphorus and molybdenum. And a diet lacking in those elements meant a deficiency of certain vitamins."

"To read Voisin's words, said Castro, was to see dialectical materialism in action. The decadence of ancient civilizations was brought about by great urban concentrations that had

led to the exhaustion of the land, to the production of vitamin-deficient foods. Through the sewers of Rome and Babylon had flowed the fertility of the soils. And as the farmlands became exhausted, a physical and moral degeneration of the inhabitants ensued. Cubans too had concentrated too much in the cities. They must look once again to the countryside. The revolution would see that they did. Because of the planned economy, Cuba's future looked bright. 'We have a country in which everyone has learned to read and write, in which almost a million adults are studying, a country that is the master of its resources, the master of its lands.' Few countries in the world had as many advantages as Cuba. He had given each comrade in the fourth year of medical school a copy of the Voisin book on soils and disease, he said. ' made them promise to read it. . . .'"

These descriptions by Quirk of Castro's activities in advocating and promoting improvements in Cuban agriculture are verified in the transcripts of Castro speeches, as well as by farmers and agricultural professionals consulted by members of four of the U.S. agricultural delegations during the 1990's. It is abundantly clear from the information derived from Quirk's book, transcripts of Castro's speeches, and the extensive information derived from many people in Cuba by members of the 1990s delegations, that Fidel Castro not only was steadfast in his attempts to improve Cuban agriculture but to improve it in ecologically sound ways, with the goal of sustaining the health and welfare of each and every one of present and future generations of Cubans.

Another strong indication of this assessment was an unusual finding by the 1990's delegations: that of a head of state casually, and frequently, visiting farmers and farm families. On their many visits to state farms, agricultural cooperatives, and private farms delegates were struck by the many displayed photographs of Fidel Castro posing with farmers, farm families, farm workers, and cooperative members. The photographs were mostly the informal type of personal family snapshots that are commonly found in most homes. Furthermore, when discussing the photographs Fidel was generally described as a member of the family. Over and over again the story was the same, Fidel would drop by for a visit, unannounced and often either alone or in the company of one or two other visitors. Furthermore, he often came around meal time and usually would dine with them. They often described how much Fidel loved them and their fellow countrymen and how much he inspired them to be good farmers and citizens.

Another very strong indication of this assessment was discovered by members of the 2003 delegation. They reported that a senior professor at the Agrarian University of Havana told them that when he received his degree in Agronomy Fidel Castro personally gave him and every other member of the graduating class a copy of Rachel Carson's book, *Silent Spring*. This was in 1963, just as Cuba was beginning to wholeheartedly adopt a chemical intensive, highly mechanized, Green Revolution style agriculture.

Obviously, as it turned out, Fidel Castro, like those described below, was a "voice in the wind."

Voices in the Wind

The seeds of agricultural change in Cuba were present throughout the first thirty years following the Revolution; and agrarian reform had always been a priority of the Cuban socialist regime. Furthermore, from the beginning, the Revolution had sought to guarantee adequate food for every person in Cuba, as a birthright; and the desire had been to supply as much of this food as possible through production, using fewer chemicals, on smaller farms or farm cooperatives located close to where people actually live. Thus, the large industrialized and foreign-owned farms were nationalized, and the priorities of production were drastically changed. Exports, especially sugar, continued as a necessity to pay for imported goods not immediately available within the confines of the nation.

Prior to the Special Period, Cuba's Green Revolution-style, highly technified agriculture was heavily dependent on foreign imports, and 57 percent of the food consumed by its population was also being imported. This situation made the collapse of the economy at the beginning of the Special Period even worse than it might otherwise have been. Furthermore, this heavy dependency on imports for running its agriculture and feeding its people, strongly indicated that the speed and success of the country's recovery -- especially its rapid development of an even stronger, healthier and more sustainable agriculture than existed before the onset of the Special Period -- truly was an amazing achievement.

Credit for this achievement is due, in large measure, to the committment and dedication of a handful of the country's scientists and practicioners, who had been researching and advocatiing for an ecologically sound, organically-based agriculture, well before the Special Period. The commitment of this minority and the effort they made to experiment with, and develop, new forms of organic farming on a national scale enabled the government to face the agricultural crisis with a range of techniques and experimental methods that have not obtained parallel acceptance nationally anywhere else in the world.

However, before the Special Period, they, like Fidel Castro, had very little impact in moving agriculture in the direction of organic production, until it was necessitated by the 1989 economic collapse. They were voices in the wind, much the same as proponents of organic farming in the United States, during the 1960s and beyond.

However, these voices in the United States eventually led to an organic movement, resulting in widespread organic production -- albeit on a small scale -- and the marketing of certified organic products throughout the country -- usually sold at premium prices. In contrast, there was never an organic movement in Cuba in spite of the efforts of some far-sighted agricultural scientists and, especially, the tireless efforts and exhortations of Fidel Castro.

Although most small farming operations in Cuba have always been organic -- much the same as Amish farmers in the United States -- it was never touted as organic nor were the products sold for premium prices. Even now, since the beginning of the Special Period, when practically all agriculture in Cuba is organic, it is not especially touted as such within the country. Comparatively, only recently have the Amish in the United State began to tout their organic production and to market it as such.

Six of the Cubans whom the author worked closest with, are representative of the small number of agricultural research scientists and academicians who had been advocating for many years that the country adopt a more organic, ecological, and sustainable agriculture. In this regard, they were representabive of small numbers of like professionals and agriculturalists in practically every country of the world, who were attempting to put the brakes on a conventional agriculture which was wasting resources, polluting the environment, driving small family farmers out of business, and was unsustainably heading for an uncertain, disasterous future. Also like the progressive, insightful advocates in the other countries they were essentially voices in the wind. However, like in other countries, they were successful in getting sustainable, agroecological concepts included in academic curricula, in research and development, and in helping to convert some farmers to more organic, agroecological, sustainable practices. In Cuba, this was mostly confined to small family farms, private cooperatives and experiment stations, and did not include the prevailing and much larger state farms.

About the only component of the new reformed agriculture which was not researched by these agroecologically-bent scientists was animal traction. They were well aware that most private farmers -- some organized into cooperatives, and collectively farming approximately ten percent of Cuba's agricultural lands -- farmed with oxen. However, before the Special Period, they did not see the need to replace tractors with oxen on the other 90 percent of the land. They were focused on making agriculture more organic in nature: more like natural ecosystems in terms of the recycling of nutrients and water.

One of the Cuban research scientists the author worked especially close with, was a professor and recognized by his colleagues as one of the leaders of the renascence. He was the country's leading expert on Voisin rational pasture rotations; and taught members of the delegations about this sustainable pasture system and showed them several examples of it in Havana and Matanzas Provinces. On the outskirts of Havana he maintained a family garden which served not only as a source of food for his family and neighbors, but also as a model garden for others to imitate. He intentionally did not use the raised-bed organoponico-style garden so that the productivity of the two types of gardens could be compared. He had published many papers on results of his organic agriculture and rational pasture rotation experiments. He was also the person who helped the author find the grave of Andre Voisin.

Another professor with whom the author and most other members of the delegations spent time was a well-known agroecologist. Another recognized leader of the renascence, he was especially involved with defining, teaching and supervising the implementation of the country's new model of agriculture. He was a great source of information about the characteristics of the country's agriculture; before and after 1989. He was especially effective in explaining the differences in the prevailing philosophy of agriculture during the two periods. He too, had a long history of sustainable agricultural research.

Two very valuable sources of information to the delegations were involved with biological control research since the late 1970's. They both were heavily involved internationally with this research, and were quite knowledgeable about progress being made in this field everywhere in the world. Cuba was indeed fortunate to have them on hand to lead the great expansion in biological control research, development, and production which was necessitated by the Special Period. Members of the 1990s delegations were probably most impressed with this component of the reformed agriculture than any other component. Cuba's progress in this critical field of sustainable agriculture was very impressive, indeed; and remains impressive.

Another research scientist, who was an organic farming researcher and advocate well before the Special Period, also was a very valuable source of information to the delegations: particularly on research and development in animal and human nutrition and on the medicinal uses of cultured as well as wild plants. Like the other scientists her work continued apace from the start of the economic crisis, and she became an important leader in the critical development of her nation's post 1989 agriculture.

Another leading member of the reformation was heavily involved with many aspects of agroecogical research before 1989; and was especially well known for his research and development work on innovative recycling of organic matter and composting. A leading advocate of biofertilizer production and utilization, he was very effective in his leadership on the use of earthworms for soil renovation as well as for processing organic wastes into compost (vermicomposting). Early in the Special Period his work lead to production of a superior vermicompost which was being sold in the export market in addition to being greatly expanded throughout the country for local use. He was also a leading researcher and developer of agroforestry and a leading advocate of its rapid expansion -- particularly in watersheds: which would serve to greatly expand food and fiber production while at the same time improving protection of these valuable lands from erosion and conserving the precious water emanating from them.

This very versatile and dedicated scientist also became one of the most popular TV personalities in Cuba, with two very popular shows. The first, and more frequently shown, were short (usually 5 to 15 minutes) productions on agricultural subjects (mostly for the benefit of city dwellers): such as urban gardening, waste recycling, composting, vermiculture and vermicomposting, food preservation, foods and nutrition, conserving water and energy, etc. The second was a weekly, hour-long nature program on ecological and evironmental subjects; in which productions valuable to the nation's natural resource restoration, preservation, conservation and protection were aired: such as ecosystem functions, ecological land use, watershed protection, water use and conservation, forests and forest restoration, soil conservation, wildlife conservation, agroforestry, agroecology, rational pasture rotations, etc.

I was fortunate to develop a close relationship with this humble man, who was loved by the Cuban people and greatly admired by his colleagues; many of whom told me that he was probably the most important and effective leader in the successful reformation of the nation's agriculture. Moreover, he was very knowledgeable about the influence of Andre Voisin on Fidel Castro. Relatedly, he gave me many insights on Castro's attempts to get the nation's educational, research, and development institutions, along with farms, state farms and farm cooperatives, to follow the principles of Voisin. He was a very valuable source to members of the delegations on the philosophy and details of the renascence of Cuban agriculture.

Members of the delegations frequently heard from these scientists the old adage, "necessity is the mother of invention;" and this was one of the guiding principles in their research and development work. In traveling around the country we saw numerous innovations, many which were particularly ingenious and impressive. Moreover, each year, over the three-year period of the delegations and 5-1/2 year period of my visits, progressively revealed even more innovative developments. Many of these were especially impressive because they had been quickly and cleverly developed from ideas received by these scientists from the many agricultural experts (including members of our delegations) who were visiting the country to review progress of the agricultural renascence taking place.

These are but a few examples of dedicated scientists who were conducting organic, agroecological, and sustainable agricultural research well before the Special Period. When the economic crisis hit, Cuba was indeed fortunate to have them, as well as others like them, to provide the research base upon which to quickly model and build a successful alternative agriculture and to provide the leadership to guide the country confidently along its path.

Rescued by the Peasant Farmers

On my second trip to Cuba I was fortunate to have the opportunity to spend several days with a university/experiment station agricultural extension specialist. This specialist was quite familiar with the agricultural experiment station and cooperative extension systems in the Land-grant universities of the United States; having earned his Ph.D. at one of these universities. He informed me that the agricultural universities in Cuba had a structure and organization similar to those in the United States.

We met frequently at the university and at several of the experiment stations, but for two days he drove me around Havana, Mantanzas and Pinar del Rio provinces to visit small private farms and private farm cooperatives. The objective was to meet farmers who had been farming independent of the government, many since the beginning of the revolution, for 30 years or more; and to especially learn about their role in helping their nation to successfully develop and establish the new model of agriculture. Many of the farmers I met were second or third generation farmers, most farming land that had been in their familes back to their fathers or grandfathers time.

One of the farmers told me that for the past year he had a difficult time in keeping up with his farm chores because of demands made on his time by university and government agents seeking information and advice to help with the renovation of agriculture which was taking place. He was even giving talks to groups of professionals, students and farmers who visited his farm, and to classes at the nearby university. Another told me that he was descended upon by university and government experts to study the rigging of his oxen, the tillage implements pulled by the oxen, and the techniques he used in working the oxen. He was enlisted by the government to train oxen and oxen handlers on his farm. Later he was given some more land and expanded his farming operation to take advantage of the additional oxen teams, implements, and the extra labor represented by the students he was training.

Early in the Special Period, the country had to put a moratorium on the slaughter of cattle, particularly steers, and on their conversion into tractable, well-trained oxen; and on the gathering of animal traction implements and paraphernalia from throughout the country. Most of the implements and paraphernalia were found as nostalgic decorative pieces around homes in both rural and urban areas.

The president of a very successful tobacco farming cooperative, in Pinar del Rio Province, was very enthusiastic in describing the characteristics of his cooperative to members of four of the 1990s delegations. The farms of this cooperative -- which included several experimental areas, in which they collected research data in cooperation with university and government scientists -- had always been farmed organically. Furthermore, they used animal traction for their plowing and tillage up until approximately 1980, when they began to shift to tractor traction. Then, from 1980 until 1990, they used a mixture of animal and mostly tractor traction. Then, early in the Special Period, they parked their tractors, converting, almost exclusively, to animal traction. In his opinion, as an expert in using both types of traction, using oxen was far superior, more enjoyable, and infinitely more sustainable. Furthermore, he said, there was a bonus, which had been forgotten during the time in which they were using tractors for most of their traction needs: farming was quieter and more peaceful using oxen, and they could again enjoy the singing of the many birds in the area.

Also, he told us how he and other members of his cooperative were very active in helping the government in transitioning from tractor to animal traction. His cooperative had some of the most advanced animal traction implements and oxen yoking apparati, and some of the most expert oxen trainers and drivers in the country. A bonus from doing this was already being realized. That is: from their work with agricultural engineers, some new, greatly improved animal traction implements had been developed and were also being used on the farms of the cooperative. Moreover, it was already evident that these implements were great improvements over the ones they replaced.

On several occasions I spent up to eight hours per visit on one of the most progressive private farming cooperatives in Havana Province, The president of the cooperative had a masters degree, and was a fountain of information about the history of agriculture in Cuba, and he was especially knowledgeable about the Special Period -- having been involved with the transformation of the country's agriculture from the beginning. Given his training and special knowledge, and the fact that his cooperative was essentially a model for every component needed during the transformation, beginning years before the onset of the Special Period, he was an exceptionally important resource person to help guide the transformation. Early in the Special Period, he began working on his Ph.D. in biological control, because of the especial importance of this field to the kind of sustainable, agroecologically based agriculture which he was helping to establish in Cuba. Interestingly, although he eventually earned his Ph.D., he proudly considered himself a peasant farmer; as did the other farmers in his cooperative.

This cooperative served as a model for the reformation of agriculture throughout the country; and rightly so. Even before 1989 the cooperative was exceptionally successful; and practically self-sufficient. It grew nearly every food crop in Cuba, raised nearly every type of animal; had its own dairy, slaughter house, butcher shop, leatherworks, metalworks, machine shop, and many other support facilities. Farming operations were done with oxen; although a few tractors, which were acquired before the Special Period, were used for especially heavy work. They had a very functional office complex: with administrative and record-keeping rooms, several meeting rooms and a large assembly hall. They kept very detailed records, including productivity data and charts. The cooperative basically recycled everything: with large compost operations, including a worm nursery and related vermicomposting. It had a large biological laboratory and production facility for the rearing of beneficial insects and the production of biofertilizers and biological control agents (beneficial bacteria and fungi). Production of composts and other biofertilizers, beneficial insects and biocontrol agents more than met the needs of the cooperative, with the excess being sold to farmers outside the cooperative.

The onset of the Special Period required immediate and drastic changes on most of Cuba's agricultural lands. In contrast, operations on this cooperative, like those on most of the private farms of Cuba, did not require any changes; and only a few were made. Most of the changes were mostly simple refinements -- based on the very rapidly emerging results of "Special Period research and develpment" --intended to make the operation even more efficient and productive than before. One very noteworthy change was the adoption of the ubiquitous organoponicos for the production of vegetables grown mostly for sale to the communities near the cooperative. By 1995 these very productive, raised-bed structures were beginning to be seen throughout the city of Havana and in other urban and near urban areas; and, by then, the cooperative had built numerous of these units on their lands: including one six-acre plot which was covered with them. This large plot was used almost exclusively for the growing of vegetables for sale to the local communities.

It is clear from the foregoing that the so-called peasant farmers constituted the fulcrum on which Cuba's reformed agriculture was raised.

The Amish

Although I knew a little about Amish farmers and had a general knowledge of their farming practices, it wasn't until I took a Rural Socialogy course during my senior year of college that I began to learn details of Amish lifestyles and farming modes. A senior research project I did in that course was an eye-opener with regard to the truth about Amish farming practices; particulary with regard to how they compared to prevailing conventional practices. As I began to learn more about the Amish I was motivated to launch a comparative evaluation of traditional versus conventional agriculture in terms of: productivity; efficiency; profitability; environmental impact; soil and water conservation; and, most importantly, sustainability. Since then I have continued along this path over the entirety of my career in the quest to understand the essential elements of a truly sustainable agriculture.

Briefly, the research project indicated, in broad terms, that the Amish farms compared to the conventional farms: were more efficient; more profitable; and more conserving of soil and water resources. The two types of farms had about the same levels of yields per acre. The Amish farms had a positive environmental impact whereas the conventional farms had a negative environmental impact. The Amish farming systems were clearly much more sustainable. The profitability comparisons were particularly informative. The conventional farms had a very high debt burden whereas the Amish farms had zero debt; and this, together with the much greater cost of inputs (not counting labor) on the conventional farms resulted in the net income per acre being approximately five times less from these types of farms than from the Amish farms. Of course, the amount of labor input was much greater per acre on the Amish farms, but this was largly discounted because labor inputs were viewed in very different ways between the two types of farms. Therefore, labor inputs were not included in the comparisons.

Two years following this senior research project on Amish agriculture, I attended the first annual Farm Science Review at the Ohio State University. The review was intended to bring together, for a few days every year: agricultural researchers from the university and agricultural experiment station; venders of agricultural services, machinery, equipment, fertilizers, seed, and other products; and farmers: to display, discuss and review the latest in agricultural research, development and technology. The founders of the review, as well as all participants, were very pleasantly surprised at the resounding success of the event. Many thousands of people attended: mostly farmers and farm families.

The biggest surprise of all, however, was that nearly a third of the attendees were Amish families. They came mostly from Ohio and adjacent states, especially Pennsylvania; but some came from as far away as Iowa. Almost all travelled by public transportation: mainly by trains and buses; including many chartered buses.

Not only did the Amish attend in large numbers, but, according to every vender and displayer, they were the most inquisitive and asked the most questions. Moreover, their questions were intelligent and most of the venders and displayers made a point that the answers they gave to the Amish questioners appeared to be well understood.

As I circulated among the displays I was particularly attracted to the displays of agricultural machinery and equipment: the latest models of tractors, harvesters, seeders, plows, cultivators, etc...; mainly because of the throngs of Amish men and boys around them. This posed a big question, why would the Amish, who farmed with horses and horse-drawn implements, be interested in gasoline engine powered machinery and implements? However, this question was quickly answered when I found out that most of the Amish at these displays were blacksmiths and blacksmith apprentices. Moreover, like they were at all of the other displays, the Amish were quite noticeably inquisitive and full of questions. Furthermore, the displayers were particularly impressed that most of the questions were about the machinery's and equipment's hydraulic systems -- questions that hardly any of the non-Amish visitors asked.

The Amish blacksmiths and farmers were clearly interested in information about the hydraulic systems which they could use in making equipment and implements which would make farming with horses and other draft animals easier and more efficient. As it turned out my questioning of all of the displayers at the review revealed that this was what attracted the Amish to the event: they were looking for ideas which could be adapted to their farming systems; to make them more productive: they weren't interested in replacing their practices with conventional ones; but merely in adapting aspects of conventional practices which would improve traditional ones.

For several months following the initial Farm Science Review the Amish who attended were the talk of the College of Agriculture. I took this as an opportunity to add to my knowlege of Amish agriculture and its comparative characteristics with conventional agriculture. I spent some time speaking of these things with the two extension agronomists who were the organizers of the review. To paraphrase their comments about the Amish is quite revealing. Their pre-review ideas about Amish farmers and farming can be summarized as follows: backward, quaint, parochial, peasant, insular, ignorant of advances in agriculture, and totally mired in 18th century farming practices. In stark contrast their post-review ideas can be summarized as follows: progressive, sophisticated, efficient, thrifty, profitable, innovative, adept in applications of appropriate technology, and expert in adopting and integrating advances in agricultural research and development into their sustainable farming practices. One of them put into words what was obvious to every non-Amish person attending the review: "It was clear to me that the Amish farmers and blacksmiths were looking to adapt as much as possible of the newest advancements in research and development which could be integrated into their system of farming without compromising it. It was also clear to me that they have been doing this for some time back into the past. In my lifetime I have never had such a misconception about something as I had about the Amish."

Later on I had occasion to spend some time with a few Amish blacksmiths when I contracted with them to design and manufacture some metallic research tools and equipment. I was amazed at the depth and range of their knowledge and skills of their trade. I eventually came to the conclusion that they could make anything possible within the limits of the capabilities of their shops. Between the blacksmith and leatherwork shops, found in all Amish communities, every tool, implement and, harness equipment needed for plowing, cultivating, seeding, and harvesting could be, and usually were, hand-made in these shops. Moreover, the things made there were of the highest quality and exceptionally well designed. Some of the field sampling tools they made for me -- based on a description of what I wanted to use the tools for -- were so well designed and manufactured, and, more importantly, worked so well in the field, that I and two of my colleagues, published a descriptive article in a scientific journal so that other field scientists could benefit from them.

Unfortunately there has been practically nothing written about the details of Amish agriculture. Furthermore, the little that has been written is very general, and practically devoid of details. Usually such accounts are included in popular-type articles about the general characteristics of the Amish people: their communities and ways of living; and these accounts usually are found in rural socialogy oriented publications, with very limited circulation. Part of this lack of published details about Amish farming practices can be attributed to the provincial nature of their communities, which strongly eschew interaction with outsiders. From my experiences in interacting with Amish communities, I was generally viewed with uncooperative suspicion: as an unwelcome outsider.

In contrast to my experiences in interacting with Amish communities, my experiences with the Cuban people -- in my research about their agriculuture -- was diametrically the opposite.

Thus, details of Amish agriculture have been generally unavailable to the Cubans, and most of what have been available, have been brief, indirect accounts in cooperative extension and non-government organization reports, such as those put out in the U.S. by the Rodale Institute. In a similar fashion, the little that has been written about the Cuban agriculture reformation is generally lacking in rigorous, systematic data compilations and detail; and has not been published as widely as needed to make the information as useful to the agricultural communities of other countries; which might be inclined to use the Cuban model, but need more detailed information in order to do so.

The Amish story is one which is very important to communities, such as the Cuban people, who are in the process of adopting, or who would like to adopt, sustainable agricultural practices based on agroecological principles and techniques. It should give them confidence that not only do such practices work, and are sustainable, but to adopt them should not be viewed as retrogressive to their agriculture. On the contrary, such changes should not only be viewed as progressive but also as the only way to have a truly sustainable agriculture. The story is included in this chapter for these very reasons.

Amish agriculture provides an excellent model for a very productive agriculture which is not only sustainable but also, relatedly, has positive environmental impacts. However, from my experiences with the Amish they could care less. They just want to make a good living and to be left alone. But everyone else not only should care but should strive to emulate it. The same is true of Cuban agriculture: other nations should strive to emulate it. There are strong similarities between Amish and Cuban agriculture; not because the Cubans copied from the Amish: on the contrary, they developed their agriculture independently of the Amish. But it is turning out to be similar to Amish agriculture for the simple reason that generally its the only model which works.

The main value of understanding Amish agriculture to Cubans, is that it should give them confidence that their agriculture is on the right track: that the Ecological Green Revolution type agriculture which they are developing should be highly successful and sustainable.

The great challenge: getting what Cuba has wrought in developing a truely sustainable agriculture accepted as modern and progressive rather than quaint, peasant and regressive.

The Drain of Urban Areas

During my youth there was still a very close relationship between towns and cities and their adjacent farming areas. Farmers hauled their produce to town and returned to their farms loaded with waste products to feed their hogs and other animals or to incorporate into their soils. Furthermore, there was a lot of gardening and small animal raising taking place within the towns and cities, and a great deal of vegetable and fruit raising on the lands immedialtely adjacent to them. Altough it wasn't ecologically ideal, since nutrients were being flushed down the toilets and there was a small (compared to now) energy drain; it was much more ecolgically sound than today. A lot of the farming around towns and cities was being done with draft animals or small tractors. A majority of the populations lived in rural areas: in agricultural communities of farms and small towns.

Now towns have coalesced into cities, cities have grown apace, and there is comparatively very little interaction between farms and urban centers. Farm products are transported to cities, consumed there, with larger amounts of nutrients being flushed down a much greater number of toilets, and waste being sent to dumps instead of being recycled back to the farms. Both the farms and the cities consume comparatively much greater amounts of energy than before. For the most part, gardens and small animal raising operations have disappeared from the cities and larger towns, and have even nearly disappeared from areas immediately adjacent to them. Also, for the most part, draft animals and small tractors have been replaced by larger, more powerful tractors on the farms. To make matters worse, from the point of view of energy drainage, is the common use of motorized lawn mowers, nearly the size of the farm tractors of 60 to 70 years ago, for mowing the lawns of the ubiquitous large grassy areas around the homes in suburban and exurban areas. Furthermore, a great majority of the populations now live in cities, exacerbating the organic matter, nutrient and energy drain of the cities. The cores of many of the larger cities, especially those of multimillions of inhabitants, have become almost completely devoid of green life, even trees; making matters immeasurably worse.

In his 12/8/64 speech, Fidel Castro commented on the drain of urban concentrations and indicated that the issue needed to be addressed in Cuba. The following two excerpts from this speech are insightful on these points.

"We must turn our sights toward the fields. Professor Voisin points out that some of the causes for the decadence of civilizations are precisely those great urban concentrations. He explains that just these great urban concentrations have led to the exhaustion of land, to the production of vitamin-deficient food."

"The decadence of ancient civilizations was brought about by great urban concentrations that had led to the exhaustion of the land, to the production of vitamin-deficient foods. Through the sewers of Rome and Babylon had flowed the fertility of the soils. And as the farmlands became exhausted, a physical and moral degeneration of the inhabitants ensued. Cubans too had concentrated too much in the cities. They must look once again to the countryside. The revolution would see that they did."

It is clear from Casto's speeches that he was very much interested in decreasing urban populations -- particularly in Havana (with more than 20% of the nation's population) -- and increasing rural populations. Relatedly, he was of the opinion that every citizen should understand the importance of agriculture to the welfare of the nation and to have a great respect for farmers. Preferably, in addition to learning to appreciate agriculture, all citizens should be involved with food production at times during their lifetimes. Most rural dwellers should be involved with agriculture full time while urban dwellers could be involved part time: cultivating gardens and providing labor during critical periods of need, such as crop harvesting times.

Some of the programs which the government promoted to decrease the drain of urban areas before the Special Period included: urban gardening; agroforestry green belts; work-study programs at elementary and secondary schools; periodic agricultural work brigades; new town programs; and alternative military service.

Like in most cities throughout the world, there had always been gardening activities in the cities of Cuba; particularly in the more sparsely populated areas. However, these gardens contributed very little to the nations food production; especially in the larger cities. Furthermore, other than the exhortations and urgings from Fidel Castro, there was very little movement toward expanding urban agriculture through the expansion of gardening per se. On the other hand, there was a strong, government-led effort to expand urban agriculture through the establishment of agroforestry greenbelts in the larger cities; especially Havana. The program called for the the planting of huge numbers of fruit and nut trees, as well as fast growing conifers and the more valuable hardwood trees, within a wide green belt around and through parts of the cities. Within the green belts, other green activities -- mainly vegetable production -- were to be expanded and intensified. Although the program was started with a great deal of fanfare and enthusiasm; it mostly fizzled out before reaching a level where it might be sustained. Although it was mostly a failure, it stimulated an increase in gardening and, more importantly, the plans, and the limited experiences which resulted, were very important to quick starting the establishment of urban agriculture and agroforestry when the economic crisis hit.

Likewise, although there was only very limited response to government requests that all elementary and secondary schools established gardens to educate students in the art and science of food growing; the efforts provided a strong basis for the very successful establishment of gardens and work-study programs after 1989.

From the beginning of the revolution agricultural work brigades in Cuba have drawn considerable attention throughout the world; especially those that were formed to harvest the nation's huge sugar crop. The annual sugar harvest actually attracted large numbers of foreigners; who flocked to Cuba to join these harvest brigades. Although such brigades consisted mainly of people who lived in the cities, who were employed part-time for periodic critical needs in the countryside; the overarching desire of the government -- especially of President Castro -- was to encourage people to relocate to the countryside and become permanently employed in farming. However, only a very small percentage of brigade members responded to this desire. The result was quite different after 1989, when large numbers of occasionally part-time city dwellers became permanent, full-time workers on the many large state farms that were growing vegetables and meats so sorely needed by the nation.

Although the "new towns" program began before the Special Period, its growth was very slow until afterwards. This program had the aim of getting people out of the cities and into the countryside, either to work in agricultural pursuits or in support roles. The idea was to build new small communities within agricultural areas to be populated by farmers; and farm tool makers, agricultural suppliers, school teachers, nurses, doctors, and other types of workers needed to make a viable and desirable community; that would be more or less self-sufficient, and with the productive capacity to provide significant amounts of agricultural products to the general population of the country.

Before the Special Period, young people had alternative options, particularly in agriculture, in lieu of mandatory military service. The government particularly encouraged young men and women to accept alternative service and to populate the new towns, as well as the already established agricultural centers; with the hope that they would choose to make their careers in agriculture; or in support roles in agricultural communities. The hope was that some of the men and women would choose to marry after their service obligation; and would raise families in the new towns.

With the onset of the Special Period the cause that Castro had espoused, as an essential component of Cuba's agriculture attaining its full potential, went from desire to necessity. The necessity was: to get the entire population to understand, appreciate, and support the nation's agricultural enterprise; with a large percentage of the people involved in full or part-time production of enough wholesome and nutritious food to sustainably meet the needs of all the people. Thus, de-urbanization and urban agricultural activities became even more important to achieve than before the Special Period; and to achieve them as quickly as possible. Therefore, all of the programs directed toward these ends, which were started before the Special Period, were expanded and intensified.

Urban agricultural expansion and intensification since the onset of the economic crisis has already been described and discussed above. Agroforestry has been established and greatly expanded throughout the country, especially within watersheds and within cities. The great expansion of urban gardens, mostly in the form of the very highly productive, French-intensive-style organoponicos, have finally made urban areas in Cuba greener than ever. Moreover, the production in urban areas is significantly contributing to the overall agricultural goals of the nation.

Before the economic crisis, gardens at elementary and secondary schools, to support agricultural work-study programs, occured mostly in small towns and rural areas. Now they occur on the grounds of nearly every city school as well. They constitute a significant part of the overall urban agricultural program.

In place of work brigades of temporary workers, the country opted for a more stable work force to support mostly the larger agricultural production units: the large state farms. This work force was formed from city dwellers, who served on the state farms for periods ranging from less than a year to two years or more. As the Special Period progressed, many members of these work crews opted to remain in agriculture, with many eventually becoming independent or cooperative farmers. All in all, this transformation of the work brigades into individual and cooperative farmers has expanded and stabilized agricultural production; and made it much more sustainable.

One of first things done at the start of the Special Period was to generally suspend construction activities in the larger cities and towns in favor of increasing construction activities in the rural areas. Construction of new towns continued, and construction of buildings to support the nation's agriculture took priority over all other construction. Relatedly, populating the countryside with farmers and a supporting cast of teachers, doctors, veterinarians, implement manufacturers, biological control technicians, and others continued apace. Nearly all alternative military service obligations were taken in the agricultural sector; and continued to meet the intended result of inducing young people to opt for careers in the agricultural sector. The government program of helping beginning farmers to get started, by providing them the needed tools and facilities in the form of grants and (mostly) long-term, very low interest loans, has very much strengthened the inducement.

Cuba has clearly been successful in decreasing the adverse drain of its cities on the country's resources. If the nation continues on its present path we may well see the day the drain is decreased to the the point that its cities become more of an asset than a liability to the health and welfare of its citizens and their descendants.

CONCLUSION

The great success in agricultural production throughout the world is generally attributed to the scientifically based, highly technical developments which began with the Green Revolution of the 1970s and 1980s. During those years farmers of cereals (mainly rice, wheat and corn), and a few other globally traded crops dramatically increased their yields with new hybrid seeds, chemical fertilizers and pesticides, and increased irrigation. Today Green Revolution technological development continues apace, with the newest technologies revolving about genetic engineering -- making greater and greater demands on soil, water and energy resources; requiring even greater inputs of chemical fertilizers and pesticides; to grow an increasing variety of genetically engineered plants and animals; and heading down a path which cannot be sustained, and even may be dangerous. Promoters of agriculture based on Green Revolution types of technologies, usually disdain organic and sustainable methods as "low yield" and incapable of feeding a growing population.

Cuba previously embraced the technical Green Revolution philosophy. It's agriculture was characterized by high-tech, chemical- and energy-intensive methods until 1989. Cuba's first green revolution lasted as long as needed chemical and mechanical inputs were available: until their economy collapsed. Since then, Cuba's scientists and farmers have been pioneering a new ecological green revolution: one with far fewer synthetic and fossil fuel inputs, and far more inputs of human ingenuity.

Without fertilizers and pesticides, Cubans turned to organic production methods. Without machinery parts and gasoline, Cubans turned to oxen. Without transport, Cubans started growing food just about everywhere: on patios, and in vacant lots, school playgrounds, and back yards. During the initial period of "withdrawal" from its first Green Revolutuion, yields of most food crops were low; but now yields from its new, Ecolgical Green Revolution, have surpassed the highest previous averages. Thus, it might be said that the Ecological Green Revolutions is the greener of the two green revolutions.

The radical restructuring of Cuban agriculture from a system modeled on California to one similar to that promoted by Rodale and other organic farming visionaries, resulted from the collapse of the Soviet bloc in 1989. The subsidies the Soviet Union had long provided for the chemical inputs and fuel that sustained the island's agricultural production were dramatically reduced or suspended as a result of the collapse. This forced Cuba to implement, on a national scale, organic farming techniques which had been tried only on a limited basis in the West. Cuba was able to do so in a short period of time mainly because of the dedication of a handful of its scientists who previously, for more than a decade, had researched, examined, and advocated technologies favoring an alternative, chemically-free agriculture. The commitment of this minority and its effort to experiment with and develop new forms of organic farming on a national scale enabled the government to face the agricultural crisis with a range of techniques and experimental methods that have not obtained parallel acceptance nationally anywhere else in the world.

For the first time, a large-scale, mono-cropping, export-oriented farming system was converted to an alternative food production system using low-input, sustainable techniques. The rapid speed and great success of the conversion were due mainly to three factors; which together form the roots of the nation's agricultural renascence: Fidel Castro, whose leadership, wisdom and untiring efforts, especially since 1964, attempted to convince the agricultural community of the efficacy of appying the principles of Andre Voisin for sustained productivity and good health of the population; a small number of scientists and practicioners, who, for a long time, had been advocating for an ecologically sound, organically-based agriculture; and a small number of so-called "peasant" farmers who had never abandoned wisdom nor the appropriate technologies of animal traction, organic recycling and fertilization, and biological pest and disease control.

While Cuba has long been, and still is, in many ways, a special case, there are important lessons to be learned for the region from its current experiences. Throughout the Caribbean and Latin America the dominant industrial model of agriculture is in a state of socio-economic and environmental crisis. The Green Revolution seems to have run its course, as yield increases have leveled off, and in many cases are dropping due to insect, disease and weed resistance to pesticides; soil compaction, erosion and salinization; and water shortages. Prevailing economic prescriptions have failed to reverse the trend toward increased rural improverishment and marginalization of small-scale farmers, or to absorb the excess labor migrating from the countryside to overpopulated cities: which exacerbates impoverishment of the countryside and decay of the cities. Relatedly, policies have failed to address the ever-expanding environmental crisis by not promoting badly needed de-urbanization and widespread adoption of green activities and sustainable farming practices.

The evidence is overwhelming that industrial agriculture, which prevails throughout most of the world, is rapidly, and unnecessarily, expending, damaging, or poisoning our natural resources. It is justified by its promoters and practitioners as the price that must be paid to meet the food needs of an expanding world population, and excused by society as a whole as the price of progress; even though these attitudes cannot be logically nor morally supported. This same scenario was being played out in Cuba prior to the advent of the Special Period; and if it had not been for this economic crisis, it is likely that it would still be playing.

Cuba is showing that it is possible to meet food production goals, promote sustainable agriculture, and provide viable economic alternatives for rural communities. What is required is a simple set of alternative macroeconomic and sectoral policies. Cuba has shown us that with proper encouragement, support and incentives from government policies, resource limited, small-scale farmers are very capable of achieving high levels of productivity: higher, in fact, than those of large-scale producers. Additionally, Cuba is demonstrating that if agrichemical inputs are kept expensive, or are scarce, rather than subsidized, farmers, regardless of previous practices and experiences, also are quite capable of achieving high productivity with alternative, sustainable practices. Thus, following the Cuban example holds great promise that other Caribbean and Latin American nations also can achieve food security, environmental recovery in rural areas, and revitalization of rural community economies by: protecting food production and loosening price controls; removing direct and indirect subsidies for Green Revolution technology; reforming land tenure; and redirecting research and extension of alternative practices, using participatory and farmer-to-farmer methods.

The emergent model which defines the radical reformation of her agriculture clearly shows that Cuba is on track toward today's most progressive and sustainable agriculture, and it should be vigorously promoted as a model for the entire world to follow. Those who believe that land stewardship is a requirement for sustainable agriculture realize that eventually agricultural practices worldwide must either fail or follow the model used by Cuba, the Amish and other sagacious organic agricultural practitioners. Those who believe that following the industrial model of agriculture not only is unsustainable, but also grossly irresponsible with regard to obligations to future generations, realize that the sustainable model being refined in Cuba offers hope that every country can meet its needs and also leave its natural resources in a condition that will ensure that future generations also will have a fair opportunity to meet their needs in a sustainable manner.

A considerable amount of space in this chapter has been devoted to the sections on Fidel Casto's attempts to improve Cuba's agriculture; the influence of Andre Voisin; and the Amish; compared to the other sections. The reasons for this are: it is so unusual for a head of state to personally devote so much time and energy to the study and promotion of agriculture as did Fidel Castro, particularly in the promotion of sustainable agriculture; the relationship which developed between Andre Voisin and Fidel Castro is an amazing story, particularly as it impacted the President's thinking and the ultimate influence it had on the reformation of the country's agriculture; and the discussion of Amish agriculture is very important from the standpoint of demonstrating that agriculture based on the new Cuban model is not "peasant," quaint and backward, but, to the contrary, is what a modern, vibrant agriculture should be if it is to be sustainable in meeting the needs, and maintaining the health and welfare, of all the people.

In conclusion, the importance of its agricultural renascence to Cuba is obvious. Cuban citizens have been striving to create a self-relient agriculture that will simultaneously meet their food and fiber needs, generate export income, and provide food security for future generations. The reformation's importance to the rest of the world is obvious to people who realize that energy and chemical intensive industrial agriculture is not sustainable. The new strategy's importance is also obvious to people who realize that something akin to the new Cuban model of agriculture is the only hope, if there is any hope at all, for the citizens of resource-poor countries to have the opportunity for healthy and decent lives.

ACKNOWLEDGEMENTS

The following persons were sources of information, derived mainly in discussions held at various times and in various places in Cuba. Those indicated with an asterix were major sources, and there were many other Cubans and non-Cubans, not listed, who also were sources of information. All but six of the non-Cubans listed were members of one or more of the five U. S. agricultural fact-finding delegations to Cuba.

Cubans: Felix Ancizar*, Juan Antonio Blanco*, Roberto Caballero Grande, Antonio Casanova*, Ricardo Delgado Diaz, Demetrio Diaz, Raul Espinosa*, Jose-Manuel Febles, Fernando Funes*, Roberto Garcia Trujillo*, V. Bruno Henriguez, Alberto Hernandez Jimenez, Ricardo Herrera, Marta Monzote*, Luis Garcia Perez*, Enrique Perez Marin, Pedro Quintero*, Jorge Ramon Cuevas*, Gina Rey, Boris Sanchez*, Humberto Vasquez*, Julia Vasquez, Julio Viera.

Non-Cubans: Earl Alexander*, Miguel Altieri*, Marta Astier*, Manoel Baltazar, Medea Benjamin*, Nanda Berman, Martin Bourque*, Larry Burkham, Judith Carney*, Robert Carran, Scott Chaplowe, Ruth Collier, David Crohn, Carl Davidson*, Jeffrey Dlott*, Katherine Dowling, Nichole Englund, Lou Falcon*, Michelle Frank, Greg Frankel, Jim Grieshop*, Lon Johnson, Nazreen Kadir, Holly Kaufman*, Jaime Kibben*, Amy Lewellen, Keith Loague*, Juan Martinez, Lena Miller, Kirsten Moller, Julio Monterrey, Catherine

Murphy*, Lari Mussatti, Joseph Oliva, Rachel O'Malley, Laura Orlando*, Ivette Perfecto*, John Perkins*, Anja Puggard, Thomas Regan*, Carmen Rodriguez-Barbosa*, Peter Rosset*, Nancy Sableski, Miyoko Sakashita, Nina Shishkoff*, Brian Schultz*, Randy Selig, Jim Smith, Pamela Stricker*, Richard Strong*, Chris Teo-Sherrell, Anne Turner, John Vandermeer*, Robyn Van En, Mark Van Horn, Miriam Volat, Lowell Wagner*, Matthew Werner*, Fred Wood*.

REFERENCES

Altieri, Miguel A. 1993. The implications of Cuba's agricultural conversion for the general Latin American agroecological movement. *Agriculture and Human Values*, Vol. X, No. 3, p. 91-92.

Alvarez, Jose and William A. Messina, Jr. 1993. Potential Cuban agricultural export profile under open trade between the U.S. and Cuba. *Agriculture and Human Values,* Vol. X, No. 3, p. 61-74.

Carney, Judith A. and Richard Haynes. 1993. From the Editors: Low-Input Sustainable Agriculture in Cuba. *Agriculture and Human Values*, Vol. X, No. 3, p.1-2.

Castro, Fidel. 1964. Casto Speech Inaugurates Voisin Lectures. Medical Association Building in Havana. *Havana Domestic Radio and Television Service,* 12/8/64.

Castro, Fidel. 1964. Castro Speech at Voisin's Funeral. Havana *Domestic Radio and Television Service,* 12/22/64

Castro, Fidel. 1965. Castro Speech on the 6th Revolution Aniversary. Jose Marti Square. *Havanà Domestic Radio and Television Service*, 1/2/65

Castro, Fidel. 1966. Castro Speech to the First Middle-Level Technicians to Graduate from the Soils, Fertilizers, and Animal Husbandry Technical Institute. Havana University. *Havana Domestic Radio and Television Service.,* 12/19/66

Castro, Fidel. 1991. Castro Speech at the Seventh Congress of Education, Science and Sports Workers. Havana Palace of Conventions. *Havana Radio Havana Cuba,* 12/22/91

Deere, Carmen Diana. 1993. Cuba's national food program and its prospects for food security. *Agriculture and Human Values,* Vol. X, No. 3, p. 35-51.

Dlott, Jeff, Ivette Perfecto, Peter Rosset, Larry Burkham, Julio Monterrey, and John Vandermeer. 1993. Management of insect pests and weeds. *Agriculture and Human Values,* Vol. X, No. 3, p. 9-15.

Funes, Fernando, Luis Garcia, Martin Bourgue, Nilda Perez and Peter Rosset (Eds.). 2002. *Sustainable Agriculture and Resistance*, Food First Books, Inst. for Food & Devel. Policy, Oakland, CA.

Gersper, Paul L. 1998. The importance of organic (sustainable) agriculture to the attainment of food security and a sustainable economy. In Erstad, R. and D. Funkhouser (Eds.), *Proceedings of Conference on the Ethics and Culture of Development: Building the Sustainable Economy, Havana, Cuba,* Amer. Friends Serv. Comm., Philadelphia.

Gersper, Paul L., Carmen S. Rodriguez-Barbosa and Laura F. Orlando. 1993. Soil conservation in Cuba: A key to the new model for agriculture. *Agriculture and Human Values,* Vol. X, No. 3, p. 16-23.

Gersper, Paul L. and Peter Rosset. 1996. The Caribbean environment: Agricultural issues. p. 14-16 in Collis, D. S. (Ed.), "The Caribbean Environment: Issues of Mutual Concern."

Georgetown University Caribbean Environment Conference Summary Document, *Center for Latin American Studies,* Washington, D.C.

Hamilton, Hal. 2003. A different Kind of Green Revolution in Cuba, *Ag World Wide* (participant in the February 2003 Food First delegation to Cuba).

Kaufman, Holly. 1993. From red to green: Cuba forced to conserve due to economic crisis. *Agriculture and Human Values*, Vol. X, No. 3, p. 31-34.

Kibben, Jaime (Director). 1995 . *The Greening of Cuba.* Food First Video, Inst. of Food & Devel. Policy, Oakland, CA.

Levins, Richard. 1993. The ecological transformation of Cuba. *Agriculture and Human Values,* Vol. X, No. 3, p. 52-60.

Murphy, Catherine. 1999. Cultivating Havana: Urban Agriculture and Food Security in the Years of Crisis. *Devel. Rpt. No. 12, Inst. for Food & Devel.* Policy, Oakland, CA.

Perfecto, Ivette. 1994. The transformation of Cuban agriculture after the cold war. *Amer. Jour. Altern. Agric.,* No. 3, p. 98-108.

Perkins, Jerry. 2003. *Organic Farming Flourishes in Cuba, Des Moines Register* (participant in the February 2003 Food First delegation to Cuba).

Perkins, John H. 1993. Cuba, Mexico, and India: Technical and social changes in agriculture during political economic crisis. *Agriculture and Human Values,* Vol. X, No. 3, p. 75-90.

Quirk, Robert E. 1993. *Fidel Castro - The full story of his rise to power, his regime, his allies, and his adversaries.* W.W. Norton & Company, Inc., New York and London.

Rosset, Peter and Medea Benjamin (Editors). 1994. *The Greening of the Revolution - Cuba's experiment with organic agriculture.* Ocean Press, Melbourne. Principal authors: Medea Benjamin, Larry Burkham, Judith Carney, Jeffrey Dlott, Paul Gersper, Julio Monterrey, Ivette Perfecto, John Perkins, Carmen Rodriguez-Barbosa, Peter Rosset, Nina Shishkoff, and John Vandermeer. Contributors: Nanda Berman, Orville Coil, Carl Davidson, Jeanne Haught, Juan Martinez, John McConkey, Cesar Morales, Catherine Murphy, and Jeff Schatz (All except Medea Benjamin were members of the first U.S. Scientific Agricultural Delegation to Cuba,. November 1992).

Shishkoff, Nina. 1993. Plant diseases and their control by biological means. *Agriculture and Human Values,* Vol. X, No. 3, p. 24-30.

Snyder, Brian. 2003. *Cuba: a Clue to our Future?* Newfarm, PA Assoc. for Sust. Agric. (participant in the February 2003 Food First delegation to Cuba).

Vandermeer, John, Judith Carney, Paul Gersper, Ivette Perfecto and Peter Rosset. 1993. Cuba and the dilemma of modern agriculture. *Agriculture and Human Values,* Vol. X, No. 3, p. 3-8.

Werner, Matthew and Jorge Ramon Cuevas. 1996. *Vermiculture in Cuba.* Biocycle, June issue, p. 57 and 61-62.

In: Latin American Issues and Challenges
Editors: L. Naciamento and G. Sousa
ISBN 978-1-60692-349-8

Chapter 2

IMPLICATION OF U.S. RICE EXPORT PROMOTION PROGRAMS: THE CASE OF SELECTED LATIN AMERICAN COUNTRIES*

Dae-Seob Lee*†, *Yiqian Wang and P. Lynn Kennedy
Department of Agricultural Economics and Agribusiness,
Louisiana State University Agricultural Center, LA, USA

ABSTRACT

The U.S. domestic rice market will not likely be able to absorb projected increases in U.S. rice supply. Without export development, rice production would be constrained by limited U.S. domestic consumption. The main objective of the study is to analyze the effect of promotion programs and exchange rates with respect to rice exports to the three major U.S. long grain rough rice importers in Latin America. Ordinary Least Square (OLS) estimation is conducted as the first step. In addition, a Generalized Method of Moments (GMM) fitness test is conducted to correct the efficiency problem in the OLS. The study showed promotion expenditures to be significant only for Mexico and Honduras. The average return of each one dollar investment would result in $5 and $39 in the Mexican and Honduran markets using the Argentine exchange rate, and $3 and $45 in these respective markets using the Uruguayan exchange rate.

Key words: Latin America, export promotion programs, U.S. rice exports.

---

* A version of this chapter was also published in *Perspectives on International Agricultural Trade and Development*, edited by Dragan Miljkovic, published by Nova Science Publishers, Inc.. It was submitted for appropriate modifications in an effort to encourage wider dissemination of research.

† Corresponding author: Dae-Seob Lee, Assistant Professor 101 Agricultural Administration Building, Dept. of Agricultural Economics and Agribusiness, Louisiana State University, Baton Rouge, LA 70803. Tel. (225) 578-0345. Fax (225) 578-2716. Email: dlee@agcenter.lsu.edu

INTRODUCTION

More than 20 percent of total agricultural products in the United States have gone to export markets during recent decades. Export markets have become an important element in government decision-making related to economic development in the U.S. agricultural industry. The value of exports for agricultural products has grown rapidly over the past two decades. U.S. agricultural export revenues accounted for 20-30 percent of U.S. farm income during the last 30 years and are projected to remain at this level (USDA/FSA, *Fact Sheet*).

Assuming constant or increasing returns to scale in rice production, combined with improved technical expectations, the domestic rice markets would not be able to absorb the total domestic rice supply (Figure 1). Without export development, rice production would be constrained by the domestic rice consumption level.

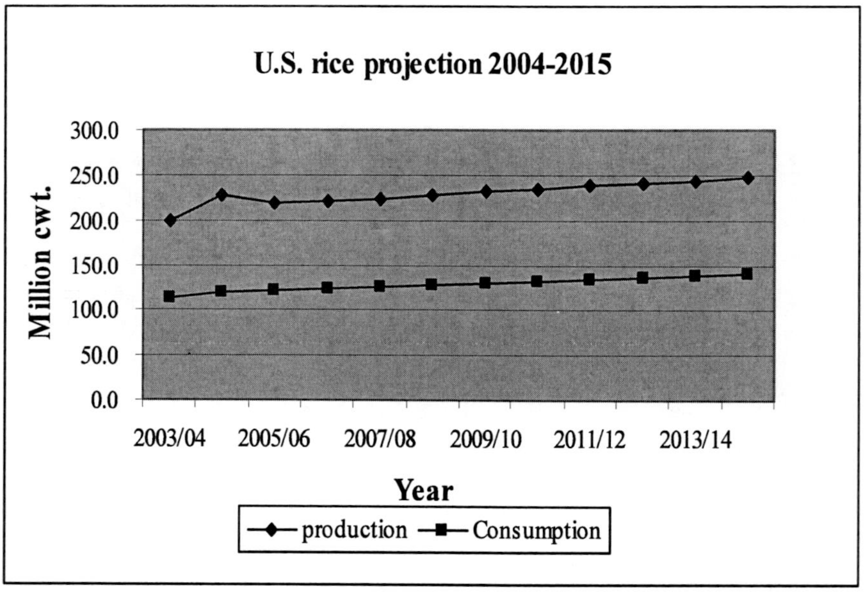

Source: USDA; 2005 USDA projections. Rice Outlook (2005), USDA

Figure 1. Rice Production and Consumption in the United States: 2004 - 2015

If the government fails to provide an acceptable support price, rice farmers could be driven out of business. Comparatively, the cost of a price-support policy would be much higher than the cost of export promotion projects, such as The Foreign Market Development Program (FMDP) and the Market Access Program (MAP). Those promotional policies for rice, with additional regional trade agreements and world trade agreements being considered, would create more opportunities for U.S. rice producers with an additional gain in social welfare.

Much of the literature focuses on specific commodities in different countries and regions and adopts various methodologies: seemingly unrelated regression (SUR) (Ward and Tang, 1978; Fuller, Bello, and Capps, 1992), single equation based econometric analysis (Binkely, 1981; Halliburton and Henneberry, 1995), and cross sectional time series analysis (Rosson, Hamming, and Jones, 1986; Le, Kaiser, and Tomek, 1998). Instead of focusing on specific methodologies, some studies analyzed the effects of exchange rates on U.S. export promotion program and expenditures (Schuh, 1975; Rosson, Adcock, and Hobbs, 2001; Adhikari et al., 2003).

The exchange rate is an essential element that influences the trade and competitiveness of U.S. agricultural products. Stable exchange would affect the long run U.S. agricultural economy. The existence of unpredictable fluctuation of exchange rates is an important source of risk to farmers and ranchers, processors, and traders. However, as a key force that influences the competitiveness of U.S. rice exports to the selected Latin American countries, competitors' exchange rates are considered in this study to understand how the competitors' exchange rate fluctuations would impact the U.S. rice exports to the selected Latin American countries. Empirically, own exchange rates are not included in the study because the prices of importing countries' rice are deflated by the importing countries' CPI and converted into U.S. dollar which reflects own exchange rate effects.

Over the past decade, the United States has lost substantial market share in Sub-Saharan Africa and the Middle East. However, rapid expansion in U.S. rough rice exports has offset much of the decline. Growth markets for rough rice exports are mainly in the Latin American region. Four countries in Latin America have been listed among the top ten U.S. rice buyers during the past 15 years. They are Mexico, Brazil, Costa Rica and Honduras. With the exception of Brazil, the others share common characteristics. U.S. rice exports to any of these three countries has taken more than 90% of the countries' import market share during the past fifteen years, along with an increasing import trend and a decrease in domestic production. Furthermore, during 1989-2003, the ratios of U.S. exports with respect to the total domestic consumption in Mexico, Costa Rica, and Honduras are 48%, 26%, and 60%, respectively, compared to approximately 2% for Brazil (USDA/FAS, *FATUS data base*). Therefore, this study focuses on these three countries: Mexico, Costa Rica, and Honduras.

The main objective of the study is to analyze the effect of promotion programs and exchange rates with respect to rice exports to the three major U.S. long grain rough rice importers in the selected Latin American Countries. Specific objectives are to develop a theoretical framework to analysis the economic factors which would affect the import demand in the three importing countries, to develop a model to estimate the import demand for Mexico, Costa Rica, and Honduras, and to evaluate the effectiveness of the promotion programs in expanding rice exports in the target markets.

The outline of the study is organized as follows: the next sections provide general information regarding U.S. rice trade with selected Latin American countries. The theoretic framework and procedures are then presented. Finally, the results and implications of the promotion programs are discussed.

U.S. Rice Trade With Selected Latin American Countries

Rice production and marketing is a multi-billion dollar activity in the United States. Rice is produced on over 3 million acres in the U.S. and accounts for $1.4 billion in farm revenues. Almost half of the rice produced in the U.S. is exported (USDA/ERS, *Outlook and Situation Yearbook*), which makes it critical for U.S. rice producers and exporters to fortify and develop international market activities (USDA/FAS, *Attaché reports*).

In terms of individual countries, U.S. exports of long grain rough rice to Mexico and Central America has become the major growth market. With none of the major Asian exporting countries allowing rough rice exports, the United States is the only major rice exporter that exports rough rice. The primary market for U.S. rough rice is Mexico, and Central American countries. Argentina, Uruguay, and Guyana ship small amounts of rough rice to Latin America. Under this situation, U.S. rough rice exports have expanded substantially since 1990/91, accounting for more than 30 percent in recent years (USDA/ERS, *Rice Outlook and Situation Year Book*).

The United States currently has a virtual monopoly on rice trade with Mexico, with an average of about 70 percent of Mexican rice imports coming from the United States during 1999-2003. Close geographic proximity and the existence of regional trade agreements, as well as sanitary and phytosanitary restrictions on Asian rice enacted by Mexico in 1993, solidify the monopoly power of the United States in this market (Zahniser and Link, 2002).

The North American Free Trade Agreement (NAFTA) benefits U.S. rice exports to Mexico, with a decreasing tariff for milled, rough, and broken rice. Before NAFTA, Mexico imposed import tariffs on U.S. rice, 20 percent on brown and milled rice and 10 percent on rough and broken rice. In 1990, the tariff rate for milled and brown U.S. rice was raised from 10 percent to 20 percent in response to demands from Mexican millers. Under NAFTA, Mexico was gradually lowering these rates to zero over the 9-year period that ended on January 1, 2003.

Honduras and Costa Rica are the primary U.S. rice importers in Central America. The United States has over a 90 percent share in both markets. Honduras had a dramatic decrease in its domestic production, which resulted from less government support and higher production costs compared to the price of importing rice. Rice imports from the United States increased during the past five years, with 90 percent of total domestic rice consumption being supplied by the United States. Costa Rica has kept a constant production level during 1989-2003, and domestic production is still a major source of satisfying domestic consumption. U.S. rice holds a nearly 99 percent import market share in Costa Rica.

Costa Rica and Honduras prefer rough rice imports to milled rice imports in order to support their domestic milling industries. According to the CAFTA agreement, Costa Rica gives a 50,000 metric ton (MT) duty-free quota to U.S. rough rice, increasing by 2 percent annually; the quota for milled rice is 5,000 MT, growing at 5 percent annually. Honduras provides U.S. rough rice a 90,000MT duty–free tariff-rated quota (TRQ) with 2 percent annual growth, and an 8,500MT duty-free TRQ for milled rice with 5 percent annual growth (USDA/FAS). Rice is a sensitive commodity to bring into trade negotiation, given that the domestic milling industries are highly protected in the targeted countries. This policy would provide little benefit to the U.S. milling industry although it provides the largest gains to U.S. rice producers. However, this current policy would benefit the U.S. rice industry if the sanitary restrictions are relaxed in the future. Asian exporters would still not receive market access, since they are not seeking to export rough rice.

U.S. Rice Export Promotion Programs

The United States Department of Agriculture (USDA) has four general categories of export promotion: consumer promotion, trade servicing, technical assistance, and export credit guarantee programs. Consumer promotion focuses on the retail level market. The intent is to raise the consumers' awareness for the products, build lasting preference, and increase the final consumption level through marketing activities. The Foreign Market Development Program (FMDP) and the Market Access Program (MAP) are the primary source of support for federal rice promotion (USDA/FAS).

The Foreign Market Development Program (FMDP) was created in 1955 and includes the Cooperator Market Development program (CMDP) and the Export Incentive Program (EIP), also administered by the Foreign Agricultural Service (FAS) of the USDA. The goal of the program is to develop, maintain, and expand long-term export markets for U.S. agricultural products, primarily through trade service and technical assistance programs. The program fosters a trade promotion partnership between USDA and U.S. agricultural producers and processors who are represented by non-profit commodity or trade associations called cooperators. Under this partnership, the USDA and cooperators pool their technical and financial resources to conduct market development activities outside the United States.

Since 1993, the Market Access Program (MAP) replaced the former Market Promotion Program (1991-1993) and the Targeted Export Assistance Program (TEA) (1986-1990). The MAP is a cost-share program that uses Commodity Credit Corporation (CCC) funds to support U.S. producers, exporters, private companies, and other trade organizations' promotional activities for U.S. agricultural products.

The U.S. Rice Federation (USARF) annual report indicates that their promotional activities in Mexico have resulted in a 200 percent increase of U.S. rice consumption in restaurants and doubled the U.S. rice long grain exports to Mexico from 1998 to 2003, including a 24 percent increase in 2001-2003 (USARF, www.usarice.com).

Through industry groups like USARF and the U.S. rice producer association (USRPA), U.S. rice producers, millers and exporters have joined together to develop export promotion effectiveness, increasing the international market demand of a variety of U.S. rice forms and types, including rough, brown, white, parboiled, and long, medium, and short grain.

THEORETICAL FRAMEWORK

This study assumes that, based on the different domestic and general import situations (imports from United States and the rest of world), the efficiency of promotion programs would differ among these three countries. The primary hypothesis to be tested is that U.S. export promotion expenditures have had a positive impact on the rice imports of selected Latin American countries. To test this hypothesis, two sets of econometric models have been applied. First, the single equation model tests the effect of the promotional programs and competitors' exchange rate fluctuation for each country. Analysis of exchange rate fluctuations shows how the competitor's exchange rates affect U.S. rice exports to the selected Latin American countries. The single-equation structural demand equation has been a popular method and remains in use for three reasons. The first reason is that demand for the studied commodities can be modeled independently with variables deemed necessary to determine demand for the commodity. Second, the data required is quite flexible. The final advantage is computational ease. Another popular method in the literature is the Almost Ideal Demand system (AIDs). The independent variable of AIDs is market share (Jan, Huang, and Epperson, 1999). However, the U.S. share of rice imports in three of the four countries is over

90% in the period studied (1989-2003). This implies that, AIDs may not be appropriate in these cases.

Binkley (1981) suggested that single-equation methods are appropriate for estimating import demand when the supply faced by importers is exogenous, i.e., the importer is a price-taker. He also suggested that in many cases in which demand (supply) are estimated, use of single-equation methods are justified on the basis that because of the highly elastic nature of supply (demand), simultaneous effects are of no practical consequence. In addition, economic theory offers little guidance on appropriate measures of variables which are included in the import demand function or on the appropriate functional form. An appropriate model is defined as one which generates unbiased and efficient elasticity estimates. Therefore, the precise specification of import demand is largely an empirical issue (Thursby and Thursby). This condition could be recognized in international rice trade where most of the rice producing countries are the major consumers, and leave only a small margin to be traded on the world market. In previous research, a single equation model has been specified to analyze the impact of promotion programs on export demand for several agricultural commodities, such as grapefruit (Fuller, Bello, and Capps, 1992), almonds (Halliburton and Henneberry, 1995; Onunkwo and Epperson, 2001), pecans (Epperson, 1999; Florkowski and Timothy, 1999; Onunkwo and Epperson, 2000), and poultry meat (Jan, Huang, and Epperson, 2002).

Ordinary Least Square (OLS) estimation is normally conducted as the first step to observe the relationship between explanatory variables and dependent variables. It holds strong estimation power in econometric analysis. The collinearity, heteroscedasticity, and autocorrelation tests are conducted to determine the efficiency of the single equation system result. A Generalized Method of Moments (GMM) fitness test is conducted to correct the efficiency problem caused by heteroscedasticity in the OLS.

The models considered in the study for the single country analysis are shown in equations (1) and (2), respectively.

$$y_{i,t} = \beta_0 + \beta_1 tds_{i,t} + \beta_2 tdc_{i,t} + \beta_3 pr_{i,t} + \beta_4 pw_{i,t} + \beta_5 pro_{i,t} + \beta_6 uex_{i,t} + e_{i,t} \tag{1}$$

$$y_{i,t} = \beta_0 + \beta_1 tds_{i,t} + \beta_2 tdc_{i,t} + \beta_3 pr_{i,t} + \beta_4 pw_{i,t} + \beta_5 pro_{i,t} + \beta_6 aex_{i,t} + e_{i,t} \tag{2}$$

where the subscript t refers to time, and subscript i represents the importing countries, Mexico, Costa Rica or Honduras. β_0 is the intercept and $e_{i,t}$ is the error term. The dependent variable $y_{i,t}$ represents the total import amount of U.S. rice exports to selected country i in year t.

For the explanatory variables, $pro_{i,t}$ denotes the promotional expenditure invested on country i in year t deflated by the United States CPI index; $pr_{i,t}$ and $pw_{i,t}$, denote the unit import prices in importing countries' currency for rice and wheat, respectively, deflated by the importing countries' CPI and converted into U.S. dollars; $tds_{i,t}$ denotes the total importing countries' annual domestic supply, including the initial stock and the domestic production. $tdc_{i,t}$ denotes the total importing countries' annual domestic consumption. $uex_{i,t}$ and $aex_{i,t}$

denote the real exchange rates of the competing exporting countries' currency in term of the U.S. dollar (Uruguayan Pesos and Argentine Pesos; See Table 1 for variable description).

Table 1. Variable Description

Variable	Source	Unit	Description
Y	USDA/FATUS	1,000 MT	Volume of U.S. exports.
Pro	USARF and USRPA	$1,000	Annual promotional programs expenditure, adjusted by the U.S. CPI (Consumer Price Index) [a]. TEA/MPP/MAP and FMDP included.
Pr	USDA/FATUS	$/MT	Export unit value [b] of rice-paddy, milled, adjusted by the U.S. CPI [a].
Pw	USDA/FATUS	$/MT	Export unit value [b] of wheat, unmilled, adjusted by the U.S. CPI [a].
TDS	PSandD	1,000 MT	Total annual domestic rice supply of the importing country, the sum of initial stock and domestic production.
TDC	PSandD	1,000 MT	Total annual domestic rice consumption of the importing country.
UEX	ERS	index	The real annual exchange rate between the Uruguay pesos and U.S. dollars.
AEX	ERS	index	The real annual exchange rate between the Argentina pesos and U.S. dollars.

Notes: a. CPI base year 1995 = 100. b. The Unit Value is calculated by dividing the sum of the value by the sum of the quantity converted to the FAS unit of measure to three decimal places (USDA/FATUS)

DATA

Annual data for the period 1989 through 2003 were used to estimate the export promotion effects. The Federal promotion program expenditure data (FMDP and MAP) used in the model was obtained from the USARF and USRPA, who are the only two recipients of the USDA/FAS promotional programs funds during the study period.

The data represent the aggregate expenditures distributed by the United States Department of Agricultural (USDA). Since MAP programs are processed by market-year (July-June) and FMDP programs are processed by calendar year, the MAP data were adjusted into a calendar-year basis data set by applying a two-year moving average method. Then, the total MAP and FMDP expenditures are summed to represent the rice export promotional expenditure. Only federal promotion program investments were included in the study.

The rice export, import, and unit values are obtained from the publication Foreign Agricultural Trade of the United States (USDA/FATUS). The export unit value derived from the total import value and quantity of each importing country is used as a proxy for the U.S. rice export price in each market. The CPI for the importing countries and the United States are collected from International Financial Statistics, published by International Monetary Fund.

ESTIMATION RESULTS

The parameter estimation of the export demand equation for U.S. rice is shown in Tables 2-4 for Mexico, Costa Rica, and Honduras, respectively. In general, F-values for most of equations are significant, and the measures of goodness-of-fit for the estimated equation are high. The adjusted R^2 value for Mexico, Costa Rica and Honduras are 0.97, 0.93, and 0.97, respectively.

Table 2. Parameter Estimation for Mexico

	OLS		GMM	
	Equation (1)	Equation (2)	Equation (1)	Equation (2)
Intercept	-688.29*	-991.02**	-688.29**	-991.02**
	(-2.07)	(-2.95)	(-3.02)	(-2.54)
Rice Export Price	-0.78	-0.72	-0.78*	-0.72*
	(-1.50)	(-1.16)	(-2.09)	(-1.91)
Wheat Export Price	1.08**	1.54**	1.08**	1.54***
	(2.32)	(2.92)	(2.65)	(4.25)
Total Mexican Domestic Rice Supply	-0.29	-0.435	-0.29	-0.435
	(-1.03)	(-1.24)	(-0.96)	(-1.01)
Total Mexican Domestic Rice Consumption	1.48**	1.70***	1.48***	1.70**
	(3.26)	(3.38)	(4.06)	(2.45)
Promotion Expenditures	0.014	0.009	0.014*	0.009
	(1.59)	(0.90)	(1.85)	(1.08)
Exchange rate Argentina Pesos: U.S. dollars	77.62**		77.62***	
	(3.34)		(6.00)	
Exchange rate Uruguay Pesos: U.S. dollars		11.55**		11.55**
		(2.52)		(2.30)
Durbin-W	2.806	2.611	2.806	2.611
F value	65.37***	48.61***	-	-
Adj. R^2	0.9650	0.9533	0.9650	0.9533

Note: Single asterisk (*), double asterisk (**), and triple asterisk (***) denote rejection of H_0 at 0.10, 0.05, 0.01 significance levels respectively

The Durbin-Watson statistic tests and the collinearity diagnostics tests do not indicate problems with autocorrelation and collinearity for the three markets. The heteroskedasticity test is obtained from the White test statistic. The null hypothesis for the test is that the variance of the residuals is homogenous. However, the chi-square value ranges from approximately 10.0-13.0, compare with the critical value 27.58. This indicates that there is a heteroskedasticity problem for the model. With the presence of heteroskedasticity, the covariance matrix is incorrect; the estimation is unbiased and consistent, but inefficient.

Table 3. Parameter Estimation for Costa Rica

	OLS		GMM	
	Equation (1)	Equation (2)	Equation (1)	Equation (2)
Intercept	-193.69**	-263.42**	-193.69**	-263.42**
	(-2.33)	(-3.01)	(-2.50)	(-3.28)
Rice Export Price	-0.08*	-0.094*	-0.08***	-0.094***
	(-1.84)	(-2.27)	(-3.96)	(-5.17)
Wheat Export Price	0.53**	0.65***	0.53***	0.65***
	(2.82)	(3.58)	(4.12)	(4.17)
Total Costa Rica Domestic Rice	-0.22	-0.13	-0.22	-0.13
Supply	(-0.94)	(-0.60)	(-1.38)	(-0.85)
Total Costa Rica Domestic Rice	1.02***	1.06***	1.02***	1.06***
Consumption	(3.40)	(3.76)	(3.32)	(3.85)
Promotion Expenditures	0.17	0.18	0.17	0.18
	(1.27)	(1.44)	(0.98)	(1.08)
Exchange rate	15.64*		15.64**	
Argentina Pesos: U.S. dollars	(1.97)		(2.81)	
Exchange rate		3.45**		3.45***
Uruguay Pesos: U.S. dollars		(2.31)		(4.10)
Durbin-W	2.983	3.188	2.984	3.188
F value	8.66***	9.91***	-	-
Adj. R^2	0.9265	0.9325	0.9265	0.9325

Note: Single asterisk (*), double asterisk (**), and triple asterisk (***) denote rejection of H_0 at 0.10, 0.05, 0.01 significance levels respectively

With error variance relationship unknown, the GMM method is applied as a remedial measure to solve the problem. The correction to the standard error uses the Newey West correction.

For the most part, the estimated parameters displayed signs consistent with prior expectations. The own-price parameters are consistently negative and significant for the three countries; the demand and price are inversely related. The price for wheat has a positive sign, which indicates that wheat is a substitute for rice in these three markets. Generally, the import demand of the three countries is more responsive to own-price than promotion expenditures. The estimation of the wheat price suggests that wheat is an elastic substitute for rice in Mexico and Costa Rica, but less elastic for the Honduran market. This result partially supports a previous study which focuses on Mexican rice import markets (Salin et al., 2000).

The results indicate a negative relationship between total domestic supply and export demand. The greater domestic production and initial stocks, the less that rice would be demanded from the foreign market. Honduras shows a significant relationship between the domestic supply and import demand (-0.34/-0.56). The total domestic rice supply also shows a negative relationship in Mexico (-0.29/-0.435) and Costa Rica (-0.22/-0.13). The positive parameter estimation for total domestic consumption shows the demand for rice imports would increase with an increasing total domestic consumption level.

Table 4. Parameter Estimation for Honduras

	OLS		GMM	
	Equation (1)	Equation (2)	Equation (1)	Equation (2)
Intercept	-31.62	-61.19*	-31.62	-61.19*
	(-0.89)	(-1.87)	(-1.22)	(-2.23)
Rice Export Price	-0.12**	-0.11**	-0.12**	-0.11**
	(-3.12)	(-3.24)	(-2.57)	(-3.20)
Wheat Export Price	0.03	0.084	0.03	0.084
	(0.18)	(0.65)	(0.23)	(0.86)
Total Honduras Domestic Rice Supply	-0.34	-0.56**	-0.34*	-0.56***
	(-1.42)	(-2.46)	(-2.04)	(-3.73)
Total Honduras Domestic Rice	1.83***	1.89***	1.83***	1.89***
Consumption	(6.83)	(7.98)	(9.33)	(10.09)
Promotion Expenditures	0.033	0.042	0.033**	0.042**
	(1.26)	(1.77)	(2.46)	(2.68)
Exchange rate	8.79*		8.79**	
Argentina Pesos: U.S. dollars	(2.04)		(2.75)	
Exchange rate		1.29		1.29***
Uruguay Pesos: U.S. dollars		(1.56)		(4.01)
Durbin-W	2.850	2.951	2.850	2.951
F value	64.82***	81.86***	-	-
Adj. R^2	0.975	0.972	0.965	0.972

Note: Single asterisk (*), double asterisk (**), and triple asterisk (***) denote rejection of H_0 at 0.10, 0.05, 0.01 significance levels respectively

The promotion expenditures are positive and significant in the Mexican and Honduran markets. This indicates that each dollar of promotion expenditure generated a positive quantity of rice exports from the U.S. rice exporters to those two importing countries. However, it is important to note that only the federal government money is included, which may exaggerate the promotion programs' effect. If the promotion programs' expenditure is the same as the private group expenditures, the return of promotion programs could be divided by two to obtain the actual dollar return per dollar invested.

The exchange rate of the competitor is positive and significant. This suggests that a strong competitor currency would benefit U.S. rice exporters. The strong currency would increase U.S. exports. If we assume that rice produced in Uruguay and Argentina is the same quality as U.S. rice, if price differences are not large, then an appreciation of the Uruguayan and Argentine pesos would increase the demand for U.S. rice. Both countries are experiencing a strong currency against U.S. dollars, which may be part of the reason the United States holds such a large market share in the three importing rice markets after competition from Asian markets is eliminated.

Table 5. Elasticities Estimation for Own Price and Export Promotion

		Own price elasticity	Promotion Expenditure Elasticity
Mexico	UEX[a]	-0.97*	0.0134**
	AEX[b]	-0.96*	0.0240*
Costa Rica	UEX[a]	-5.15***	0.153
	AEX[b]	-5.09***	0.136
Honduras	UEX[a]	-0.838**	0.036*
	AEX[b]	-0.62	0.031*

Notes: Elasticities are calculated by the method of OLS with log-log model, show in each cell in three lines from up down respectively. Single asterisk (*), double asterisk (**), and triple asterisk (***) denote rejection of H_0 at 0.10, 0.05, 0.01 significance levels respectively, a: The elasticities are derived from the model with Uruguay exchange rate, b: The elasticities are derived from the model with Argentina exchange rate

The elasticities for own price and promotion are derived through transforming the previous model into log-log form. The results are shown in Table 6. The own price elasticities for Mexico are -0.97 and -0.96 for the model using the Uruguayan exchange rate and the Argentine exchange rate, respectively. Every one percent increase of the promotion programs would result in a 0.96 percent decreasing in the import demand. The promotion expenditures elasticities differ in the two equations, which are 0.0134 and 0.0240 for Uruguayan and Argentine equations, respectively.

For Honduras, the own price elasticities are -0.828 and -0.615, and the promotion expenditure elasticities are 0.036 and 0.031 for Uruguay and Argentina equation respectively. Costa Rica has very high price elasticity levels, with -5.15 and -5.09 for Uruguayan and Argentine exchange rates, respectively. The Costa Rica market acts more sensitively than the other two, since the U.S. rice import ratio only account an average 26 percent in the studying period. The promotion elasticity is higher than other two markets, 0.153 and 0.136 for Uruguay and Argentina, respectively.

The promotion expenditure return could be calculated using the elasticities obtained from this section. The average marginal return on promotion expenditure for each country could be obtained by multiplying the elasticity by mean value of export expenditures, and then dividing by the mean value of export promotion expenditures. Based on the elasticities derived in table 5, the return ranged from 3 to 5 dollars for the Mexican market, and the from 39 to 45 dollars for the Honduran market with respect to each one dollar investment in promotions from 1989-2003. However, this method simply provides the gross return without considering the production and export cost, and is overestimated by not including the private sector's promotion investment.

Table 6. Estimate of Lag Distribution: Decaying Promotion Effect

	Mexico		Costa Rica		Honduras	
Lag variable	Estimate	t value	Estimate	t value	Estimate	t value
lPro_0[a]	0.42	1.77	-0.14	-1.1	0.19***	108.07
lPro_1	0.25	1.01	0.02	0.33	0.07***	53.59
lPro_2	0.14	0.52	0.12	0.85	-0.01***	-7.29
lPro_3	0.08	0.36	0.13	0.91	-0.06***	-33.86
lPro_4	0.08	0.77	0.07	0.81	-0.07***	-44.23

Note: lPro_0, lPro_1, lPro_2, lPro_3 and lPro_4 represent the lag distribution from 0 to 4.

PROMOTION PROGRAMS LAGS

Lags in consumer behavior in response to advertising programs would occur between current sales and future sales. The effect of the advertising programs is assumed to show significant not only in the initial year, but has a finite declining procedure. Because of the habit persistence and lags in consumer behavior, time lags must be considered in the model. Distributed lags analysis is a specialized technique for examining the relationships between import demands and advertising programs that involve some delay.

As with other domestic advertising, international promotion programs also hold a decaying effect. A consistent investment in promotion programs would effectively increase the rice consumption demand and maintain the market share in the targeted importing countries in long run. Given factors in addition to the domestic market, the international promotional programs could require more work to analyze.

The polynomial distributed lag models are applied to the analysis of the impact of generic promotion on the demand for rice in three targeted markets. The current year promotion programs have much more impact on the rice import demand for Mexico and Honduras, then decay for the following years. For Costa Rica, there has been a slow lag time for the promotion programs to take effect. A possibility for this result is that the Costa Rican market is a mature market for rice consumption with a much higher per capita consumption level than compared to the other countries. A mature market could already have its own taste, consumption patterns, and loyalty to a certain type of rice. It would take a longer time for the new supplier to adjust to the market and learn its characteristics. The strategies to gain market share in such a market would be a consistent persuasive advertising pattern to attract and switch the consumer appetites and purchasing habits. However, only the estimated results for Honduras are significant, with the first year promotion effect of 0.19, decreasing to 0.07 in the second year. The insignificance of the results maybe due to data limitations; a short time-series of fifteen observations would inflate the error term and decrease the t value (Table 6).

IMPLICATIONS

The study showed promotion expenditures to be significant only for Mexico and Honduras. The average returns to Honduras show effectiveness of the promotion programs. This does not necessarily imply that promotion programs do not work in the other two markets. Given the returns over the promotion expenditure, the promotion programs should be continued in the targeted markets. The increase in the demand for U.S.-grown rice in those markets would continuously become a source of expanding U.S. rice sales.

Also, for markets with different levels of per capita consumption, the promotion programs should be designed separately. For the Mexican and Honduran markets, the promotion programs should continuously focus on promoting demand for U.S. rice. In markets which already consume large quantities of rice, the emphasis should be left on gaining more market share from local producers and other rice exporters. Given this, further study focusing on the price elasticity and other exporters' competitiveness would be important.

The U.S. rice exports to the three targeted countries, Mexico, Honduras and Costa Rica, hold over 90 percent of the import markets in recent years. If this situation changes due to the release of the previous sanitary restriction on Asian-grown rice, the Asian exporters could become strong competitors in those markets. The existing cost and price advantage of Asian rice exporters may shrink the current U.S. rice market share in the Latin American market. If the rice imported from the Asian markets are substitutable for U.S. rice, then price would become a dominant decision-making element for consumers and importers in importing countries. However, there is no indication as to when this sanitary restriction could be eliminated. Even if this restriction were eliminated, Asian access to this market may be limited due to preferential treatment received by U.S. producers under the NAFTA and CAFTA agreements. Given that rice is a sensitive commodity in the region, it is difficult to predict trade liberalization that may occur through the World Trade Organization negotiations.

MAP and FMDP focus more on the generic advertising than on brand sales, which means that although the consumption demand increased, the advertisers may not benefit from the money spent on promotion. Local rice producers and other exporters could easily act as free-riders and reduce the newly-gained market share. It may give promotion expenditure more flexibility by allowing promotional monies to be spent not only on generic advertising but also targeted at the brand level. Brand loyalty could be a more consistent motive than the general knowledge of the benefits of rice, such as better nutrition, ease of cooking and combining to local food taste.

CONCLUDING REMARKS

An import demand equation for the U.S. rice was estimated, with special focus on the two major export promotion programs: Foreign Market Development Program (FMDP) and Market Access Program (MAP). The Ordinary Least Squares method was used to estimate the equation based on annual exports to Mexico, Costa Rica and Honduras from 1989 to 2003. These countries represent the major export markets for U.S. long grain rough rice, which became the fastest increasing rice export market. Their preference for rough rice distinguishes their position in the world rice market, which would benefit U.S. rice exports.

The empirical analysis consists of three parts. The first part contains the regression estimation results and the interpretation of the promotion expenditure and exchange rate pass-through from competitor's currencies. In the second part, the elasticities for the own price and promotion expenditure were derived. Finally, the lagged effects of the promotion programs are tested to investigate the trend of the long-run decaying positive promotion effects. The empirical evidence from the regression analysis is supportive of the promotion programs and exchange rate effect of competitors' currency fluctuation with respect to U.S. dollars.

In the econometric model, the validity of the promotion effect for those importing countries was estimated. In addition, various lag lengths were considered, in addition to the original value of the promotion expenditures, in an attempt to test the promotion effect in the current year and long run. The results indicate a tendency for promotion to have the highest effect on current import demand in the Mexican and Honduran markets. In the case of Costa Rica, the promotion programs may come into effect in the long run. The results generally support the hypothesis that the promotion programs have a positive impact on U.S. rice exports to Mexico and Honduras, and Costa Rica to a lesser extent. Nevertheless, future research may include the supply and demand systems in world long grain rice trade, which would provide further understanding of the rice markets in the Latin American region. Details on the long grain rice production cost in the exporting countries and importing countries, the transportation costs, trade policies, and importing market's rice market development could be considered in future studies of the market.

REFERENCES

Adhikari, M., L. Paudel, J.E. Houston, and B.N. Paudel. 2003. "Measuring the Impacts of U.S. Export Promotion Program for Wheat in Selected Importing Regions." Selected Paper for Southern Agricultural Economics Association Annual Meeting, Mobile, Alabama, February 1-5.

Binkley, J. 1981. "The Relationship between Elasticity and least squares bias." *The Review of Economics and Statistics.* 63:307-309.

Epperson, J.E. 1999. "The Effectiveness of U.S. Promotion Programs on the Export Demand for U.S. Pecans." *Journal of Food Distribution Research.* 30:169-170.

Florkowski, W.J. and A.P. Timothy. 1999. "Promotional Programs and Consumer Purchasing Decisions: Pecan Demand Models." *Applied Economics.* 33:763-770.

Fuller, S.F., H. Bello, H, and O. Capps. 1992. "Import Demands for U.S. Fresh Grapefruit: Effect of U.S. Promotion Programs and Trade Policies of Importing Nations." *Journal of Agricultural and Applied Economics.* 24(2):251-260.

Le, C. T., H.M. Kaiser, and W. Tomek, W. 1998. "Export promotion and import demand for U.S. red meat in selected Pacific Rim countries." *Agribusiness: an International Journal.* 14(1):95-105.

Halliburton, K. and S. Henneberry. 1995. "The effectiveness of U.S. Nonprice Promotion of Almonds in the Pacific Rim." *Journal of Agricultural and Resource Economics.* 20(1):108-121.

International Monetary Fund (IMF), *International Financial Statistics*. Washington DC. Various issues.

Jan, M.S., C.L. Huang, and J.E. Epperson. 1999. "U.S. Export Demand for Poultry Meat Products: A Bayesian Approach for Almost Ideal Demand System (AIDS) Model Estimation." *Journal of Food Distribution Research*. 30(1):172-183.

Jan, M.S., C.L. Huang, and J.E. Epperson. 2002. "Estimating the Effects of Non-Price Promotion on Export Demands for U.S. Poultry Meat." *Journal of International Food and Agribusiness Marketing*. 13(1):61-82.

Onunkwo, I.M., and J.E. Epperson. 2000. "Export Demand for U.S. Pecan: Impacts of U.S. Export Promotion Programs." *Agribusiness: an International Journal*. 16(2):253-265.

__________. 2001. "Export Demand for U.S. Almond: Impacts of U.S. Export Promotion Programs." *Journal of Food Distribution Research*. 32(1): 140-151.

Rosson, C.P. III, M.D. Hamming, and J.W. Jones. 1986. "Foreign Market Promotion Programs: An Analysis of Promotion Response for Apples, Poultry, and Tobacco." *Agribusiness*. 2(1):33-42.

Rosson, P., F. Adcock, and A. Hobbs. 2001. "Exchange Rate Impacts on U.S. Agriculture and the Potential Role of Dollarization." A study provided for the American Farm Bureau Federation.

Slain, V., G. Williams, M. Haigh, J. Malaga, J.C. Madrinan, and K. Sheaff. 2000. "Structure of The Mexican Rice Industry: Implications for Strategic Planning." TAMRC International Market Research Report No. IM 2-00.

Schuh, G. E. 1974. "The Exchange Rate and U.S. Agriculture." *American Journal of Agricultural Economics*. 56(1):1-13.

U.S.A. Rice Federation. http://www.usarice.com.

U.S.A. Rice Producer Association. http://www.usriceproducers.com.

U.S. Department of Agriculture-Economic Research Service (ERS). *Rice Situation and Outlook*. Washington DC: U.S. Department of Agriculture, Various issues.

U.S. Department of Agriculture, Foreign Agricultural Service (FAS), *Attaché reports*. Washington DC: U.S. Department of Agriculture, Various issues.

U.S. Department of Agriculture, Farm Service Agency (FSA), *Fact Sheet*. Washington DC: U.S. Department of Agriculture, Various issues.

Ward, R.W. and J. Tang. 1978. "U.S. Grapefruit Exports and Japanese Trade Restrictions." *Southern Journal of Agricultural Economics*. 10(1):77-82.

Zahniser, S. and J. Link. 2002. "Effects of North American Free Trade Agreement on Agriculture and the Rural Economy." USDA/ERS Agricultural and Trade Reports. WRS-02-1.

In: Latin American Issues and Challenges
Editors: L. Naciamento and G. Sousa
ISBN 978-1-60692-349-8

Chapter 3

FROM ARGIROPOLIS TO MACONDO: LATIN AMERICAN INTELLECTUALS AND THE TASKS OF MODERNIZATION

Emil Volek
Arizona State University, Tempe, USA

In the current crisis, … intellectual work (needs to be) understood as public service and as civilizational obligation.
Alfonso Reyes, Notas sobre la inteligencia americana (1935)

ABSTRACT

In the 20th century, Latin American attempts at self-analysis have gotten bogged down in the imaginary invention of the Latin American "being" or have been derailed by scores of foreign blueprints and local revolutionary myths. This chapter focuses on the attitudes of Latin American *intelligentsia* towards modernity and the tasks of modernization of their countries after the Independence. Between the 19th and the 20th centuries, in accord with the changes of the European *intelligentsia* positions, the advocacy for modernization in Latin America has been substituted by the search for the mirage of cultural identity. The postulate of an absolute otherness for the continent has led to the splendors and misery of the *macondismo.* The projects espoused by Domingo Faustino Sarmiento, José Martí, José Enrique Rodó, José Vasconcelos, José Carlos Mariátegui, and Octavio Paz are discussed in some length as a critique of the road to the *macondismo* and of its consequences for the continent.

INTRODUCTION

The Spanish-speaking part of Latin America will soon begin celebrating two hundred years of Independence (the River Plate region and Mexico both in 2010). The first one hundred years of "progress" were greeted with a big patriotic splash (Salas), in May of 1910 in Argentina and in October in Mexico. Yet the oligarchic republic was already in full-blown crisis in Argentina, where the 1916 elections would radically change the political landscape by sweeping into power the populist Radical Party under Hipólito Irigoyen, while in Mexico, the Revolution would explode just a couple of weeks after the rigged November reelection of the perennial Porfirio Díaz. This quick turn of events was symptomatic of the region's crisis of modernization.

Signs of exhaustion of the 19th century model of modernization as introduced to Latin American countries were all over the place. What served well for the developed center did not bring the expected miracles to the underdeveloped periphery, yet the accumulation of wealth in some of these countries was spectacular. However, wealth in the hands of a few would only aggravate conflicts with the emerging pauper mass society. At the turn of the century, the River Plate region reached the peak of illusion of general prosperity, accompanied by the delusion of being a world power.[1] The First World War would feed the last orgy of this classical liberal *laissez-faire* model, followed by the coup de grâce administered to it by the changed world landscape and by a series of economic crises in which the free trade world collapsed.

The situation was further complicated by the exhaustion of the 19th century "scientism" (embodied in the philosophy of Positivism) that was, to top it off, used in some quarters as appendage to oligarchic politics (for example, the notorious "scientific Government" of Porfirio Díaz covering his old-fashioned dictatorship with the fig leaf of "modernity"). Among the legacies of Positivism, there was especially one strand of inquiry that brought many sleepless nights to Latin America: the pseudo-scientific theory of races. This was a sensitive issue for a continent multiracial by definition. Actually, Latin America struggled with this "problem" since the very beginning, when the closely watched *pureza de sangre* produced the unwieldy "castas" system for those who did not qualify upfront (Lomnitz). In the context of the sputtering modernization, the race theory offered many useful explanations for the failure. Besides the Church, the Indian was declared the main obstacle to modernization. Different "shock treatments" were devised to deal with the "sick" and "degenerate" race. The vogue of "raw naturalism" in literature added intensity to the hues in the negative image of the Indian. An additional problem was the alleged maleficent miscegenation that supposedly drew together the worst from the original races. The *mestizo* was the pits. At least the Indian had had some glorious history. Only the white Creole and the arduous process of "whitening" of "inferior" races were the solution for the problem.

However, the "scientific" theory was running afoul of the already well-established romantic image of the *noble savage* and of the romantic critique of the civilization in all its forms (especially the modern). This sentimental tradition pushed for a sweeping celebratory revaluation of the Indian as well as of his next kin, the *mestizo,* as closest to nature (whatever that might be).[2]

---

[1] Emir Rodríguez Monegal (1969) has explored the "literary" effects of the obscene wealth of the River Plate oligarchy at the turn of the century, when, among other things, new local forms of "trickle down" economy were discovered (for example, when the allegedly almost naked heiress of a huge *pampa* ranching fortune enjoyed throwing one pound sterling bills from the balcony of a centric hotel and residence of diplomats). The delusion of power will weigh heavily on the Argentine social imaginary, self-image, and on that country's troubled quixotic relations with the United States throughout the 20th century (Escudé).

[2] The traditional imaginary, aided by History, focuses on an Indian woman usually raped by some white fellow or, later, by a *mestizo*, who quickly fade away from the picture of the Hispanic "Sacred Family," consisting of the mother, the kid, and the absent father as the norm. The *Boom* and the *Postboom* novel of the 1960s and 70s

Cultural traditions in conflict created a whole range of opposing ideological options to choose from. The exhaustion of the positivist "scientific" paradigm opened, now unhindered, the gates of sentimental romanticism, again. The recent vogue of the "subaltern" enlightened by the halo of romanticized mythology will be just another avatar in the *noble savage* line of opportunistic political transformations.

The first serious attempt at modernization of the region, in the second half of the 19th century, coupled with the influx of new European immigrants (more pronounced in the Southern Cone), was bound to provoke a conservative-nationalistic backlash. Yet, what should those nations be? What might their anchors vis-à-vis the immigration onslaught and emerging urban mass society be? All self-respecting high-end intellectuals got to work on this all-important pipe dream.[3] In all of their concoctions of the nation, diverse strands of conservative Romanticism from France and Germany came to the fore and stressed *culture* over *modernity.* The only problem with this critique of modernity, copied from Europe, was that France and Germany continued to modernize, in spite of the misgivings of their intellectuals, while Latin America did not figure out the crossroads.

After a brief hesitation about what that "culture" should be, "classic" or "romantic," the romantic interpretation regained ground. Romantic culture relied on the nature and on the "natural man" to do its chores. What did not come "naturally," from the heart or from the inside of a society, need not bother to come at all. Particularly unwelcome was everything modern, always encroaching from outside, upsetting venerable traditions and patriarchal ways of life. In the River Plate region, the *gaucho* was brought back from the grave and ascended from a bandit to the symbol of nationhood;[4] in his absence, even the good old *criollo* small-time ranchers would do, defending their leisure and guitar-playing as they were against the entrepreneurial upstart *gringos* (at that time, the Italian immigrants) who were intruding upon their territory. In this story, plotted to the tune of the manly, *macho,* local traditions, it is the Creole man and the *gringo* woman who reconcile their differences in holy matrimony.

This defensive "cultural turn" would weigh heavily on Latin America and her imaginary throughout the 20th century, even long after the elite intellectual *letrado* is overwhelmed by the mass society from the 1920s on. The humanistic culture would become the prime if not the sole object of educational pursuits. Everything suspect of "practical" use would be shunned. In those few unavoidable cases, reading novels and poetry would be a necessary redeeming feature. The high European culture would become the standard to emulate or simulate (the travel to the source would be highly appreciated and would be recognized as anointment sign for leadership roles). Narcissistic cultural self-centeredness would become the ideal of the intellectual priesthood. The defense of the presumed virginal cultural identity–

---

added a new ending to this story: the "mama" works her way up to become shrewd owner of a luxury brothel in the capital, and the white guy now pays a hefty price to "repossess" her and get other, especially political, favors. Many a revolution will be generated in the beds of these deep-rooted cultural institutions.

3 The process of inventing modern nations as "imagined communities" is broached in Anderson (1991). In Latin America, the imagination goes in one direction in the 19th century and in another in the 20th. Only the romantic sentimental melodrama works as the thread uniting both. What strikes the foreigner—especially the one coming from the subdued rationalistic modernity—as refreshing "intensity" and "depth of feeling," is the conventional expected cultural expression there.

4 *Gaucho* was many things at different times: originally, a *criollo* squatter on the free and vast *pampa;* a celebrated freedom-fighter during the Independence wars; a hated supporter of *caudillos* in the ensuing civil wars; a rebellious and disturbing element on the privatized and modernized *pampa* in the later peace times; a forced conscript in the wars with the *pampa* Indians, in an effort to extinguish both.

hidden somewhere deep down—from the ravages of modernization and from foreign interlopers would saddle even the left of all shades as it was emerging in subsequent revolutionary cycles after First World War.

In his *Identity and Modernity in Latin America,* the Chilean sociologist Jorge Larraín has argued that, among Latin American intellectuals, there has been a manifest tendency "to consider modernity as something external and in opposition to identity" (2000: 206-7). Thus, a broad polarity of "alternate periods" may be established: "modernity in periods of expansion" and "identity in times of crisis" (207). However, for Larraín himself, both the modernity and the cultural identity constructions are historical processes and, as such, are intimately intertwined. In this way, he argues, both processes and the pendulum swings characterizing their respective hegemony in different periods have jointly become parts of Latin America's troubled modernization efforts and of her no less troubled self-affirmation constructs. This chapter will focus on the saga of the Latin American intellectual (the *letrado,* the *pensador*) in these processes and on his contributions to the topsy-turvy roads of "self-invention" of the Continent as a distinct cultural entity.

At Independence, due to the fact that Latin American societies were deeply conservative, the task of modernization in the new countries in formation fell into the hands of the elite "enlightened" intellectuals. After the first failures of nation building, an impressive generation of "public intellectuals" stepped forward (in Argentina, the Generation of 1837). The ensuing battle between liberals and conservatives for the Latin American "soul" produced a heated debate over the "true Americanism" that is still paradigmatic today, although the particular roles of the parties involved changed surreptitiously at the turn of the century when the old liberals adopted the conservative agenda and vice versa (O'Gorman).

However, as the 19th century paradigm of modernization ran its course, the public intellectual was replaced by a generation of *literati.* The new crop of intellectuals turned their back on modernity and modernized...literature. José Martí and José Enrique Rodó would mark the beginning and the end-point of this u-turn. Under the influence of diverse strands of conservative Romanticism, the search for some "deep-rooted traditions and underground spiritual dimensions" of America (the *América profunda*) got underway, and a new image of Latin America began to emerge, coalescing in García Márquez's metaphor of Latin America as a postmodern and kitschy *Macondo,* substituting for Sarmiento's utopian futuristic vision for the region as a modern *Argirópolis.*

As a consequence of these processes, the intellectual became a major liability and challenge for the 20th century Latin America.

The overall decline of the intellectual and his many all too human weaknesses in turbulent modern times have been amply explored (in Molnar, Johnson). In this chapter I will focus on the Latin American specimen in his historical milieu, but, whenever needed, I will contextualize his journey within contemporary intellectual currents. Obviously, I will not be able to offer the whole story of the Latin American intelligentsia in the last two hundred years. A reopening of some key questions and vistas must suffice.

The Argentine Generation of 1837

This is the most talked about generation in Latin America (for basic historical overview see Shumway), the one most celebrated, most maligned, and most stereotyped. In many ways, however, this generation has been surprisingly poorly read.[5] Its members embodied the modernization ideal, and were judged accordingly: since their side won, temporarily, they were called to write the official history of the country; but as their project stalled and came under attack, waves of "revisionist" history began pounding on them. In Argentina, the heated debate pro and con continues to this date unabated.

Judging from their first writings, these intellectuals—still in transition between Enlightenment and Romanticism—were a surprisingly pragmatic bunch. They were conscious of the failure of the previous "ideological" generation that only led the country into fratricidal wars. Another limitation of that generation, as they saw it, was that everybody was coming with his own preferred idol and wanted to impose dogmatically his partial interpretation; in contradistinction, they were for a systemic solution, and this could not be a mere copy of anything. Further, they proposed themselves as beyond the old conflicts between the *unitarios* and the *federales*,[6] but, unfortunately, they happened to raise their heads in times of consolidated dictatorship of the "federalist" General Rosas.

Juan Manuel Rosas created a perfect and long-lasting reign of terror in Argentina. He was slow in showing his true colors. He began as the "Restorer of the Laws," which was rightfully appreciated by many in those war-torn times. Yet then, under the guise of "federalism," he slowly but surely dominated among the provincial *caudillos*, and so de facto "centralized," the country from his bastion in the Buenos Aires province. One cannot fathom Argentine history without understanding what the city of Buenos Aires has meant for that country: as the only big maritime port, all commerce with the world had to pass through it and, as a consequence, Buenos Aires has maintained an economic stranglehold on the country, which has ended up organized around this one city, and has resented it ever since. Yet all attempts to defeat this Goliath have failed so far.[7] Due to its geographic and economic position, Buenos Aires has also been the face of the country to the world. Rosas used this privileged situation fully to his advantage.

Another striking feature of his government was the intimate involvement of his family in the state affairs. To assure that the "people" supported him enthusiastically, his wife had organized the "Mazorca" vigilantes movement (*mazorca* appears to be playing on "corn," but its meaning was coming ominously from the cries of Rosas' supporters, "más horca," "more gallows"), and his daughter had graciously mastered a web of spies constituted of the black women servants in the patrician households: the *unitarios* were held by their throats, and were in danger of having them slit at the least provocation, suspicion, or whim. Those patriotic times had even ready special music for the occasion ("La resbalosa"), favored at sending to afterlife enemy prisoners by cutting their throats... It was not the time for the faint-hearted.

Rosas also hijacked opportunistically the idea of "Americanism" and did not hesitate to use the conflicts with foreign powers to play on the "natural" patriotic disposition of his

---

5 Some recent poor readings outside of Argentine context have been aided by tons of Theory (as in Alonso or Sommer).

6 *Unitarios,* the patrician liberals concentrated in Buenos Aires, advocating centralized government, under the guidance of their city, of course; and the *federales,* the conservatives from the countryside and from the provinces, fought for the federal organization of the country and for equal rights of all parts. Geography and economics complicated the liberals vs. conservatives struggle.

7 Reference is made to the title of Ezequiel Martínez Estrada's famous invective against the city, *La cabeza de Goliath* (1940). Attempts at reconfiguration of the country will be repeated, but Buenos Aires would always come on top at the end. This has led to an uneasy feeling that a proper political arrangement for Argentina has not been found yet. A number of Latin American countries are in the same predicament, however.

people. Surviving the French and the English blockades only added to his *americanista* cachet. To top it off, the high patriotic sentiment was used for other good practical and "patriotic" purposes: in order to force everybody to show off support for him and to further intimidate the designated "enemies" (the "savage *unitarios,*" as the official slogan went), a special dress code was imposed: the European decadent tailcoat was out, the American manly poncho was in, among other strictures (Sarmiento 2003: 226). Esteban Echeverría (1805-1851) captured this atmosphere of sheer terror in his magnificent short story "El matadero" (The Slaughterhouse, written in 1838-1840, published posthumously).

Rosas himself was an ascetic and his trip was the power; but power corrupts and the lofty principles allegedly defended turned more and more on his personal whims. That was what did him in at the end, and the fact that he was defeated not by the *unitarios* but by his fellow *federales* impacted the political moves in the following period. His attitude toward the country, typical in Latin America to this day, was that the State was his personal patrimony with which he could dispose as he pleased. All in all, his dictatorship was to be prophetic in many ways, and would be closely imitated by many victorious political movements based on "organized" popular support, both in Argentina and in Latin America up to this day. And Latin American intellectuals would be intimately involved on both sides of the "barricades" (whatever they symbolized at different times).

The Generation of 1837 wanted to serve their country even if that country was Rosas. Its members tried to look at the "bright side" of the dictator as the "savior" from chaos. The will to compromise and the *americanista* stance is clearly felt from the initial works of Juan Bautista Alberdi (1810-1884) and Esteban Echeverría. Alberdi's philosophy of law, formulated, in 1837, in his *Fragmento preliminar,* is especially explicit in the praise of Rosas. It is amusing to see that Alberdi looks for assistance to Aristotle, Montesquieu, Rousseau, Volney, including Moses and Jesus Christ (1954:72), in order to somehow define positively the people who support the strongman. Since so many follow him, he cannot be a despot, so goes the reasoning.[8] But Rosas mistrusts these intellectuals. Echeverría had only recently returned from Paris! His head was full of Romanticism and of utopian socialism. Alberdi wanted to put the State apparatus on sound legal and institutional basis gleaned from best thinkers from Antiquity to present. All this sounded strange and subversive to the dictator. He yearned for unconditional support, not for "intellectuals." It was time to show them who was the Law.

The "literary salon," used for political gatherings of like-minded friends, is closed, the group tries to go underground[9] but is soon dispersed; some abandon the city, many flee for their lives to Montevideo and exile. Another route to exile from the provinces leads to Chile. But it will be a long wait for the fall of the dictator; some will die before it is over. Exile

---

[8] This gesture of compromise will be pasted over by its protagonists and by the official historiography; but it will be used by the "revisionist" history to rehabilitate the dictator. To the contrary, the "progressive" dictators of the turn of the century will be savaged by the "novel of the dictator" of the *Boom* period, whose authors would side with other contemporary "progressive" dictators, however. This pattern of reversal and double standard will be typical of Latin American historiography and *hommes de lettres.*

[9] Echeverría—first a reluctant leader of the Generation, yet predetermined for the leadership role by his stay in Europe—founded the association of "Young Argentina" (1838), patterned on Mazzini's "Young Italy." Like many groupings of its kind, while of fairly little practical significance at its time, it became increasingly important by the democratic social project developed from there, mainly in exile, and by its impact on the writing of other intellectuals of the Generation (Alberdi, Sarmiento), and later on their work after the demise of the dictatorship.

radicalizes them. If "Americanism" is represented by the dictatorship, then one has to be "anti-American." If the cure for that barbaric Americanism is the European-style civilization, interpreted as *democracy,* then *this* is the real Americanism.[10] One "Americanism" looks backwards, the other one looks forwards, and not to modernization only but, perhaps even more, to the *quality* of the society South America should become. This democratic heritage cannot be missed in Echeverría, of course, but it is all but erased from the accounts of the other leading intellectuals of the Generation in the "revisionist" histories of all stripes.

This is also the forward looking ethos coming out of the strange mixture of genres all amalgamated in *Facundo: Civilización y barbarie,* written feverishly by Domingo Faustino Sarmiento (1811-1888) in a couple of weeks in 1845. More than just a political pamphlet, *Facundo* is an anatomy of the country, pieced together from her history, from her culture, from her people and the physical environment that has shaped them, from some prototypical biographies of *caudillos;* the analysis and the testimony[11] are then contrasted with a prophetic blueprint for her magnificent future, and all this is rather sketched out than calmly argued, and written with passion and with fascination for what is coming out of the fiery pen. The narration is full of anecdotes, the text is full of diverse texts hastily pieced together, the description is full of dialogue with the readers, or with Westerners who, typically to this day, do not make the effort to understand Latin America and let themselves be easily seduced by the exotic "Americanism," or even defend it against those who understand the Americanism in a different way, such as the Generation of 1837. Sarmiento is enraged by the condescending attitude of some Westerners towards the "others," and towards the Americans in general. Even if they were just looking for consumers for their manufactured goods, their supporting the backward and impoverished America is counterproductive, he fumes (2003:236-7).

Sarmiento is in no mood to just copy others:[12] he sees grand future for his country and is ready to *challenge* the world. He is a proud American, personally, to the point of arrogance (in accord with the well-known stereotype of the Argentine). He is an American who sees the *Americanism* in a different way. He is not interested in saving some identity, in protecting some such thing from the dangers coming from outside; his concern is rather with the *problematic inside.* Much has been said about his alleged wholesale rejection of the provincial "barbarism." Yet once he steps down from his fiery rhetoric to reality, he is readily pointing out that what is *really* happening is much more complex than what his title might suggest. Alberdi will add additional nuances in his *Bases*. And this Generation, once the dictatorship is over, will be very careful to make peace with the old foes.[13] After all, the liberation comes from the *federales* side. And, on second thought, it was a nasty brawl, but

---

[10] The "revisionist" historiography of all stripes has successfully obfuscated this equation of "Europe/civilization = democracy" made by the Generation of 1837, and has instead harped on the "foreignness" introduced against the grain of and to the harm to Latin America. Postmodern criticism in the U.S. happily regurgitates this partial slippage.

[11] It is interesting to see that as new genres appear on the horizon of Latin American literature, they reveal novel aspects of *Facundo* (for the *testimonio* and its contradictory idelogical underpinnings see Volek 2002).

[12] The accusation of some will to slavish imitation is another useful misconception brandished by the "revisionist" historiography that has spilled over into the current postmodern mindset in the U.S. academy.

[13] A good example of this effort is José Mármol's novel *Amalia,* whose serialized version savaging the *federales* is stopped after Rosas' defeat at Caseros, in February 1852, and the novel is rewritten and sanitized for the sake of country's unity (this did not spare the author physical abuse by the relatives of some *federales* depicted in the novel, an unsuspected danger of writing a contemporary "historical novel").

within the limited family of the Argentine elite that was finally coming together. Yet this "happy ending" will put its limits on the social project for the country nurtured in their dreams by the Generation. They won on the intellectual side, but did not win over the country as a whole.

At the end, "barbarism" will stick only to the primitive tribes of the *pampa* Indians. Yet it will be precisely under Sarmiento already as the president of the Republic that the Argentine Congress will approve a treaty, in 1870, with the Ranqueles nation. This "detail" is usually missed in the literature on Sarmiento, since he tends to be linked with the U.S. model of dealing with native tribes interpreted as advocating extermination of the Indians. However, since "legality" in Latin America tends to depend on the current strongman, in the late 1870s, General Roca and future president will make the decision on the "final" solution to the problem. But it would be disingenuous to pin the blame backwards on Sarmiento as it is usually done.

Something similar happens with the call to open up the country for the European immigration. This is now interpreted in a way that the new human stock was supposed to replace both the "barbaric" Creoles from the provinces and the "savage" Indians from their lands. Nothing would be farther from the truth. Sarmiento, in *Argirópolis,* and Alberdi, in *Bases,* think about the European immigrants as the living teachers, who would take along native populations more easily through the processes of modernization. In addition, higher density of population is, for them, a precondition for development and for a better future. And more: in order to attract immigrants of all creeds, speeding up of the process of religious democratization is required.

Facundo is a testimony to his author's personal and generational struggle to understand the complex reality of his country, to fathom the possible future, and to direct his actions to bring it about. Born out of the red hot politics, *Facundo* will be recognized by friend and foe as one of the highest and lasting *literary* achievements in Latin America of all times, and will become a cultural institution, for many, substituting for the Argentine reality of its times. Unfortunately, many will not read beyond the title.

What is actually striking is that the works of this Generation, such as Sarmiento's *Facundo* or Echeverría's *El matadero,* written from the birth pangs of a modern nation, managed to capture so much of the already ingrained matrices of that culture-in-formation that they strike one to be as relevant today as they were yesterday. (The same is true, for example, for Sarmiento's observations on the U.S. way of life in his travel notes.) And also their democratic project has remained as alive and as incomplete today as then.

Without historical context and without taking into account that the Generation of 1837 was pushed into exile by certain ruthless "Americanism," the alleged "anti-Americanism" of this Generation cannot be properly understood. The revisionist history, starting from Martí as a matter of fact, muddles the issues by decontextualizing them, and gives especially Sarmiento bad rap. Actually, modern and anti-modern ideologies clash here. The reader may choose sides, but may also simply put facts into their own perspectives, understanding that the charge of "anti-Americanism" comes from a certain vantage point and values that are not impervious to challenge.

Travel will be another eye-opener for this Generation. In the 19th century, Latin American travelers went usually quickly through the U.S. to make their pilgrimage to other main points on their agenda in Europe or in the Middle East (Onís). Sarmiento will travel extensively to and through the U.S. and *also* to Europe. He will not come to the U.S. with the usual European bias. He will look and compare. In a reversal of roles, he comes to modernity as a prospector searching for what might be most suitable for his own country. He pays attention to what is advanced and to what is promising; the fact that he is coming for inspiration rather than for the pastime of digging some dirt on this country, may have confused some readers, who complain that he idealizes the U.S. Let us also remember that the River Plate region was not only the last Vice Royalty created in the Spanish Colony, but remained always at the margin of the colonial system (just think about the now clear absurdity of having Buenos Aires being administered from Peru through the Andes). As such, River Plate was less burdened by aristocratic traditions. This is one more reason why Sarmiento, himself a "self-made man," feels much closer to the U.S. than to the Europe of that time. He will be able to return to the U.S. in about fifteen years, to compare notes, already as the Argentine Ambassador, and will leave this country as the Argentine President.

At a closer look, the "outside" shapes up differently than how it is imagined from the books. Sarmiento is a sharp, critical observer. He embodies a "can do" spirit of his times. While it could be argued that the Independence left the country in a typical postcolonial morass, the transhistorical thread linking the 19th and the 20th century postcolonialities is fairly tenuous. The historical situation, the issues, and especially the attitudes were different. The liberal Generation of 1837 is highly critical of the Hispanic colonial heritage surviving after Independence, and the backward contemporary Spain is ridiculed. In their anti-Hispanic fever, some hotheads would demand cutting off all links to that culture (from the Spanish peninsular usage, to orthography and even to the language itself, proposing French as the substitute). But it was hard sell to the Hispanic *criollos,* and beyond touting the values of French culture not much else happened.[14] Sarmiento himself does not adopt any injured posse against the West at large; although he protests against the European "Latin Americanism"—to use the current term—and its blindness, including the stereotypical condescending vision of "Americanism," he himself sees each country as he has experienced it. He looks for what he can find of good and usable there. He has no ideological hangovers like the postmoderns.

At that time, it was normal to consider human history as a pretty violent business. Sarmiento himself does not have to wait to read Darwin: he has seen it all. Therefore, he does not demonize the outside: he is not naïve enough to think that all is friendly there, but he has faith in himself and in his country. And more: he speaks as a proud *American,* proud that the ex-colonial northern part of America is more developed than the Europe as he saw her, and even proud to challenge both Europe and the U.S. His call "Let's become the U.S. of the South," means just this: we have enough resources and potential to become as strong and as prosperous as the most developed nations on the Earth, and not to slavishly copy anything.[15] His optimistic exuberance is without bounds at that time. Obviously, he was not hampered by any "postcolonial" or "dependency" theory of today, and the attempts to plot him onto those

---

14 Yet even this incremental "little" has produced, over time, some significant differences: for example, in comparison with the rest of Spanish America, a greater tolerance in the schools of the local popular usage (the *voseo*) has opened up space for the distinct River Plate colloquial speech style.

15 His detractors deliberately confuse "learning from" and "slavish copy." The idea that Latin America has copied "too much" has become a *topos* in Latin American thinking since Martí. The Generation of 1837 has recognized, more shrewdly, that the error of the previous generation was rather to copy *poorly,* and dogmatically at that. After all, imitation is part of the learning process. However, when Latin American intellectuals were returning home from the burning Europe, in the late 1930s, they were coming with the idea that Latin America had "come of age" and had nothing to learn from anybody else any more (for example, the Uruguayan Joaquín Torres García).

and other tales only produce tortured discourse (good example of this in Sommer and Alonso). There are distinct perils in projecting today's theories, ideologies, and feelings backwards on the historical times oriented towards different values than the wholesale anti-modern attitudes prevalent in the studiously pessimistic postmodern culture.

The exile and the travel was an important learning time. The dictatorship fell in 1852, but the country continued in turmoil for almost another decade, when, within the Federation, Buenos Aires won a special place, again. By that time, Sarmiento had jumped the federative ship and pinned his futures on the city of his highest prophecy. Alberdi did not, was shunned by the victors, and spent almost the rest of his life in another exile, in Europe. His most important legacy were his *Bases,* put together in 1852, which came to constitute the rationale of the Argentine Constitution as the vehicle for modernization of the country. All in all, the Generation of 1837 had to wait twenty-five years to put their words to deeds, and had to compromise, again.

Today, it is easy to blame them for the shortcomings of the age, or for the modern project itself, or to twist them at will in accord with some "theories" in vogue today. Yet doing this tells more about the authors of these critiques than about their objects of study. Notwithstanding some rhetorical excesses—mainly due to the polemical nature of some of their better known writings—, this group of intellectuals has come up with a very generous plan of action for their country. The democratic ethos, coming from the Saint-Simonian utopian socialism, was pervasive in their thought. It was not necessarily their fault that the blueprint was not fully put into effect. But even the intent, the accidental road of their lives, and the ferment of ideas they left behind, anchored Latin America to the ideas that change was possible and that modernization mattered as a road to democratization of their societies.

The End-of the 19th Century U-turn: The Prophets' Time

Paradoxically, the question of identity comes to Latin America in the mid-19th century on the wings of the French imperial project, launched by Louis Napoleon, to harness the Mediterranean countries behind the *latinité* cultural-political cause and create a defensive block opposed to the threats of two great powers lurking on the horizon, Russia in the East (the French must have felt pretty chastised by the defeat that precipitated the first Napoleon's fall) and the U.S. in the West (as the representative of the Anglo-Saxon dominated area). In Spanish America, *latinité* has had the advantage of de-coupling the liberated colonies from the detested Spanish metropolis and relating them to an entity of a "higher" status, represented by France, with which their elites have been finding more and more affinities. While Russia was far away, the threat has been increasingly seen in the U.S. However, the short-lived French adventure in Mexico, in the 1860s, has muddled this picture. Fortunately, towards the end of the 19th century, this misadventure has been almost forgotten, while the threat of the U.S. has grown larger ("América y el problema de su identidad", in Zea 1991: 196-209).

1898 was a pivotal year: the U.S.-Spanish war brought home the threat from the North, and Spanish America, after the distance of many decades, felt free to embrace the old metropolis and strengthen old ties, now, however, on equal footing. With Rubén Darío, poetry in Spanish flowed freely between the continents, and Spanish Americans were elated by this "return of the caravels": now *they* were adding to the Spanish culture. As if they were making up for the lost time, the closeness of the cultural elites on both sides of the Atlantic at that time was remarkable. In Spain, the shock of the loss of the last colonies turned the cultural elite, the Generation of 98, inward, into the search for the Spanish soul as the depository of historical strength that would guarantee future revival of the country. While conditioned by the local events, this search for her soul ran in Spain parallel to the conservative nationalistic movements in France and in Germany. Spanish America was to add to her search for identity within the broader context of Hispanism and *latinité,* a new feature: anti-imperialism, directed against the northern neighbor. One of the earliest and most vocal speakers for this stance was the Argentine Manuel Ugarte (1875-1951), in *El porvenir de la América Española* (1910).[16]

However, internally, *latinité* only pasted over the multi-racial character of Latin American countries, and, in Spanish America specifically, it simply rearticulated the old hegemony of Hispanic heritage there to make it more palatable (as Vasconcelos will point out). *Latinité* worked best in contrasting the "Saxon" North America with the "other" America, whose characteristics remained to be determined.

The Cuban José Martí (1853-1895) is a transitional yet pivotal figure. He sensed the quick pace of modern times and the need to adjust. But during his long exile in the U.S., he also could see how this country was preparing for her entry onto the world stage as a great power (Zimmermann). Reading the daily press, he could feel the disdain for everything Hispanic. In his thinking, the need for modernization was derailed by the fear of the North. He worked hastily for the liberation of Cuba as a means of stopping the future expansion of the U. S. in the Caribbean and in South America. He thought that the free Cuba and the united Latin America would together create a bulwark contributing to world balance and to peaceful coexistence of nations. The growing sense of urgency, on the one hand, stimulated some wishful, utopian thinking, pasting over complex realities by exorcising inconvenient facts (in racial issues, among others), and, on the other hand, led to feverish political activism. Since the late 1880s, Martí was getting more and more radicalized in his views. While continuing to stress democratic ideas, his rhetoric became more visceral and lethal and, as such, could easily be misused. He died in combat in the first days of the rebellion. His death as a martyr of the Cuban freedom froze his image into a patriotic symbol, used freely by everybody at will (Volek 2006).

Martí has condensed his thought on Latin America in his essay-poem in prose "Our America," published in 1891. It is actually a collection of slogans that turn around a small number of poetic symbols-leitmotifs that, together, organize the piece into a kind of contrapuntal "musical" structure. The need for modernization elicits an ambiguous response: modern ideas need to be introduced, but they must be grafted carefully on the trunk of our republics (Martí: 18).[17] However, what that "trunk" might be? What is the dosage of the new and the old? There is also something essentialist about the "trunk" image and something funny about the trees free-floating in the air. On balance, Martí is more concerned about the loss of identity than about the urgency of modernization. On the one hand, he speaks

---

[16] There is a curious re-edition of the book, under the title *El porvenir de la América Latina,* in late 1916 or early 1917, in Mexico, courtesy of Servicio de Informaciones Alemanas. The Latin American anti-imperialism has had and will have many interested external supporters.

[17] Due to his high-strung rhetoric and liberal use of symbols and images, it is extremely difficult to translate Martí. It is easy to miss cues. The English translation in his *Selected Writings* (Penguin, 2002) is deplorable on all accounts.

admiringly about the new, modern Latin America rising before his eyes—while the U.S. is floundering terminally;[18] on the other hand, he thinks that the failure of modernization so far is due to the excess of imitation. Importation of foreign books is not "civilization" but only "false erudition."

Spanish American reality is not readily accessible through foreign books and needs to be studied in its own right. The American university should pay attention. Martí appears to follow in this the steps of Andrés Bello and of Emerson; but then the slippage begins: Apparently, it is more important to teach the history of the Incas and the Aztecs than the history of Greece. The question put in this way, then, is, What is "ours"? Foreshadowing some "postcolonial" attempts of today, Latin America's historical road would be "re-routed." The link to Western culture would be cut and some metaphorical "roots" would be implanted instead. Due to only a very limited knowledge of ancient Amerindian cultures at that time, imagination would have its feast, as can be seen in Martí himself and later in Vasconcelos or in Mariátegui, for that matter. When Alfonso Reyes wrote his poetic evocation of the Aztec culture, "Visión de Anáhuac," in 1915, he had to translate some indigenous texts from English. While the situation has improved, it is still far from satisfactory even today. The point here is not the importance of study of the indigenous cultures, but the diagnosis of the formation of Latin American societies that is proposed in Martí's formula. The "postcolonial" de-occidentalization of Latin America (Mignolo) somehow tries to erase history and return to the point of rupture; the funny thing is that this project is hatched based on tons of European theories. The *topos* of "restitution," real or imaginary, runs through this pipe dream.

Martí also presupposes that the knowledge of the reality will by itself lead to a better government. History does not readily support this expectation. In his time, a good example of some such "scientific government" was the one under Porfirio Díaz, with whom Martí eventually reconciled and was related to through his dear friend and "brother" Manuel Mercado, who was one of the highest officials of that government. Martí even contradicts himself when he notices that many dictators actually came to power using these "natural elements." But who would dare to point out contradictions in a poem-sermon of a Saint?

The romantic celebration of nature and of the "natural man" follows. From here comes the famous attack on Sarmiento: "No hay batalla entre la civilización y la barbarie, sino entre la falsa erudición y la naturaleza" [There is no battle between civilization and barbarism, but between false erudition and nature] (17). Not only this statement shows that Sarmiento's ideas are twisted beyond recognition, but Enlightenment values are simply supplanted here by romantic ones, as if Romanticism was less imported to America from Europe, and as if Enlightenment was less important to America. However, the exchange of values within the opposites is striking and foreshadows the "romantic turn" coming in the 20th century (with Ezequiel Martínez Estrada, Eduardo Mallea, the "romantic" *barbudos* and other "subcomandantes," among others).

From the "nature" comes the "natural man." "Natural men have vanquished artificial intellectuals." And another twisted parallel: "The autochthonous mestizo has vanquished the exotic *criollo*." Martí is desperately looking for some anchor for his unifying vision of America. The Indian does not qualify, yet, since his image is marred by the 19th century's racial theories. On this account, Martí mentions in passing "silent masses of Indians" (16) and

[18] The U.S. in terminal decadence will be an important *topos* of Latin American thought throughout the 20th century.

"the clotted blood of the Indian race" (17). On the other hand, there was the paradox of the Creole formulated already by Simón Bolívar: "European in America, and American in Europe." In this version of the story, the "exotic Creole" pays for all the broken china in Latin American history. In his search for the "trunk," Martí opts for the supposed middle ground: the *mestizo,* and plays the card of "nuestra América mestiza" (19). This is a powerful metaphor and a bold revaluation of *mestizo*, but the symbol of "mestizo" again only pastes over the complex racial, social and cultural realities of Latin America (see, for example, the discussion of the Indian/Ladino problematic in Guatemala, in Morales, or the recent debate over "transculturation" and "hybridization"). The metaphor was raised to a status symbol in the Cuban Revolution, and at one time there was no Latin American intellectual who would not call himself *mestizo,* of course, in that lofty sense of the word only.

The *mestizo* as the proposed "trunk" for the tree grafting purposes offers a symbolic, yet illusory solution to the problem considered. This "trunk" has not served well neither for diagnosis of Latin American racial realities, much less as a stimulus for the needed modernization. Finally, Martí's "Americanism" ends up being uncomfortably close to that of precisely those retrograde forces in the past he denounces, and yet nurtures at home. The Revolutionary Cuba as a gigantic museum of the 1950s is a sad monument to this "Americanism" and to the simulacrum of an "alternative" modern project that has not panned out.

Intellectuals as Prophets, Continued

At the turn of the century, a young Uruguayan, José Enrique Rodó (1872-1917), puts on mask of an old and venerable teacher addressing the young Latin American generation. His message, full of self-indulgence, is that of Culture and Beauty, the ideals of self-cultivation and disinterestedness for which he goes back to the ancient Greece and to the modern Kantian aesthetics. The *fin de siècle* aestheticism is proposed as a tangible ideal for the continent. Rodó denounces the vulgar utilitarianism of the century (that of Industrial Revolution) and the mediocre and "poorly understood democracy," both neatly represented by the "spirit of Americanism," as the Europeans have chosen to call—not without some resentment—the relentless modernization processes they saw invading their sacred space from the U.S. While in Europe this reaction was directed against something real, or imagined as really happening at an ever-increasing pace, in Rodó's America, this critique was rather preemptive if not empty—or confused. The oligarchy, at the height of their power, was not utilitarian at all, but was squandering fortunes on sumptuous consumption. And the masses were not "utilitarian" either, but were struggling to survive, living many times in infrahuman conditions.

Where his rhetorical outburst has touched a sensitive chord was when he attacks the alleged contemporary *nordomanía* that threatens to "delatinitize" Spanish American "genius of the race" (read: culture and identity). His *Ariel*—freely borrowing from and turning into symbols the characters of Shakespeare's *The Tempest,* a literary-allegorical game made popular by Ernest Renan at that time—has appeared just two years after the 1898 war and the changes in mood this war has generated. For his "analysis" of the U.S. in crisis and decadence, Rodó has marshaled all the French writers who had something critical to say about this country. The rhetorical barrage is most impressive; historical accuracy much less.

Rodó readily acknowledges that "certain material welfare" is needed for a society, but he does not bother to dwell on how it might be achieved in the South—certainly not by imitating the North, which would only take from the originality of the "people who are yet forming and modeling their national entity." His solution lies in the future: the two peoples should coexist until a synthesis can be reached and "the definitive American of the future," "a new human type," is constituted (Vasconcelos will read these lines with special care). And he has a remarkably simple recipe for that synthesis: since Latin America is spiritually superior, the North American utilitarian Calibans will be serving the cause of the southern spiritual Ariels. And, well in the spirit of the times, all this is predetermined and will happen exactly as the young-old sage has envisioned it.

This message of heroic self-cultivation appealed to the oligarchic and upper-middle class elite, but had little to say to the pauper masses in the streets and in the countryside. Yet all appreciated the pep talk and especially the severe critique of the North. Once this ingredient is on hand in Latin America, the more outlandish the better, any discourse is on safe ground there (and increasingly also here).

With his ideal aimed inside, towards the preservation of a historical heritage of "race" and culture, Latin American intellectual has turned his back on modernization. Why struggle for modernization if his world is already spiritually superior? And worse, if modernization would mean doing what North Americans do. Standing at the crossroads, the present is felt as untenable, the modernity ahead is disqualified; what remains open to do is to search for identity as a safeguard against change or as a reencounter with the proper self that would somehow mythically "complete" itself, or to search for all kinds of touted alternatives to modernization. Nostalgia of an ancient Arcadia and wishful utopia are the extremes of this search.

Martí and Rodó, though so different and even opposed, are the two intellectual switchmen who together set the rails for the 20th century train of the Latin American thinking in an opposite direction to the best minds of the 19th century (this u-turn is celebrated in Miller as search for an "alternative modernity"). The road to paralysis and to Macondo has been wide open. The next stop is "Universópolis."

The Mexican José Vasconcelos (1882-1959) will turn his reading of Martí's *mestizo* and of Rodó's *Ariel* into a new prophetic concoction in *La raza cósmica,* published in 1925. Vasconcelos also starts from the premise that "Saxonism" in America must be stopped by the Latin race. He focuses on the synthesis theme that fell somewhat flat in Rodó and works out a detailed plan for History to follow. In one line of his thought, he feels with satisfaction that the Latin civilization is superior, for him, because it has more easily sympathized with strangers, and that this has been translated in assimilation of the Indians rather than in their extermination (in the North). This spiritual endowment gives the South a special mission for all humanity: conduct the transformation of the four existing races into a new one, a truly *cosmic* race. Vasconcelos is not interested in the *real mestizo* (Mariátegui will take him to task for that), since his aim is to build a bright future. He has been greatly influenced by theosophy that played with the fifth, Aryan race, and he freely blends this with the "fifth sun," the final historical period announced in Aztec mythology (D.H. Lawrence's *The Plumed Serpent,* 1926, will reflect some of this ferment).

The fusion into a cosmic race has different consequences for different races. For example, the Indian's road to the future leads through modern culture and through Latin civilization only. The white race, on the other hand, has already fulfilled its mission by creating conditions for the racial fusion and now will serve merely as the bridge to the future. All other races, then, in this theory, would need to go through that bridge of "whitening." However, stated in this way, it would be just vulgar Positivism that Vasconcelos' Atheneum Generation of 1910 vehemently denounced; the process as outlined must, then, be much more complicated than that.

To achieve that, in his second line of thought, Vasconcelos differentiates three stages of development. He skips the first two (including the basic, "material," "the empire of the need") as of little interest to concentrate on the third, the "spiritual and aesthetic" stage, governed by the "superior norms of feeling and fantasy" (Vasconcelos: 37). And the free play of fantasy it is. This third period will be determined, according to him, by three supreme laws: those of Spirituality, Beauty, and Love. Love will be spontaneous, without norms, but—the 1960s must wait yet—it still comes without the "low appetites." This definition will confuse some of his acolytes. Antonieta Rivas Mercado, who will sacrifice everything for the prophet, will get burned on this ambiguous creed, and will lose her fortune, her family, and her life. The prophet will be untouched by her plight and will lend her with magnanimity his pistol to commit suicide.

Beauty will have its rigors, too. Vasconcelos imagines that this categorical imperative will produce a kind of aesthetic eugenics: the ugly will not wish to procreate, and the blacks and the other less than beautiful lineages and inferior races will be redeemed and improved slowly in this way. The union of the black Apollo and a blond Venus is heartily recommended, but the marriage of a black woman with a white man is viewed with "profound horror" (41). Mendel's laws of heredity will guide the gradual process of perfection of the species.[19]

In his imaginary trip to the future, Vasconcelos stumbles on the tropics: if Hegel viewed them as total degeneration of order (even birds sing out of tune there because they cannot hear themselves in the noise, he opines), the Mexican prophet sees in them future paradise. According to him, the world of the future will belong to those who will conquer the Amazon region. If the English do it, they will sure found some ugly "Anglotown." However, if the cosmic race consolidates her civilization in that "promised land," as is convenient for her to do, she will build there a mighty city called "Universópolis," a new center of the world of the future (34-35). In any case, the Latin civilization of America is already a "reserve of all Humanity" (49).

This lofty babble of a foremost Mexican educator flew to the heads of a generation of Latin Americans and was the rage of the 1920s. It still reverberates in contemporary Chicano culture. One wonders if any of them has read beyond the title.

One young Peruvian was impressed by the intent of the cosmic *mestizaje* message, but thought that the project stood on its head. He tried to put it on its feet, and then some. His name was José Carlos Mariátegui (1894-1930). He spent several crucial years in Europe (mainly in Italy) on government stipend and returned home, in 1923, as a convinced Marxist revolutionary. The stay in Europe, like in so many other cases of Latin American intellectuals, qualified him as the natural leader of his generation (maintained through the influential journal *Amauta,* 1926-1930, he edited), until the "real" Marxism struck.

Mariátegui was returning home with a complete, detailed theory. The only problem was that the Peruvian reality of that time did not respond to its expectations. There was barely any

---

[19] Yes, some selective "science" is needed to spice up utopias, too, scientific or not.

revolutionary proletariat and not much of a nationalistic bourgeoisie either, to do the expected chores. He realized that he had to learn first more about his country, and he used the Marxist theory (emphasizing class division, ownership of means of production, and five stages of social organization, from the "primitive communism" to the future socialism and full-fledged scientific communism), as he got acquainted with it in Italy, to interpret it. Again, the theory was allegedly "scientific" and the course of History was predetermined. What, then, to do to fit the unresponsive reality into the infallible theory? His *Siete ensayos de interpretación de la realidad peruana,* pieced together, in 1928, from his journalistic production, was a by-product of that learning phase. One of the limits of that interpretation is that economics is presented as the root-cause of everything; but it was a novel partial approach to the Peruvian reality at that time. Yet turning the Andean *ayllu* into some type of *kolkhoz* would perhaps help the survival of the Indian communities on the highlands, but would hardly solve the problems faced by them in a multi-ethnic, anomic, underdeveloped Peruvian society and in the modern world.

Simultaneously, Mariátegui began prospecting Peruvian reality for revolutionary potential. Soon he discovered the *indigenista* movement, created by the *mestizo* intelligentsia on behalf of the Indian (Lauer), and was attracted to the Indian himself. Peru at that time was still sharply divided into the lowland area along the seashore (*la Costa*), inhabited by the Creoles, *mestizos,* blacks, mulattoes, and Oriental immigrants, and the Andean high plateau (*la Sierra*), inhabited mainly by the Indians. Mariátegui did not know the *Sierra* firsthand and had to rely on friends, on messengers, and on the *indigenista* writers (Leibner). These *chasquis* seem to have exaggerated the revolutionary ferment in the highlands. Luis Valcárcel, in his miscellany *Tempestad en los Andes,*[20] 1927, celebrated the "new Indian" who, contrary to the 19th century doxa, was now, according to him, taking his destiny into his own hands.[21] Mariátegui published this work in his series and wrote an enthusiastic preface to it. Soon, seeds for revolt were popping up everywhere. If the proletariat was not there, the Indian would do. However, this revelation would not chime well with the coming "true" Marxism, as Mariátegui will learn one year later.[22] Yet by the time of *Siete ensayos,* Mariátegui is ecstatic about the Indian, especially, since he also discovered "historical evidence of Inca's communism," so evident for him that it did not need any proof (Mariátegui: 79). After all, Marxist theory of historical stages would suggest something of the kind. For Mariátegui, then, it was just a short step from one communism to another. And another myth has been born.

After the emphasis put on the Indian, logically, others have to suffer. In the segments on the *indigenismo* and *mestizaje* (385-400), the "sociological analysis" shows some surprising slippage from "economy" and "class struggle" towards popular psychology and visceral judgments. The *mestizo* of the highlands is considered more or less positively since he is apparently quite close to the Indian, who conserves faithfully his ancestral "biological material" (388), contrary to the *mestizo* living in the lowlands, who is prone to assimilate to

[20] The title "The Storm over the Andes" is borrowed from Vsevolod Pudovkin's early Soviet revolutionary film "The Storm over Asia," from the same year 1927.

[21] It is interesting to note that Valcárcel, in his story of emancipation of the Indian, can still recognize fairly favorably the multifaceted work of the U.S. Evangelical Churches in the Peruvian highlands. This candid recognition would be unthinkable in the later, anti-imperialist climate of the "cold war."

[22] Actually, the discovery of revolutionary potential in the peasant Indian would put Mariátegui in line as a precursor of the heresy of Mao Tse-Tung.

the whites. The Chinese embodies the "decrepit Orient" (395), and the black and the mulatto are criticized because they fail to identify with the Indian. Their contributions to the national culture, envisioned as constructed around the Indian by Mariátegui and by the *indigenistas,* are "almost always negative and out of place" (398). These misfits in the utopia of a unified nation, dreamed up under the banner of socialist revolution, must have forgotten that the Indian and the Incas were the "natural state" of mind of the Peruvian progressive *intelligentsia* of the times. The real *hybrid race,* contrary to what Vasconcelos claimed, has never worked out, since negative sediments prevail and cause "sordid and morbid stagnation" (398). According to Mariátegui, the socialism with its class consciousness is the only way to solve these problems in the future (387). The utopia of socialism looms large on the horizon.

This happy tinkering with the Theory in the 1920s came to an abrupt end in the mid-1929 when the Comintern's commissars arrived to Buenos Aires to impose Stalin's interpretation of the philosopher's Word in South America. Mariátegui's *Siete ensayos* was found wanting, this time for too much emphasis on culture, his Marxism was suspect of eclecticism and of wrong authorities, and the reality he espoused as well as the revolutionary hero he proposed for the task were seen as incompatible with the now firmly established orthodoxy (Flores Galindo). Mariátegui got increasingly isolated as his comrades in arms, one by one, surrendered to the prevailing sentiment that one could not be a revolutionary outside of the Moscow-based Comintern umbrella. Mariátegui vowed to explain himself in a new book, in which he would outline his proposal for the course of action, but it has never been found and, more probably, has never been written. With all probability, it would have been deemed heretic anyway. The revolution did not need intellectuals, only faithful *apparatchiks* (this cycle would be repeated in the 1960s). The premature death spared the Peruvian from the need for recantation and saved him for future rehabilitations that happily paste over this sad history.

Following Georges Sorel, Mariátegui has reclaimed the power of the myth for the revolution. But in putting his wager on the Indian as the foremost "revolutionary element," he has got ensnared in his own mythmaking and wishful thinking. On top of that, Stalin's envoys came in time to impose a different orthodox blueprint. Mariátegui's promised alternative plan for action fizzled.

What he managed to do in his short life is sketchy. His socialism aims at social justice rather than at modernization. The well-meaning redistribution of wealth was the main thrust, not its production: socialism would somehow take care of that "detail." As far as the Indians were concerned, his plan called for the restitution of the land to the Indian communities. As an act of justice, this is fine indeed. But it would hardly be sufficient as a solution. Besides, underlying this idea of restitution is also the myth of the Inca's alleged prototype of communism. Somehow, the future looks backwards. And the "socialist revolution" seems to be the magic wand that is supposed to solve by one stroke all remaining problems. Today we are wiser.

At the end, the *indigenismo* movement and the Indian, designated as the new revolutionary force yet apparently unchanged by the historical processes, played the role of the Trojan horse of ethnic and cultural identity. Even the Marxist drive for modernization, so clear in all its brutality in Russia, has been undercut in Latin America by the "cultural" and identity turn.

We could go on dissecting the diverse projects proposed by the Latin American intellectuals, some more thoughtful and impressive than others (for example, the work and the intellectual and political trajectory of the Mexican Octavio Paz).[23] But, on the whole, we have seen enough already. What is striking is rather the fact that these "trips" of imagination might be celebrated by contemporary academy as some serious search for "alternative modernity" (Miller among others); these must be signs of confused postmodern times (see Volek 2008).

By the 1950s, the splendid run of the grand intellectual—the "specialist in generalities," as he was caustically called by some—has ended, and the *homme de lettres* has been superseded by the host of specialists in social sciences and humanities disciplines (Devés Valdés 2000-2004). But the professionalization itself has not solved the problems either, since reality has happily continued to be made fit to most diverse theories, only in an apparently more "scientific" and sober frame (for a partial account of the theories applied in that period, see Vidal).

The explosion of the mass-media and of the entertainment industry in the 1970s has introduced a host of TV and other media-stars, also substituting for the traditional intellectual. The globalization has presented other challenges: on the one hand, we can see considerable proliferation of NGOs and research groups vying for Western support (even the Mayan shamans have organized their own NGO, see Morales), some more clearly political (the "solidarity" networks); on the other hand, Western funding sources may tend to look for "proven" values (i.e. the entrepreneurial research "celebrities" able to marshal local talent for personal advancement), for compatible agendas, or even for messages the romantic and complex-ridden West would like to hear.[24] This feedback loop of expectations is bound to create new distortions.

In the 20th century, Latin American attempts at self-analysis have gotten bogged down in the imaginary invention of the Latin American "being" or have been derailed by scores of foreign blueprints[25] and local revolutionary myths. A generation of young Latin Americans was massacred or sent to exile on trying to repeat the "Cuban model" (the "focus" theory as espoused by the *Che* and "explained to children" in Régis Debray's *Revolution in the Revolution,* 1967). The Revolution glorified action and guns over pens and independent minds. The intellectual readily accepted the task to "serve" and to uphold the served orthodoxies, of populist governments, of revolutionary movements, of splinter groups... The encounter of the exiles with the "real socialism" was sobering and perplexing. Since the 1970s, Cuba was losing her luster. The final watershed came with the fall of the Berlin Wall in 1989. A number of Latin American intellectuals, especially those working in the sociology of culture, began assessing the balance of the Latin American thought in the "lost" century. A new term emerged to characterize it: *macondismo.*

---

[23] On Octavio Paz (1914-1998) see, in this line of critique, my piece (Volek 2005).

[24] This new dependency on Western foundations is criticized by Petras and Morley (1990); but the foil of their complaint is the nostalgia for the "heroic" intellectual of the 1960s.

[25] Up to the 1950s, the one and only blueprint considered as valid was furnished by the Soviet model; from the 1960s on, fragmentation ensued: the Cuban model was followed by the Chinese, then Vietnamese, etc. Latin American left went regularly for "orientation" to the embassies of these countries and made pilgrimage to the source. In Peru, the group going to the Albanian embassy was considered the absolute thing. Latin America *made in* Albania, that's really something!

Macondo and Macondismo

"Macondo" as a symbol of Latin America was coined in Gabriel García Márquez's celebrated novel *One Hundred Years of Solitude* (1967).[26] This novel–beyond its convoluted storyline and genealogies—may be read as a grand allegory of Latin American history and of the misadventures of this continent in modern times. The work of art, powerful as it may be, became valued as a heuristic instrument for the interpretation of Latin American reality as such (became valued as a way of "understanding" without understanding, as the Chilean sociologist José Joaquín Brunner argues in his already classical essay "Traditionalism and Modernity in Latin American Culture," published in 1989, and reprinted many times). Interpreting reality through the works of art is tempting, yet it has its pitfalls. Works of art are not in a "one to one" relationship with social realities nor are they necessarily determined by the social realities on the "one to one" scale. This caveat was brandished by all schools of formalist criticism in the 20th century, but was happily and quickly unlearnt by the ideological criticism that followed in the last decades of the century. In the "cultural studies" exercises, works of art—but not only works of *high* culture—have been read straightforwardly as plain mirrors of social realities.

Yet works of art can teach us quite a bit about the society and its culture. Karl Marx, for that matter, argued that he had learnt more through Balzac about the French society than through the more specialized technical literature of his time. Once we understand *One Hundred Years of Solitude* not as the Latin American reality as it apparently is but as a particular perspective that illuminates that reality in a special way, the novel becomes useful for our critical search *against the grain of macondismo.*

In *One Hundred Years of Solitude,* the caricature, the history of Latin America viewed in the distorted mirror of *magic realism*, has managed, in my opinion, to bring out more forcefully certain constitutive features latent in that history as well as in its many intellectual elaborations–I am thinking about the great Latin American intellectuals such as Sarmiento, Martí, Rodó, Mariátegui, Vasconcelos, Paz—, elaborations apparently more reasonable, reasoned, and even highly credible at certain times or in certain contexts. In other words, it may be helpful to use the artistic *condensation* we find in García Márquez's novel, condensation–term taken from the Freudian "Dreamwork"—of elements and perspectives normally disseminated throughout Latin American history and, therefore, in a certain way *concealed* in it, to refocus on and critically review that history and its intellectual elaborations.

For many readers of García Márquez, what was perhaps intended by him as a satire and exorcism of certain Latin American realities, became Latin American *reality as such* and turned, in their minds, into a revelation, embellishment, and even justification of that supposed state of affairs there: in other words, Macondo changed into *macondismo.* Phenomenology and artistic playfulness were interpreted as ontology: certain *vision* of Latin American reality (*the marvelous real,* coined by Alejo Carpentier), combined with certain poetics and aesthetics (*magic realism*), was viewed as the Latin American reality as such.

---

[26] In this segment, I am following the lecture given at the UC Merced in January 2007; in a summary form it appeared as part of a section "*Boom,* posmodernismo, macondismo" in my "Promesas y simulacros" (Volek 2008: 149-52).

The magic realism of García Márquez has exposed the "hot" popular Latin American culture to the gaze of sophisticated readers of the "colder cultures." The international success was instantaneous and explains the Nobel Prizes for Miguel Angel Asturias, for García Márquez and even for Rigoberta Menchú, as well as its absence in Jorge Luis Borges. Let's also remember that magic moment, to wit, the fact that the magic realism in García Márquez's version got its wings on the coattails of the Cuban Revolution of 1959: for the tired moderns, discontent with their dull everyday lives, the 1960s seemed to offer a poetic utopia, on the heels of the romantic *barbudos* descending as biblical prophets from the mountain and of the dancing and chanting crowds in the streets of Havana at the beginning of the Revolution. Latin America, then, was interesting not only for its persistent pre-modern features, but also for its fleeting promise as the harbinger of a better future for all mankind. For the tired Western moderns, "life is (always) elsewhere," and at that time it was–and for some still is—in Latin America. The magic moment passed quickly, but it is always difficult to "let go" and face the reality.

Magic realism was not always like this, however. In its beginnings–in Miguel Angel Asturias, in Alejo Carpentier, in José María Arguedas, or in Juan Rulfo—magic realism was an artistic and critical exploration of certain archaic and pre-modern, marginal cultural worlds and also of certain cultures that were immersed in time warps within modernity yet were outside of the horizon of the modern rational everyday life, such as the indigenous, the Afro-Caribbean, or the Andean *mestizo* worlds, or the Mexican Creole culture. It was serious business, because the aesthetics of magic realism was chosen as an instrument for discovering and revealing the aesthetic and human values of marginal ethnic cultures. For these early masters, what was *exotic* for the European Avant-Gardes, was recognized and recovered by them as part of their own local realities, and indeed obliged them, and others, to redefine and enrich the concept of national cultures, identified until then mainly with the Hispanic heritage. The role of the *negrismo* movement in the redefinition of the Caribbean national cultures is well known. The same goes for the *indigenismo* in the Andes. In the latter case, we have seen how the pendulum went to the other extreme. The literature of magic realism, at that time, anticipated the social emancipation of minority cultures. In that sense and in that phase, magic realism was actually revolutionary artistic method, because it pried open cultural spaces that had been closed for those marginal ethnic realities for a long time.

The new, postmodern metamorphosis of magic realism leaves this serious *modern* business behind, and opts rather for the surface. *One Hundred Years of Solitude* is actually on the edge between these two incarnations of magic realism. In the postmodern version, the lens of the traditional popular Creole culture, enhanced by fantasy, has made the reality of Macondo gracious, even hilarious, and has fascinated foreign readers, who have clamored for more. Yet another difference: in Carpentier, for example, we find "sexual acts," some even marked by what would be today viewed as overbearing—and rather unbearable—traces of *machismo* (only perhaps Mario Vargas Llosa would indulge in them today), or in Asturias, the sex has telluric and cosmic dimensions; but there is not much eroticism in their works. In its *light,* postmodern version, the new magic realism is all about fantasy, eroticism, and humor, and is spiced with only tiny dosages of reality, or such that do not upset the new framework of the genre.[27]

---

[27] The current of "magic realism" in literature and in film has been notoriously poorly theorized in Latin American criticism and now in the criticism at large. Among other persistent confusions (the origin of the term, the

It is *this* Macondo that *has become* Latin America for our times. Due to the self-assurance, charm, and diligence of Isabel Allende and her followers, this new magic realism has turned into a full-fledged cultural industry. It offers Latin America (including Hispanic culture in the U.S.) reduced to *kitsch* and packaged for export. Through the concept of "hybridization" the *magic real* has been recognized as *postmodern* and as such, in spite of García Canclini's protestations, has come to be an apology for Macondo. For some, Latin America has been *always* postmodern (they must have been counting from the first *chingada* of the Conquest, I guess).

In this reading of the continent, reality and analysis were substituted by fantasy, notwithstanding some good intentions and gestures. Secular failures of the region were celebrated as achievements, as idiosyncrasy, as authenticity, as inscrutable mystery, and, last but not least, as spiritual superiority. Why bother about the struggle for modernity and modernization if the *macondista* "hybrid" was already postmodern *avant la lettre?* And another point of false self-satisfaction: "we" have won over the laborious moderns just by being "us" (whatever that "being us" may mean), without having to change a bit or do anything for it.

This is a very comforting attitude, perhaps way too comforting (let's recall Karl Marx's stark diagnosis of modern changes, ending in that famous phrase "all that is solid melts into air"). There is no cheap and easy way of modernization. Yet throughout the 20th century, while her situation was rapidly deteriorating, Latin America both institutionally and intellectually was on a lookout for one magical shortcut to modernity after another, and even thought to be jumping over it, directly to postmodernity. In the Latin American conditions, the postmodern critique of modern failures and shortcomings has become an important ally of *macondismo.* In this way, the *macondismo* has emerged as the "bright side," embellished by literature, of the secular failures to modernize in the region.

WHAT IS MACONDISMO?

What does *macondismo* consist of? According to José Joaquín Brunner, this attitude has extended, on the wings of the *Boom* writing of the 1960s, "among a sector of Latin American intelligentsia that does not want to renounce making America a land of promised wonders. The land of dreams and utopias; the new world out of which an alternative rationality will emerge for the West," and let's add, for the world (2002: 15). The fundamental features of *macondismo* would be: first, interpreting Latin America through literature "as a product of the narratives that we tell to ourselves in order to mark out our identity"; second, believing that "these narratives, especially those acclaimed by foreign critics, constitute the Latin American reality—producing it as a text in which we would be called upon to recognize ourselves"; third, prolonging the traditional idea of "predominance of Nature over culture, but now in more complex ways": "Macondo would be a metaphor for the mysterious or the Magic Real of Latin America—its essence ever unnamable by the categories of Reason and by the political, commercial and scientific cartography of the moderns"; fourth, covering up with its

competing concepts), the ethnically and culturally bound magic realism (the Maya heritage in Asturias, the Mexican Creole culture in Rulfo, for example) has been happily confused with the Kafkaesque neo-fantastic literature (as found in Borges or in Cortázar, for example). My discussion here summarizes what I have written elsewhere (mainly Volek 1994: 11-24).

magically expanding wings the maladjustments "of the present-day realities of our societies" (14).

In this sense, Brunner continues, "Macondo is not only used as a metaphor for the incongruities perceived culturally in the (recent) modernization of Latin America but, more profoundly, as a representation of the continent's 'contested soul'" (16). And it is also a conceptual configuration confronting modernity and the "others." These "others" "will not be able to understand us (the Latin Americans) easily" (17).[28]

Brunner sums up his analysis:

> Macondo, it is said to us, is not Europe (and will not be) because it does not share the same rationality, nor is it the United States because it is not a market. But, moreover, *Macondoamérica* is subtly superior to anything else because it has "poetry," reveals "passion," communicates "mystery," speaks in tongues, and manifests the full powers of a Nature sheltering men under its mantle. Macondo is the final aristocratic gesture of a semideveloped continent that finally is obliged to recognize itself in Modernity. (17)

This is a devastating analysis of a culturally attractive yet intellectually flawed figuration of self-identity, developed in Latin America over the course of a century and finally coalescing in and through Gabriel García Márquez's magnificent novel.

Macondismos

We could actually speak about several *cycles* of *macondismo.* The Discovery of the New World (or rather its "invention," as Edmundo O'Gorman has called it) and the 16th and the 17th centuries would constitute one of these cycles. At least Latin Americans would not be responsible for that one: at that time, America was a European invention. Then the reaction to the excesses of imagination set in: the Enlightenment came and, with it, the relentless "scientific" questioning of everything those two centuries brought up. However, the limits of that science are now more than apparent. Towards the end of the 19th century, the pendulum would swing back, again. The *modernista* manifesto *Ariel* would protagonize this shift. As I have argued, Rodó's proposal of the aesthetic self-cultivation of the educated individual was perhaps well suited for the Bohemian and leisure class of the oligarchic elites, but was not a viable program for the hungry majority of the population. Yet the intellectuals signed on almost without exception.

From the *Modernismo* of the turn of the century on, a personal renovation and later the search for a cultural identity have been offered instead of the need for modernization. As a consequence of this shift, in Latin America, the search for modernity has been substituted by the search for the mirage of "identity" (Larraín 2000).

This "cultural turn" taking place at the end of the 19th century was not only radical but was also somewhat confusing. The Mexican historian Edmundo O'Gorman has called our attention to the disconcerting fact that the traditional "liberals" and "conservatives," in that

---

[28] Remember what José Martí has proposed in "Our America": for him, the Latin American reality is *so* original and *so* different that, as he has put it, "neither the European book, nor the Yankee book could offer a clue to the Spanish American enigma" (1891: 20). The reader is left with the impression that, in sum, "nobody understands us," and probably, "neither do we."

transition, appear to have exchanged their political and cultural agendas.[29] The mixture of most contradictory attitudes in that turn–a mixture strikingly "postmodern" *avant la lettre*—has created the breeding ground for the new one hundred years plague of *macondismo.*

This new cycle of *macondismo* has grown a cluster of rhizomatous strands.[30] Let's point out just two interlocked ones (Volek 2002: xxvi-xxvii).

In Latin America, the discontent with the perceived state of modernity there has lead to two apparently opposed attitudes. Those who see the "half-full" glass of accomplished modernity, as Octavio Paz does, look through the lens of high culture and go to History for the reasons of the present debacles. The lack of strong Enlightenment-type shake-up in the 18th century Latin America's colonies, that would have created a decisive break with the Tradition, stands out for him as one powerful motive for the present "deficiencies" of and perhaps even incapacity for modernity.

This perceived weakness is made to look worse by measuring Latin America's present up against an idealized West. Moreover, Latin Americans are put into an awkward position of striving to become yet what the others already have been for some time. Since, in addition, everything modern has been coming from outside, this leads Paz to the assertion that "to become modern, we had to sacrifice being ourselves," from which comes the conclusion that Latin America's half-accomplished modernity is just a mask, a falsification, a superficial varnish over some hidden "being" which must resurface first or be recovered eventually for the Continent to become wholesome again.

The quest for an authentic modernity thus turns into a quest for the lost self and soul. This myth-turned-history-turned-myth underlies Paz's vision of Mexican history since *The Labyrinth of Solitude* (1950). A frustrated search for the self and for identity with the "other"—two quests at cross-purpose—leaves little space for optimism for the future. Because Latin America missed out on the 18th century, it would now seem forever condemned, like the dead souls of Juan Rulfo's novel *Pedro Páramo* (1955, in part a tongue-in-cheek response to Paz), to the Purgatory of incomplete or pseudo-modernity (on Paz more in Volek 2005).

On the other hand, those who despair over the half-empty glass, or see it as irretrievably broken, look for reasons for failure in the very constitution of "being" Latin American. In their vision, the Latin American "difference" acquires the characteristics of "radical otherness." As a consequence, what was the troubling end-result of the failed identity quest in Paz, is postulated upfront here: Western Modernity has not worked in Latin America because it simply *cannot* work there. Nature and the non-Western origin of the native population, among others, have created an absolutely different reality (the *marvelous real*) that does not respond to the enticements of modern instrumental reason. The quest for modernity is hopeless, and it might be better to celebrate the resulting social dysfunctionality and anomy in a carnival *fiesta.* According to some of these Macondians, Latin American culture is forever condemned to be a carnivalesque parody of the Western culture.

These two attitudes only appear as opposed; actually they act more like "communicating vessels," being complementary and even frequently echoing each other. It is certainly not by

[29] O'Gorman writes about this in a little known book, *México: El trauma de su historia,* 1977, rarely quoted, since it is uncomfortable for everybody, including Octavio Paz and his allies, showing indirectly the weight of the old conservative agenda in their work.

[30] Useful critique of diverse strands of contemporary Latin American identity thought, although without tying it to *macondismo,* may be found in Castro-Gómez. For the comprehensive overview see Devés-Valdés.

chance that the title of Paz's essay resonates in García Márquez's novel. While the theory of "deficiencies" may be true as History, it does not explain fully the present. And similarly, while the gracious *macondismo* may be good for imaginative literature, it fails as a heuristic prism for interpretation of the complex Latin American realities of today and—worse—it works as a cover-up of the ugly undersides of these realities.

The Strange Attractors in the Identity Story

Let's try to pull together, yet from another angle, what we have been discussing about the *macondismo* so far. In the "identity story" underwritten by the Latin American *macondismo* there appear some anchors, supports, or something we might call metaphorically "strange attractors" (using the term coming from the "chaos" theory), latent points of attraction that somehow organize and so create a kind of master narrative of the *macondismo.*

According to the Chilean sociologist Jorge Larraín, the *macondismo* proposes a radical, Manichean opposition between two different cultural models and worlds: "the European rational enlightened and the Latin American symbolic dramatic" (2002: 88). The former strongly believes in instrumental reason, emphasizes abstract and conceptual discourse, and builds on logical argument. The latter "is suspicious of instrumental reason and has a religious-aesthetic approach to reality" (88); "emphasizes images, dramatic representations and rites, and appeals to sensations" (89). The two models and traditions constitute truly distinct types of rationality. In this perspective, Larraín continues, "the Latin American future would depend upon its loyalty to some traditions or principles, be they of religious or of Indian origin, which had been forgotten or marginalized by instrumental reason, by the alienated enlightened elite and by the neoliberal modernizing attempts. ... It is this essentialist conception which opposes the Latin American cultural model to the European enlightened one that was encouraged by Postmodernism in the 1980s" (89).

These two models as opposed to one another would work like the "ideal types" in the terminology of Max Weber: in different texts and thinkers, we will not find them necessarily in such a pure form. In Weber, the "ideal types" are meant as heuristic intellectual constructs created in order for us to *measure*, in a way, the specific complex and even confusing make-up of concrete social realities, realities that normally show mixed characteristics. Yet the constitutive elements of those constructs also operate as a type of latent symbolic pointers, or "strange attractors" in today's parlance, that pull the reality to the one or the other ideal model. In the intellectual production, they tend to organize discourses around certain points of gravitation. The growing radicalization of diverse currents of the Latin American thought focusing on cultural identity and culminating in the *macondismo* is a testimony to the force and to the operation of these symbolic pointers in the discourses of the Latin American thought on identity throughout the 20th century.

The *macondismo* exacerbates certain mechanisms that operate normally in all processes of constitution of personal identity or in search for an "imagined identity" suitable for the "imagined communities" in need of one (to use Benedict Anderson's term). In our case, the problem begins with the very name of that macrocommunity: América Latina (with capital letter) or latina (with small letter), Hispanoamérica, América española, Ibero-América, Indoamérica, etc., since always something is not well represented, or so it seems.[31]

In the process of the constitution of identity, several stages are generally pointed out: the mirror stage, the phase of differentiation, and that of recognition.

First, the *macondismo* exaggerates the negative value of identification with some model (be it the "mother," such as Mother Spain, Mother Europe, or the elder or *Big Brother* in the North America). It devalues programmatically all imitation, or legitimizes it only in the distant past, when Latin America has not "come of age" yet. This creates a great anxiety of influence and a twisted competition for the appearance of "originality" (Harold Bloom studied this in literature, showing how epigones struggle to pretend they are not).

While, among adults, communication, imitation, and emulation is part of a normal intercourse and of learning from each other, Latin America somehow wants to be left alone to figure out everything by herself, and then come out in a grand way and teach the marvels to the world. The promised prophecy of the new "alternative" modernity being invented there for the benefit of all mankind is a heart-felt story, yet it only manages to compensate for the destitute soliloquy.[32] The metaphor of Aureliano Buendía, who one day discovers on his own that the Earth is round like an orange, becomes an uneasy model of originality to follow.

The idea of "coming of age" emerged with great force in the 1930s (Reyes, repeated by Paz in *El laberinto*) and had some historical justification. The world was in economic crisis and in social and political turmoil. Between the condemnation of the Western (i.e. European) culture in terminal decadence, by Oswald Spengler after the quagmire of First World War, and the new war that was seen on the horizon, Latin America takes her distance from Europe as her intellectual model and teacher. Latin American intellectuals were returning home with great hopes: America would now be the future and it was exciting to work on it since everything remained to be done there.[33] This facile optimism faded after the war. While Spengler's prophecies had no impact in the North, they lingered on in the South, to revive periodically. The Cuban Revolution and the *Boom* literature of the 1960s raised the consciousness of "coming of age" and of self-sufficiency to new heights.

The anxiety of influence and the fear of becoming the same as the "other(s)" are with all probability overblown. Whatever Latin America might do, she would hardly become the same as Europe or the U.S. Actually, neither Europe nor the U.S. are strictly homogeneous even within their own confines.[34] The same fear of homogenization has impregnated many visceral

---

[31] I am not sure that "Abya Yala" that Walter Mignolo (2005) has recently half-heartedly (or half in jest?) proposed in his avowedly postmodern manifesto will be more successful as a representative and more inclusive name for Latin America.

[32] There is no doubt in my mind that new and new cycles of modernity will emerge: the human History has shown no intention to end any time soon; my doubt is, however, if the "new" modernity will come out of poverty and underdevelopment, as Latin American intellectuals seem to be inclined to believe.

[33] The Uruguayan avant-gardist painter Joaquín Torres García, returning from Europe after spending practically his whole life there, is typical in this sense: he declares that it is too late for whomever has not learnt the European lesson by that time; from now on, Latin America's "North" should be the South (1944). The Cuban Carpentier and others were coming with the same enthusiasm.

[34] Where does "Europe" begin or end? Is it now identical with the "European Union"? For some Latin Americans, Europe is France. After 1989, the striking slogan in my old country, sitting in the very heart of that continent, was "back to Europe"! Or remember the Count Hermann Keyselring, who contributed so much to the Latin American identitarian furor in the late 1920s and 30s and who has put Spain squarely as part of Africa! Ortega y Gasset who invited his thoughtful contribution to his *Revista de Occidente* was not amused…

reactions against "globalization," a process that has been going on actually since the beginning of civilization.

Second, when the similarity is devaluated, the price put on the *difference* is exaggerated. In that perspective, the Latin American "difference" achieves the status of radical otherness. I have already mentioned some implications regarding the alleged Latin American incapacity for modernity. Isn't that amazing! It is as if Latin America was more "different" than, say, Japan, Corea, or China! Yet, in Latin America, the tale of the insurmountable difference continues to be told with absolute seriousness.

On this chessboard of similarities and differences, one important complicating factor for Latin America has been its ambiguous and increasingly troubled relation with its "significant other," the U.S., both as the emerging world and imperial power and as the model of modernity. This is a huge topic, a big minefield, and I cannot do justice to it here. Suffice it to say that the effort to distance herself culturally from the Anglo protestant colossus in the North that has left its mark on the 20th century, has interfered, overtly and covertly, with the Latin America's already quite complicated attitude towards modernity and with the need for modernization. The defensive embrace of her cultural difference at the expense of modernization has been seen as fully justified both by the left and the right. Even for the most enlightened Latin American thinkers, the intent to reconcile the imperative of modernization with the rejection of the empire and the country model of modernity equals to attempt squaring the circle. It is obvious that the relentless and mainly unfortunate U.S. interventions into Latin American affairs have not been helpful.

The third step in our search for the supports of the *macondista* master narrative is the recognition phase. The right to difference in its *macondista* version has been ratified by the overwhelming reception of magic realism abroad and by the postmodernist discourse. The latter, according to Larraín, "would seem to be the only contemporary theory which allows Latin America its own voice and legitimates its right to be different" (2002: 88). There, he thinks, resides "the cause of Postmodernism's enthusiastic reception in Latin America."[35] This problematic recognition from abroad, predicated on the values represented by the *macondismo,* reinforces the negativity of those attitudes and proposes them as essential Latin American values. Postmodernist discourse and the voyeurism of the "First World" would then seem to go hand in hand in reinforcing the essentialist, fundamentalist, and oppositionist positions regarding Latin American identity. "Postmodernism seems to support the Latin American discourse which tries not to be reduced to European models and which asserts its unique character and its own specificity" (89). The irony is that even this "different" Latin America still depends on the authority of others, that of the modern world audience fascinated by the literary image of a "hot" and "exotic" culture.

Latin America, so "different" and so "original" in her own imagination, yet so marginal and abandoned on the world stage, has decided to compensate her insecurity by a prophetic discourse. Throughout the 20th century, a plague of utopian, *macondista* type of thinking has expanded on the continent like a brushfire, and even worse if it has been coming in the nihilist rhetorical forms (always some supposed ideal or death, as if there were no other alternatives possible). A continent stuck between *Macondo* or death is indeed a sorry picture, for those who can see. Without being bothered in the least by the little "detail" that Latin American

[35] Undoubtedly, Larraín is thinking about the group around Nelly Richard and the journal *Revista de crítica cultural* (1990-), in Chile.

continent has not solved yet any of its vital problems, the Latin American deep *pensadores* are set to dream up a new future, a new rationality, and a new modernity for the whole mankind. While dreaming in literature costs nothing, the social costs of operetta politics (*la política criolla*) and of day-dreaming have been staggering.

Fourth, it does not surprise us, then, that an equivocal recognition from abroad, the self-imposed mask, and the self-induced deception, assumed glibly by the industrial production of the magic realism after García Márquez's signal achievement, have provoked doubts about the legitimacy of some such identity adopted in the name of the difference for the difference's sake. A problematic recognition cannot but create a sense of *emptiness* in the subject who pretends to recognize himself in his own intellectual constructs and in the applause of others. The anxiety about the "true" identity, lost in the mayhem of history or hidden in some deep and inaccessible place, will weigh heavily on the "enigma" of the Latin American identity. The Chilean writer Antonio Skármeta has declared in one recent interview: "We do not know who we are, but we have already great literature."

This emptiness, felt intuitively inside, turns into an imperative outside: in *El laberinto de la soledad,* after searching through the diverse epiphenomena of *mexicanidad,* the proposed road to the true modernity becomes surreptitiously a mythical search for an authentic identity, lost in the vicissitudes of modern history. At the end, Octavio Paz's magnificent *mythopoeia* produced by great poet and visionary, leaves us with empty hands, and only prepares the turn towards the metaphysics of the "profound America" (such as the *México profundo,* in Bonfil Batalla), that will border on the *pataphysics* in the work of Rodolfo Kush and some of his postmodern "postcolonial" followers.[36]

In the meantime, the *macondista* search for the "Latin American (id)entity" has produced great expectations. In *The Book of Imaginary Beings,* compiled by Jorge Luis Borges, this specimen of "Latin American" has got a reserved place between *lamias* and *lemures* (see the first pages of José Vasconcelos' *La raza cósmica*). The lemurs of Madagascar have got somehow the sage's attention and have been awarded an unspecified prominent role in the early American history concocted by this great Mexican intellectual and mystic. "Cosmic" sounds now rather like "comic," and the postmodern Puerto Rican writer Rubén Ríos Avila plays on that when discussing the culture of his island in *La raza cómica,* published in 2002.

The expectation that has been created around so much emptiness, and the accepted view that "when that purported identity will be discovered"–somehow, somewhere—it will be something spectacular, connect with the phase of exaggerated difference, and give closure, in this way, to the mythic journey through the symbolic supports of the *macondista* master narrative. We have got, then, the *exaggeration of difference,* the *devaluation of similarity,* the *inflation of equivocal recognition* from abroad and the *deflation of self-recognition.* Does this ring a bell? This chain of two correlated oppositions—the four symbolic pointers brought to perfection by the *macondismo*—sure looks like the symbolic anchors of the "latent structure" of the myth, revealed by Claude Lévi-Strauss in his path-breaking study of the myth (see Figure 1).

[36] The last chapter of Kush's *América profunda,* 1962, is called "Hedor y sabiduría" (Stench and Wisdom). Kush walks through a poor, possibly Andean village, enjoying the smell of raw sewage flowing along the road, and in his deep vision fathoms a profound wisdom of ancient Amerindian cultures floating somewhere there behind the shit. Mignolo (1995) sees in his work one of the milestones towards the "post-occidentalism" (whatever that might mean).

This latent mythical structure, not unlike a set of "strange attractors," then, underlies and organizes the master narrative of the latest cycle of the Latin American *macondismo.* And like in a good myth, one exaggeration generates another, and among all, they suffocate what they were supposed to bring to life. The "waste land" of identity is echoed by the "waste land" of modernity in Latin America. Yet, like in T.S. Eliot, the *Waste Land* of modernity can be great modern poetry.

The *macondismo,* like the earlier Spanish American *Modernismo* in its heyday, appears to be the cultural flip side of the incomplete, frustrated or failed processes of modernization in Latin America. And, as a matter of fact, has contributed to that failure.

1	2	3	4
Positive exaggeration of the value of the difference	Negative exaggeration of the value of the similitude, imitation, etc.	Inflation of the value put on the recognition from abroad (feedback for the identity assumed for/by others)	Deflation of the value of the self-recognition

Figure 1.

Conclusions

After the Independence from the ultraconservative Spanish metropolis, the new Spanish American countries (Brazil's case was a bit different, yet within the same pattern) woke up in a modern world. The need for modernization and for social readjustment was evident, but the task of modernization was extremely difficult given the deep provincial and conservative mindset of the societies emerging from the colonial status. The change would have required a remarkable unity of the elite Creole class which was not the case. The chaos and the protracted civil wars afflicting almost all countries in the first decades did not help either.

The first generation of Latin American *intelligentsia* that has left a lasting imprint on the continent's intellectual and social history was the Argentine Generation of 1837. However, its legacy has been in the debate ever since. With the growing crisis of the continent and with the changing attitudes—within the postmodern cultural context—towards the modernization projects as such, the democratic intellectual heritage of that Generation has tended to be rather obfuscated. Instead, some fancy and farfetched inventions of the Latin American "being" have become celebrated as deep probes into the Latin American soul. Even the revolutionary projects of the Marxist left got bogged down in this imaginary search for national cultural anchors.

In the Latin American thought focused on the cultural identity, the emerging notion of radical difference posited as the absolute otherness has opened the doors to the 20th century *macondismo.* The *macondismo* in art and in literature, spilling into some disciplines in social sciences and in humanities, has pasted over the secular failures of the continent to modernize and has celebrated this state of affairs as some spectacular achievement. The *macondization* of the academy is a symptom of a larger postmodern malaise.

Today, the plague of *macondismo* does not only afflict a substantial part of the Latin American *intelligentsia* but has also made significant inroads in the *intelligentsia* and the academy of the First World, including "nomadic" intellectuals transplanted from all kinds of Third Worlds.

The secular crisis of Latin America obliges us to reexamine, radically, current cultural values and worn out identity concepts that have only led to paralysis of the continent. Forty years after the publication of García Márquez's *magnum opus,* it is high time to dismantle the Macondo! It will not be an easy task, since its dragon heads emerge all over the place (wherever there is talk about Latin American "enigmas," "monsters" blocking the road ahead, "original sins," or "labyrinths") and are celebrated by the most prestigious critics and academics of our times.

Today, it is high time to critically reread the *pensadores* writing on the road leading up to Macondo for what they are worth. If not now, when? There has been some help coming from Latin America in the recent decades. Philosophers (the Mexican Leopoldo Zea of the 1990s, the Colombian Santiago Castro-Gómez), historians (the Mexican Edmundo O'Gorman), students of sociology of culture (the Chileans José Joaquín Brunner, Jorge Larraín, Eduardo Devés Valdés, Javier Pinedo, the Argentine Néstor García Canclini, among others), students of communications (the Catalan-Colombian Jesús Martín-Barbero), or critical intellectuals (such as the Argentine Beatriz Sarlo or the Guatemalan Mario Roberto Morales) have all tackled parts of the problem. It is only symptomatic that much of their most incisive work has not been published in English yet.[37]

REFERENCES

Alberdi, Juan Bautista. (1954). *Fragmento preliminar al estudio del derecho.* Buenos Aires: Hachette. (Orig. ed. 1837).

———. (1915). *Las bases.* Biblioteca Argentina. Buenos Aires: Librería La Facultad. (Orig. ed. 1852).

Alonso, Carlos J. (1998). *The Burden of Modernity: The Rhetoric of Cultural Discourse in Spanish America.* New York/Oxford: Oxford University Press.

Anderson, Benedict. (1991). *Imagined Communities: Reflections on the Origins and Spread of Nationalism.* London/New York: Verso.

Bonfil Batalla, Guillermo. (2001). *México profundo: Una civilización negada.* Mexico: Conaculta.

Brunner, Jose Joaquín. (2002). Traditionalism and Modernity in Latin American Culture. In Emil Volek (Ed.). *Latin America Writes Back* (pp. 3-31).

Castro-Gómez, Santiago. (1996). *Crítica de la razón latinoamericana.* Barcelona: Puvill.

Devés Valdés, Eduardo. (2000-2004). *El pensamiento latinoamericano en el siglo XX.* 3 vols. Buenos Aires: Biblos.

Escudé, Carlos. (1995). Argentina, 1900-1950: imagen de sí misma, imagen de Estados Unidos y el conflicto diplomático. In Víctor A. Arriaga Weiss and Ana Rosa Suárez

[37] Special effort to recover some of this work done in the 1990s has been made in my edited *Latin America Writes Back* (2002).

Argüello (Eds.). *Estados Unidos desde América Latina: Sociedad, política y cultura* (pp. 231-68). Mexico: El Colegio de Mexico.

Flores Galindo, Alberto. (1980). *La agonía de Mariátegui: La polémica con la Komintern.* Lima: DESCO.

García Canclini, Néstor. (1990). *Culturas híbridas: estrategias para entrar y salir de la modernidad.* Mexico: Grijalbo.

Johnson, Paul. (1988). *Intellectuals.* London: Weidenfeld & Nicholson.

Kusch, Rodolfo. (1962). *América profunda.* Buenos Aires: Hachette.

Larraín, Jorge. (2000). *Identity and Modernity in Latin America.* Cambridge, UK: Polity Press.

———. (2002). Postmodernism and Latin American Identity. In Emil Volek (Ed.). *Latin America Writes Back* (pp. 79-104).

Lauer, Mirko. (1997). *Andes imaginarios: Discursos del indigenismo 2.* Cusco: CBC.

Leibner, Gerardo. (1999). *El mito del socialismo indígena: Fuentes y contextos peruanos de Mariátegui.* Lima: Pontificia Universidad Católica del Perú.

Lomnitz-Adler, Claudio. (1992). *Exits from the Labyrinth: Culture and Ideology in the Mexican National Space.* Berkeley/Los Angeles: University of California Press.

Mariátegui, José Carlos. (1973). *Siete ensayos de interpretación de la realidad peruana.* Havana: Casa de las Américas. (Orig. ed. 1928).

Martí, José. (1891). Nuestra América. In his *Obras completas VI* (pp. 15-23). Havana: Editorial Nacional, 1963-1966.

Martínez Estrada, Ezequiel. (1940). *La cabeza de Goliath: Microscopía de Buenos Aires.* Buenos Aires: Club del Libro ALA.

Mignolo, Walter. (1995). Occidentalización, imperialismo, globalización: herencias coloniales y teorías postcoloniales. *Revista iberoamericana* 61.170-171, pp. 27-40.

———. (2005). *The Idea of Latin America.* Oxford, UK: Blackwell.

Miller, Nicola. (2008). *Reinventing Modernity in Latin America: Intellectuals Imagine the Future, 1900-1930.* New York: Palgrave Macmillan.

Molnar, Thomas. (1994). *The Decline of the Intellectual.* New Brunswick/London: Transaction Publishers.

Morales, Mario Roberto. (1998). *La articulación de las diferencias, o el síndrome de Maximón: Los discursos literarios y políticos del debate interétnico en Guatemala.* Guatemala: FLACSO.

O'Gorman, Edmundo. (1977). *México: El trauma de su historia.* Mexico: UNAM.

Onís, José de. (1975). *The United States as Seen by Spanish American Writers (1776-1890).* New York: Gordian Press.

Paz, Octavio. (1959). *El laberinto de la soledad.* Mexico: FCE.

Petras, James & Morris Morley. (1990). The Metamorphosis of Latin America's Intellectuals. *US Hegemony Under Siege: Class, Politics and Development in Latin America.* London/New York: Verso, pp. 147-56.

Reyes, Alfonso. (1935). Notas sobre la inteligencia Americana. *Obras completas XI: Ultima Tule.* Mexico: FCE, 1960, pp. 82-90.

Rodó, José Enrique. (1977). *Ariel.* Mexico: Porrúa. (Orig. ed. 1900).

Rodríguez Monegal, Emir. (1969). *Sexo y poesía en el 900 uruguayo: Los extraños destinos de Roberto y Delmira.* Montevideo: Editorial Alfa.

Salas, Horacio. (1996). *El centenario: La Argentina en su hora más gloriosa.* Buenos Aires: Planeta.

Sarmiento, Domingo Faustino. (2003). *Facundo: Civilization and Barbarism.* Transl. Kathleen Ross. Berkeley/Los Angeles: University of California Press. (Orig. ed. 1845).

———. (1916). *Argirópolis.* Buenos Aires: La Cultura Argentina. (Orig. ed. 1850).

Sommer, Doris. (1991). *Foundational Fictions: The National Romances of Latin America.* Berkeley/Los Angeles: University of California Press.

Shumway, Nicolas. (1991). *The Invention of Argentina.* Berkeley/Los Angeles: University of California Press.

Torres García, Joaquín. (1944). *Universalismo constructivo: Contribución a la unificación del arte y la cultura de América.* Buenos Aires: Poseidón.

Valcárcel, Luis E. (1927). *Tempestad en los Andes.* Biblioteca Amauta. Lima: Minerva.

Vasconcelos, José. (1948). *La raza cósmica.* Mexico: Espasa Calpe. (Orig. ed. 1925).

Vidal, Hernán (Ed.). (2008). *Treinta años de estudios literarios/culturales latinoamericanistas en Estados Unidos: Memorias, testimonios, reflexiones críticas.* Biblioteca de América, Pittsburgh: ILLI/University of Pittsburgh.

Volek, Emil. (1994). El realismo mágico entre la modernidad y la postmodernidad. *Literatura hispanoamericana entre la modernidad y la postmodernidad.* Cuadernos de Trabajo, 9. Bogotá: Universidad Nacional de Colombia, pp. 11-24.

———. (2002). Los entramados ideológicos del testimonio latinoamericano: La Revolución anunciada, el escuro objeto del deseo, el macondismo posmoderno/poscolonial, Menchú y Stoll. *Chasqui* 31.1, pp. 44-74.

———. (2005). Anverso y reverso del laberinto: Octavio Paz, ¿fundador de Macondo? In Alma Leticia Martínez-Figueroa (Ed.). *Memoria: XIX Coloquio de Literatura Mexicana e Hispanoamericana (2003)* (pp. 35-49). Hermosillo: Universidad de Sonora.

———. (2006). José Martí: Nuestra (Macondo)América. *Caribe* 9.1, pp. 19-40.

———. (2008). Promesas y simulacros en el baratillo posmodernista: saber y ser en las encrucijadas de una "historia mostrenca". In Hernán Vidal (Ed.), *Treinta años* (pp. 129-64).

Volek, Emil (Ed.). (2002). *Latin America Writes Back: Postmodernity in the Periphery, An Interdisciplinary Perspective.* Hispanic Issues 28. New York/London: Routlege.

Zea, Leopoldo. (1991). *La filosofía como compromiso de liberación.* Caracas: Biblioteca Ayacucho.

Zimmermann, Warren. (2001). *First Great Triumph: How Five Americans Made Their Country a World Power.* New York: Farrar, Strauss, and Giroux.

In: Latin American Issues and Challenges
Editors: L. Naciamento and G. Sousa
ISBN 978-1-60692-349-8

Chapter 4

TROUBLING THE *FEMME FATALE* GENDER IN THE BRAZILIAN FILM *MADAME SATÃ* (2002)

Antônio Márcio da Silva
Dep. of Hispanic, Portuguese, and Latin American Studies, University of Bristol - UK

ABSTRACT

This chapter analyzes the film Madame Satã. It reads the protagonist Madame Satã (João)—a male homosexual—as a femme fatale to challenge the construction of the femme fatale based solely on the biological gender pair: male/female (Stables 1998: 177). It draws on Butler's (1990a) discussion of gender, which asserts that 'there is no gender identity behind the expression of gender; [...] identity is performatively constituted by the very "expressions" that are said to be its results (p.25).' This chapter highlights commonalities that link Satã and the femme fatale to argue that both pose a threat to social gender construction rules and challenge the acceptable gender roles dictated by social order.

Keywords: Brazilian Cinema, *femme fatale*, gender performativity, sexuality, film

Karim Ainouz's *Madame Satã* is a film that plays with gender representations. It presents the male/female pair as constructs of performativity rather than the 'biology-is-destiny gender formulation'.[1] Satã's performance is a mixture of the figure of the *malandro*[2] and a drag queen. These are two opposing gender performances that are conflated to confuse established male/female gender roles in a patriarchal society. This simultaneously prevents Madame Satã from being configured under the categories of a "fairy" or a "man" as 'he seemed to be

---

[1] Butler, J. (1990a) *Gender Trouble: Feminism and the Subversion of Identity*, New York and London: Routledge, p.11.

[2] The word "*malandro*" has no direct English equivalent. He is an archetypal figure who was not simply a criminal but a mastermind of the con art. He dwells in the underworld and is smooth, almost perfect, in commanding the respect and also love even of his victims. He seems to be a match to the *femme fatale*, i.e., a *homme fatal*.

both'.[3] Arguably, his[4] gender performativity becomes a 'free-floating artifice' that could be 'theorized as radically independent of sex'. This is because his gender performativity implies that '*man* and *masculine* might just as easily signify a female body as a male one, and *woman* and *feminine* a male body as easily as a female one.'[5] For James N. Green, Satã's ambiguous way of leading his life, which we would call 'gender performativity', confuses the idea of appropriate behavior for a *malandro*. His behavior makes him 'queer' not only in the sense of strange and different but also in the way he challenges 'easy classifications'.[6]

This chapter therefore discusses the representation of the *femme fatale* based on Madame Satã's gender performativity, despite his biological sex. By referring to Judith Butler's theory of gender performativity that she developed in her seminal work *Gender Trouble* (1990a), this chapter suggests new ways to read the "deadly woman". Rather than concentrating on the usual biological gender (female), it suggests exploring the deadly woman's construction through performance, ignoring if it is via a male or female biological body. Instead, it considers how a biological body—male or female (in the case of this chapter, male)—performs fatality. In Butler's interpretation, 'Performativity is not a singular act, but a repetition and a ritual, which achieves its effects through its naturalization in the context of a body, understood, in part, as a culturally sustained temporal duration.'[7] Satã's gender performativity seems to have temporal duration that shifts according to the context in which it is performed. He sees the way he manages his gender shifts as normal but society despises him for his acts, and views them as deviant and a threat to masculinity.

The film is based on the real-life story of João Francisco dos Santos (1900–1976). João was born to descendents of slaves in the northeast of Brazil. His mother sold him to a horse seller when he was eight years old.[8] His skin color is significant[9], especially when considering the time the story develops: the 1930s. For example, the whitening project[10] was a government policy in the previous decades aimed at literally whitening the nation's population by encouraging the immigration of white Europeans into Brazil. For Green (*op. cit.*), race cannot be ignored in his case, since Satã plays the figure of the *malandro* and in the Brazilian popular imaginary the *malandro* is nearly always an Afro-descendent. According to the author, the criminologists who studied homosexuality in Rio de Janeiro in the 1930s usually associated race to sexual transgression as well as to pathological behavior, which even includes murder.[11]

---

[3] Green, J. N. (2003) O Pasquim e Madame Satã, a "Rainha" Negra da Boemia Brasileira, *TOPOI*, v. 4, n.7, Jul-Dez, pp.201-221.

[4] Every time references are made to Madame Satã in this article, they will use masculine pronouns and possessives, so to avoid the s/he or his/her since that causes confusion in some parts, depending on the gender he is performing.

[5] Butler, J. (1990a), p.9.

[6] Green, J.N. (2003), p.219.

[7] Butler, J. (1990a), p. xv.

[8] Green, J.N. (2003), p.205.

[9] In some periods of Brazilian history, it seems to become the main aim of the ruling class to sweep the black race from the national territory, to "purify the race" so that Brazil became a powerful nation. That seems to have become an obssession, especially during the era so-called "Belle Epoque". For instance, in 1912, the so-called whitening project, when Carlos Lacerda calculated that in 2012 the black population in Brazil would be zero per cent of the total country's population while the mulattoes would represent only three per cent.

[10] See Skidmore (1993), p. 81.

[11] Green, J.N. (2003), p.214.

João flees to Rio de Janeiro, when he is still eight years old, with a woman who promised him work in a boarding house. Later, in Rio, when he was around thirteen, he leaves the house to live on the streets and do small jobs in Lapa's neighborhood. When he turned eighteen, he went to live in a brothel where he worked as a waiter/maid and "served" customers in ways dictated by their preferences.[12] The film, however, portrays an already adult João who is involved in crime, works in low-paid jobs (when he manages to be paid), and dreams of becoming a famous performer. The failure to achieve this dream throughout the film, he declares, becomes a key element in developing his "rage" toward everything and everyone, which is confirmed at the end of the film when he is successful in his first public performance. He states: 'I have never been happier in my entire life.'

The film is set in Lapa in Rio de Janeiro – a place portrayed with the glamour and darkness of the noir or, more accurately, the new-noir films through the cinematography, which suggests similarities of Lapa with the dark and shadowy streets of the traditional *femme fatale* films. João's (Lázaro Ramos) commune has in it the whore Laurita (Marcelia Cartaxo) and her young daughter Vitória, to whom João acts as a quasi-father (if not "mother"), and Tabú (Flávio Bauraqui),[13] a transvestite who apparently takes the role of the maid in the house and to whom João acts as a pimp. João behaves as the male figure in charge of the household and a sequence showing Tabú doing the washing suggests João's control of the house. The presence of Tabú and Laurita in the house is another important factor as, although they do not apparently have any sexual contact with Satã, it could still suggest bigamy with Satã performing the role of the heterosexual husband whose acts are violent and authoritative, and they prevent the "women" from having an "active voice" in the house. He controls the "females" and they are in charge of the housework. The 'indecently handsome'[14] petty-thief Renatinho (Fellipe Marques) is also part of the commune and becomes a kind of boyfriend to João, although João subsequently romances and assaults him.

The question Satã is asked in the sequence near the end of the film, when he suffers an unprovoked homophobic attack from a drunkard, exemplifies how the gay character's performance in the film could equal that of the *femme fatale*'s: 'Are you playing a woman or a man?' It also reinforces Gutmann and Vigoya's observation that 'homophobia in Latin America is a widespread source of violence directed at men who are seen in some sense as effeminate or are believed to have sex with other men.'[15] Satã's performance in the sequence, as in most of the film, challenges the distinction between sex and gender once such distinction, according to Judith Butler, 'serves the argument that whatever biological intractability sex appears to have, gender is culturally constructed', which 'originally intended to dispute the biology-is-destiny formulation.'[16] Hence, for Butler, gender ends up being 'neither the casual result of sex nor as fixed as sex.'[17] Gender, in Butler's interpretation, could be a 'multiple interpretation of sex'. Satã challenges the roles that a biological male is

---

[12] Green, J.N. (2003), p.205.

[13] Tabú, in English 'taboo', does not seem to be a name chosen randomly. It implies critique to the patriarchal established norms which are challenged in the film.

[14] Morris, Gary (2003) *Fists and Feathers: Madame Satã Reviewed*, available online at: www.brightlightsfilm.com/41/madame.htm

[15] Gutmann, M.C. & M.V. Vigoya (2005), 'Masculinities in Latin America', in M. S. Kimmel, J. Hearn and R.W. Connell (eds.), Handbook of Studies on Men & Masculinities, London.: Sage Publications, (114-128), p.118.

[16] Butler, J. (1990a), p.8.

[17] Ibid

supposed to play and his gender shifts suggest multiplicity of and independence from sex. His gender performativity follows personal choices rather than what society dictates as normal. In his interpretation, there was nothing wrong in being a "*bicha*". He was one because he wanted to, but, significantly, he claims he was not "less" man because of such a choice.[18]

Satã's choice of words in the phrase "become a *bicha*" echoes Simone de Beauvoir's famous sentence that 'one is not born a woman, but, rather, becomes one.'[19] Butler (1990a) argues that Beauvoir's comment indicates that someone who becomes a woman does not necessarily need to be born as female. Therefore, Satã declaring that he *became* a "*bicha*" could signify not only his performance of gender, but also that he could easily *become* "a woman" and a "*femme fatale*". According to Green (*op. cit.*), Madame Satã's behavior confused the social stereotypes associated to homosexuals or "*bichas*", since it transgressed patterns of effeminacy and mimicry associated to women. The author argues that Satã challenged the stereotypes and destabilized the beliefs people had about the appropriate behavior of Brazilian homosexuals.[20] Satã's behavior, according to Green, also gave birth to stereotypes and created anxiety—primarily about the men who would fight with him (p.212). Thus, Satã's gender performance poses a direct threat to masculinity, which is also the case with the *femme fatale*.

The point argued in this chapter after a detailed analysis of various gay characters in certain films, is that *Madame Satã* shows how gay characters could bear much in common with the "deadly woman". Considering studies on fatality, we have the *femme fatale* and the *homme fatal,* who are presented based on the traditional biological gender pair: male/female. What about the queer characters present on cinematic productions, such as Madame Satã, who have *fatal(e)* features? What should they be named: *femme fatale*, *homme fatal*, *gay* or *queer fatal/ fatale*? Where would they fit in the scholarship of gender once they need to be included in discussions about fatality – an approach hitherto to the best of our knowledge remains unexplored by scholars, especially those working on queer cinema.

There are, however, studies that deal with lesbian *femmes fatales,* for example Hart (1994), Stables (1998), White (1998) and Straayer (1998), among others. The lesbian *femmes fatales* mostly engage in a "dispute", even if indirectly, with a man over another woman. So, how could these lesbians be *femmes fatales* if they do not threaten masculinity directly? Moving from that, the gay male searching for a male lover (if not for a sex plaything as the *femme fatale* does) could be seen as a more direct threat to masculinity as the *femme fatale* is. Furthermore, gay males are usually presented as being an additional threat to society as a whole, which in the film is illustrated with the drunkard's words towards Satã, in the aforementioned sequence: 'It's because of niggers like you' (i.e. "*bicha*") that 'this place (Lapa) is going to shit.'

Besides exposing the problem João faces because of his race, such a comment also links his color to his sexual identity and reinforces what was said about him in his first sequence in the film. In it, he is portrayed in a medium shot in a police station. A male voice-over reads the bulletin and reports his crime and deviations, but also judges João's character. It is reported, for instance, that 'he hates society, once this one rejects him because of his vices.' Thus, 'gender trouble' in *Madame Satã* is stated as an important reason for the hatred João

[18] Green, J.N. (2003), p.213.
[19] Beauvoir, S. (1973) *The Second Sex,* trans. E. M. Parshley, New York: Vintage, p.301.
[20] Green, J.N. (2003), p.201.

(Satã) suffers from society. This apparently intersects with 'racial, class, ethnic, sexual, and regional modalities of discursively constituted identities.'[21] He is an Afro-descendent, lower class migrant who came from the Brazilian northeast, and is homosexual. As a result of the intersection between gender and the other modalities, as Butler suggested in another context, it becomes impossible to 'separate out "gender" from the political and cultural intersections in which it is invariably produced and maintained.'[22]

These intersections are present in *Madame Satã* and reflect gender performativity in the film. Thus, in the film, gender becomes an act that is staged and shifts according to what João's (Satã) needs are. He acts as a father, mother, husband, avenger, pimp and drag queen. Although he is generally effeminate, he also suddenly shifts and displays hard line male attitudes, as he does in the way he treats and constantly assaults Tabú.

In questioning whether gender is an act, Butler (1990b) describes performance as something that is repeated, which, she suggests, can also bear the repetition of something already socially established. She relates this repetition to the constitution of gender and points out the fact that there are bodies that enact the social performance so its signification becomes 'stylized into gendered modes'. Therefore, 'this act performed by gender also becomes public.' Once performance becomes public, and because the public usually understands gender as the biology-is-destiny male/female pair, it then has consequences since it 'is affected with the strategic aim of maintaining gender within its binary frame.'[23] However, as Butler notes, 'the body is not passively scripted with cultural codes, as if it were a lifeless recipient of wholly pre-given cultural relations.'[24] Satã, for instance, challenges cultural inscriptions as he performs "different genders" and ignores the established biological male/female gender roles society dictates. For Butler:

> If gender is the cultural meanings that the sexed body assumes, then a gender cannot be said to follow from a sex in any one way. Taken to its logical limit, the sex/gender distinction suggests a radical discontinuity between sexed bodies and culturally constructed genders (1990a: 9).

Butler further elaborates on gender performance by comparing it within theatrical and non-theatrical domains. She proposes that in the non-theatrical context such performance is governed in a more punitive and regulatory way than under social conventions.[25] Satã's performance on the stage (as a drag) is seen as pleasurable whereas his gender performance outside it, in the "real world", even though it is displayed on the same biological body, is not accepted. This is also the case in other films portraying drag queens such as the Australian film *The Adventures of Priscilla, Queen of the Desert* (1994), which is also set in a macho-orientated culture. As Butler argues, 'the sight of a transvestite on stage can compel pleasure and applause, while the sight of the same transvestite on the seat next to us on the bus can

[21] Butler, J. (1990a), p.4.
[22] Ibid, pp.4-5.
[23] Butler, J. (1990b) 'Performative Acts and Gender Constitution: An Essay on Phenomenology and Feminist Theory', in Sue-Ellen Case (ed.), *Performing Feminisms: Feminist Critical Theory and Theatre*, Baltimore: Johns Hopkins University Press, (154-165), p.160.
[24] Ibid
[25] Ibid, p. 161.

compel fear, rage, even violence.'[26] For the author, this happens because of the protection the spectator has in the theatrical realm where s/he can say, 'this is just an act'. This differentiates it and makes it distinct from what is understood as 'real'. However, on the street, she suggests, this same act can become quite dangerous since the theatrical conventions that delimit the 'imaginary character' of the act cease to exist.[27]

An example of this is the opening scene in *Madame Satã* – one of the most remarkable moments – which presents Satã's manufactured social image to the viewer. A male voice-over characterizes him: 'he has no education' and 'associates with pederasts, whores, procurers and other misfits'; 'his money can come only from degenerate criminal activities.' Therefore, 'for all these reasons, he is entirely pernicious and poses a considerable threat to society.' This characterization of Satã could be related to what Butler further argues:

> As a corporeal field of cultural play, gender is a basically innovative affair, although it is quite clear that there are strict punishments for contesting the script by performing out of turn or through unwarranted improvisations. Gender is not passively scripted on the body, and neither is it determined by nature, language, the symbolic, or the overwhelming history of patriarchy (1990b: 164).

Building on Butler's gender performativity theory, Shaw (2000) suggests that if gender is a construct from a series of repeated actions learned within cultures, then there exists the possibility of breaking from traditional performances of both the masculine and the feminine. For Shaw, subjects can then be freed from restrictions associated with their sex and consequently take on multiple gender identities.[28]

In working with the complex relationship between gender construction and culture it is important to be aware of cultural differences. For instance, it would be dangerous to make any generalized assertion of Brazilian or Latin American culture based on the culture in Lapa portrayed in the film. Cantú (2000) criticizes the scholarly relationship established on Latin American studies between gender and culture, pointing out problems such as homogenizing Latino culture as one without cultural differences. Additionally, he argues, Latino Culture is commonly represented as if it were fixed or static, which he exemplifies with the gender role stereotypes of male and female roles as being confined to machismo and marianismo sex-role models in scholarly studies. The author points out the common view of such gender roles: 'women are supposedly submissive, maternal, and virginal; men are characterized by verbal and bodily aggression, frequent drunkenness, and sexual dominance' (p.227). His argument could be complemented by Guttmann and Vigoya's (2005) suggestion that 'one obstacle that must be overcome in studying sexual passivity in Latin America is the notion that passivity is the mirror opposite of activity' (p.121). In Satã, sexual acts are very much portrayed based on this notion of passive and active perception, especially regarding homosexuality. However, Satã's sexual acts and behavior deny society beliefs and stereotypes of who is active or passive in gay sex copulation.

---

[26] Ibid

[27] Ibid

[28] Shaw, D. (2000), Men in High Heels: The Feminine Man and Performances of Femininity in Tacones Lejanos by Pedro Almodovar, *Journal of Iberian and Latin American Studies*, 6:1, (55-62), p.56.

Concerning studies on the Latino gay, Cantú (*op. cit.*) provides insights into sociological and anthropological literature – such as Almaguer (1993), Carrier (1995), Lancaster (1992), and Murray (1995) – which contribute to an understanding of Latino men's sexual identities. These identities are determined not 'by the biological sex of the sexual partner but the culturally defined roles of *activo/pasivo* (i.e. dominant/submissive) assumed by the actors' (2000: 228). These culturally defined roles of active and passive in *Madame Satã* suggest that Satã poses a threat to masculinity and becomes a source of anxiety for society. In other words, although he is seen as passive or as the *"bicha"* (the fairy), during the intercourse scenes he is portrayed as the dominant male who takes on the active role even though the men he has sex with (Álvaro, a married man, and Renatinho) behave as straight males. These performances contradict the conflicting understanding of homosexuality in Brazil, which is that if two men have sex the "gay" or "*bicha*" is the only one penetrated.[29]

James N. Green (2003), together with other scholars who have studied Brazilian sexuality such as Parker (1991), suggests that the passive and active roles performed by the homosexual subjects define their position in society. The "*bofe*" who assumes the active male role is not usually seen as homosexual while the "*bicha*" is the one who adopts the passive role and represents the assumed role of a woman in sexual intercourse. This is again based on the biological male and female heterosexual coupling. However, this is another aspect that the film challenges. Even though the real life Satã (João Francisco dos Santos) declares in an interview to the Pasquim[30] in the 1970s that he was the passive[31] one in the copulations, the film does not imply this, which apparently protects the supposed "*bofes*". In the eyes of society, for instance, Renatinho and Álvaro would definitely be seen as "*bofes*" – especially the latter, since he is married to a woman.

Thus, the two men who act straight do not comply with the active and dominant roles that would be a precondition of reaffirming their masculinity since 'as long as Latino men remain *activo* (active) or dominant in the sexual script, their masculinity, as culturally defined, remains intact.'[32] However, instead of taking such roles they submit themselves to the sexual domineering Madame Satã who poses a threat to their culturally constructed masculinity. Hence, the appearance disguises the actual acts. The idea of Satã being expected to be passive is highlighted in the opening sequence at the police station by the male voice-over: 'he is a passive pederast, who shaves his eyebrows and imitates women, even changing his own voice', but this proves to be false. The straight acting males depend on the secrecy of what happens between them and Satã, which if not revealed, give the two men security of their status as the dominant male in accordance with the societal norms. It could be argued that what they look for in Satã is what men usually look for in the *femme fatale*: to be dominated by her and to satisfy their male sexual fantasies and possibly their sadomasochist pleasures.[33]

---

[29] Kulick, D. (1998) *Travesti: Sex, Gender and Culture among Brazilian Transgendered Prostitutes*, Chicago and London: The University of Chicago Press, p.212.

[30] A newspaper in the 1970s that represented opposition to the military regime. It was considerably against homosexuality; however, it surprisingly interviewed João (Madame Satã).

[31] Green, J.N. (2003)

[32] Cantú (2000), 'Entre Hombres/Between Men: Latino Masculinities and Homosexualities', in P.M. Nardi (ed.), *Gay Masculinities*, Thousand Oaks: Sage Publications, (224-246), p.229.

[33] This is very common in the films that bring the *femme fatale* figure in the 1990s. For instance, *Basic Instinct* (1992), *Basic Instinct 2* (2006), Body *of Evidence* (1993), *The Last Seduction* (1993) and *Femme Fatale* (2002).

Males in patriarchal societies usually have the need to prove themselves to be a "man", to "act like a man", to have a "man's job" and to "dress as a man", along with having certain male attitudes. They do not want to be seen outside the male community; they do not want to be the strange and rejected element in a homophobic society so they usually hate "otherness" – that is homosexuality; but 'as basic psychology shows, what is identified as the external "*other*" is usually part of the self which is rejected and hence projected outwards.'[34] This could be an illustration of Butler's (*op. cit.*) point regarding the terror and anxiety some people suffer in "becoming gay", which concerns a fear of losing a 'place in gender' or of not knowing what s/he will be if s/he sleeps with another person ostensibly of the "same" gender.[35]

In *Madame Satã*, gender performativity moves back and forth; that is, Satã's gender shifts to a new gender performance but suddenly return to a previous state. Satã's attitudes are complex, which makes it difficult for the audience to assert his gender based on his performance. For instance, his drag queen performance could demonstrate Butler's suggestion that drag 'is meant to establish that "reality" is not as fixed as we generally assume it to be.'[36] This could also apply to the *femme fatale* who does not necessarily need to be studied based on biological sex but rather on performance, since, as for Butler, when Beauvoir asserted that one is not born a woman but becomes one, there is nothing to prove that this person is a biological female. Thus, once gender construction is theorized independently of biological sex, as Butler (*op. cit.*) suggested, an intersection between the gay male and the *femme fatale* can become possible.

The film's first sequence at the bar Danúbio in Lapa, which has a mix of shots portraying defragmented bodies, shows this. Satã's face, hands with rings and nails polished in red (which could be either of a male or female) are edited together with shots of a female body and male spectators' gazes. The men seem to be looking at both defragmented bodies. This suggests that there are male spectators for the male/female biological bodies and that the male gaze scrutinizes both. Satã's face, which is covered by a curtain, appears in close-ups, indicating a need for accessories in his performance. The camera then cuts and shows a female performer, whom the viewer sees from Satã's point of view while he mimics her. Hence, female performativity of gender can be played by both biological sexes.

During her presentation on the stage, the female performer, Vitória, recites lines about a Sultan who married different virgin girls every night. Her lines are considerably important in reassuring masculinity in the patriarchal discourse as well as emphasizing the hetero male/female pair. Vitória's use of a veil and other accessories in her performance as well as her story to seduce males and her song in French, combine with her color, white, to contrast Satã. Although Satã mimics her "European" feminine performance, he is black and male. The clothes and accessories in the sequence are important since they also show conflict between performances that could be public or private. In other words, performances that are accepted by the public as natural, such as the female's, or seen as a subversion of what is understood as being the acceptable, such as the "unnatural" effeminate male's transvestite performance. As Vitória is female, her performance is public as she does not need to hide whereas Satã does his mimicked performance in the back stage – out of the male spectators' gazes. This makes

[34] Barry, Peter (2002), *Beginning Theory: An Introduction to Literary and Cultural Theory*, 2nd ed., Manchester and New York: Manchester University Press, p.145.

[35] Butler, J. (1990a), p. xi.

[36] Ibid, p. xxv.

the "private performance" a secure mechanism that does not threaten public masculinity directly, which is also the case in his performance of active/passive roles in bed (previously mentioned in this chapter).

Satã's mimicry of Vitoria's performance occurs repeatedly in the film and could be a direct criticism of the latter's femininity as well as the sameness in her performance. According to Vitória, she has been doing the same thing for over two years and 'it is high time to finish it and change' so perhaps the public or "male" is looking for something different. This could also imply her unnatural performance of femininity. Thus, Satã's 'parodic repetition of the "original" […] reveals the original to be nothing other than a parody of the idea of the natural and the original.'[37] In *Madame Satã*, gender performativity shifts as a chameleon changes its color. The feminine (queer) performance Satã makes is sharply opposed in the sequence following the one mentioned above, which shows a shadow of a masculine figure that seems as though it is the *malandro*.

A later sequence in the film also intertwines shots of Satã mimicking Vitória's performance. This time he is cross-dressed in the female performer's clothes in the dressing room while she does her public performance. When Vitória goes to the dressing room, she undresses by handing her accessories to Satã, who the viewer finds out, works as her assistant. This suggests transference of her femininity onto him. However, in another sequence, she becomes angry when she finds him wearing her clothes and asks him who he thinks he is to be mimicking her. For Satã, it was not such an issue to have worn her clothes; however, she offends Satã by declaring that she had been advised before 'not to trust that "nigger"' because 'he was crazier than a mad dog.' Of course, Satã does not accept such treatment and destroys her costumes and accessories as revenge, which implies that he is destroying her femininity since it relies on such accessories. As Satã is offended he decides to discontinue working for Vitória and her husband Gregório.

When Satã goes to Gregório to demand payment for his work, the latter refuses to pay him and points a gun to Satã's face. However, Gregório has to stop showing off his macho power once Satã puts a razor on his genitalia and threatens to castrate him if he shoots. Thus, Satã represents two threats: one to the female, as he shows he can perform "her gender" regardless of his biological body, another because he represents a metaphorical castration of the male, manifested in his razor. The suggestion is that these are a direct result of his transgression of the established hetero gender roles, especially considering the figure of the *malandro*.

Reading Satã as a Femme Fatale

To read Madame Satã as a *femme fatale*, it is useful to consider the main mechanisms used to construct the image of the *female fatale* on screen, especially concerning her sexuality, such as the iconography of image and visual style that Place (1978) suggested as well as the language the "deadly woman" uses, particularly in more recent films. Thus, it is important to discuss the background of the presence of *femmes fatales* in artistic productions. Though she became prominent in films made in the 1940s, she also re-emerged in films of the 1990s and persists in the present decade.

[37] Butler, J. (1990a), p.31.

The notion of the *femme fatale* resonated strongly throughout nineteenth century cultural production, particularly in Europe. In literature, she usually posed a threat to the male colonizer as her representation highlighted the organization of the colonial system and the otherness of colonized peoples. By the twentieth century, the *femme fatale* was considered clichéd and rejected as a modern subject. Bade noted that she was no longer an important subject for 'serious writers and painters' who 'abandoned her to the hacks and the film industry' (1978: 36). The deadly woman therefore occupies a place in modern cinematic production, especially in America, in the film noirs of the 1940s and 1950s. In such films, she shifts from posing a threat to the male colonizer only to modern manhood in general. She plays a key role in the battle of the sexes as she challenges the traditionally male-dominated social order. However, after the zenith of the *femme fatale* fever pitch in film noirs, this representation of women did not disappear from either cinema or literature as expected (Bade: 1978). Deadly women still occupy modern film scenarios and, to some extent, literature.[38] Nevertheless, they are reconfigured and appear reshaped to fit the period. This occurs mainly with the relationship between their sexuality and money, and in terms of their possible sexual arrangements, especially concerning the insertion of same-sex intercourse in films of the 1990s, which is relevant to how Madame Satã is presented on screen and how his power is suggested by the 'iconography of image' and 'visual style'.

In *Madame Satã*, the iconography of image shows the mechanisms Satã uses to seduce men, which are 'explicitly sexual'.[39] This is different from the *femme fatale* who uses her hair, which is long unlike Satã's. As if to compensate, Satã puts on make-up and jewelry, and smokes. For example, when João (Satã) first sees Renatinho, his future lover, a shot-reverse-shot sequence shows his device to seduce him. Despite being advised not to get involved with Renatinho by Laurita, while he is dancing with her, João (Satã) puts a cigarette in his mouth and blows the trail of smoke in the air while looking seductively at Renatinho. The use of cigarette in the sequence is very significant since, according to Place (*op. cit.*), cigarettes with their wispy trails of smoke can serve as cues for dark and immoral female sensuality. In this case, one sees a biological male seducing another male by using the same device constantly used by the *femme fatale*.

Another feature of *Madame Satã* related to the iconography of image (more precisely phrased, 'iconography of violence') in *femmes fatales* films is guns. A gun, according to Place, 'is a specific symbol (as is perhaps the cigarette) of the *femme fatale*'s "unnatural" phallic power.'[40] Arguably, Satã, like the well-known *femmes fatales,* seems to have an unnatural phallic power. This power is one he and indeed the *femmes fatales* are allowed to exercise by males (perhaps related to males' masochist pleasures and need to be dominated by the *femme fatale*). Such power performativity reflects Bakhtin's interpretation of carnivalesque power[41] – the *femme fatale* is allowed to reach the domineering position and thereby subverts traditional gender roles, particularly in the sexual context. However, she does not remain in power and is punished severely both for threatening the hero's masculinity

[38] Some examples of *femmes fatales* in contemporary Brazilian literature which were adapted to recent TV series include: *Hilda Furacão* and *Presença de Anita.*

[39] Place, J. (1978) 'Women in Film Noir', in E. Ann Kaplan (ed.), *Women in Film Noir*, London: BFI Publishing, (35-54), p.43.

[40] Ibid, p.45

[41] Bakhtin, M.M. (1984) *Rabelais and His World,* trans. H. Iswolsky, Bloomington: Indiana University Press. See Robert Stam (1990) for a detailed discussion of Bakhtin's interpretation of carnival.

and for subverting acceptable female (in *Madame Satã,* male) behavior dictated by social order. She, therefore, becomes destitute and is punished, which gives a moralistic male-prejudiced message for women (and males) who transgress "acceptable" gender roles. The *femme fatale* is apparently allowed to *perform* power, as is the case with the gay characters, yet is not allowed to remain in the position of power for long and is consequently destroyed.

Regarding visual style, Place (*op. cit.)* notes how the strength of the *femme fatale* is suggested by way of composition, angle, camera movement and lighting. The author also observes how the *femme fatale* actually controls camera movement,[42] not only directing the camera but also the hero's gaze, as well as the audiences'. In *Madame Satã,* the camera movement, angles and shots are important in showing the power performance of Satã's sexuality. Besides the visual style, his performance is important since, as with the *femme fatale*, he also makes use of different devices to seduce his partners. For instance, he uses "*golpes de capoeira"* (*capoeira* moves) in a sequence where he faces a man who has a gun – the gun being a phallic symbol that gives the owner male power. However, the man is metaphorically "castrated" by Satã since the latter removes the gun from him, which also reinforces Satã's motto that a real man defends himself without using a gun. The man tried to get Laurita to have sex with him but Laurita refused, saying she had finished work for the night. The man replied: 'Since when was a hooker ever done for the night?' When Satã performs his masculinity to defend Laurita against patriarchal violence, the man does not take him seriously. Furthermore, the man confronts and abuses him, saying that what Satã likes is a 'fat cock'. However, Satã removes the gun from him with his *capoeira* moves and makes the man disappear, kicking his bum and humiliating him in front of the other people who were in the pub. Satã's attitude suggests his support for female liberation against male domination, and against females being objectified and presented as visual embellishments perpetually available to satiate men's needs.

After beating the man, Satã tells Renatinho: 'You know that it was for you that I kicked that fat pig's ass, don't you?' and slaps Renatinho's face. Thus, besides protecting Laurita, Satã also uses his power performance to seduce Renatinho, which shows how powerful he is and that although he is seen as a 'faggot', he is as much a man as any other man. He slides the "phallic" gun he took from the man down Renatinho's face while talking to him.

At some point in the film, Satã dances for Renatinho. Renatinho cannot resist and kisses him. However, after the kiss, Satã reprimands him: 'Leave this depraved, stinking world.' Satã's choice of words recalls the point Mary Douglas makes that 'a polluting person is always in the wrong. He (sic) has developed some wrong condition or simply crossed over some line which should not have been crossed and this displacement unleashes danger for someone.'[43] Thus, in Satã's understanding, homosexuality has a polluted status in society. He keeps emphasizing such a status in different references he makes to it. For instance, his paternalist discourse is present in a sequence when he reprimands Tabú for having had sex in their house. He refers to the sexual intercourse as "*suas porcarias*" (your dirty things) and gives the impression that gay sex is dirty and cannot happen in a "family house" like theirs, with the father model, the "wife", the "maid" and the child – young Vitória.

[42] Here, it should be understood in terms of how the camera focus on them, not how the director positions a camera giving the actors the space the camera can reach. It might be better understood in terms of visual presentation rather than according to the film production process.

[43] Douglas, M. (1969) *Purity and Danger*, London, Boston and Henley: Routledge and Kegan Paul, p.4, (cited in Butler 1990a: 179).

Satã's point of view mirrors Butler's suggestion that 'homosexuality is almost always conceived within the homophobic signifying economy as both uncivilized and unnatural.'[44] Douglas' and Butler's points are also illustrated near the end of the film, at the already mentioned sequence of the drunkard assaulting Satã. The man uses different words, such as dirty and shit, amongst others, which connote the polluting and uncivilized status of homosexuality.

Madame Satã also echoes the differences added to the new *femme fatale* films, summarized in Stable's (*op. cit.*) model. As the author observes, there is an introduction of three key areas in the new *femme fatale* films: repeated representations of sexual acts, transparently sexual speech and the open problematizing of the *femme fatale*'s sexuality (p.172). Satã uses violence and words related to sex while seducing the men he has intercourse with, which supports Stable's proposition. There is also a mix of male body and female imagery to make it more comfortable for his counterparts. The sequence in which he takes Álvaro, the married man, home demonstrates this. The conversation between them suggests language performativity:

Satã: So, you are looking for a dark girl and the same height as me?
Álvaro: Yeah
Satã: I've got a sister like that! Her name is Josefa. She's got big thighs, hungry lips. She's really *naughty* my sister.

Satã grabs Álvaro's hand and puts it in his own thighs then orders him:

Satã: Feel her thighs, feel them.

With his mouth, he takes the wedding ring from Álvaro's finger in a sensual and graphic sequence. Álvaro takes it from Satã's tongue and spits it away. This suggests Álvaro's abandonment of his married straight man status and also sets the scene for him to experience the pleasure of the red light district with another man. Álvaro is dominated by Satã when he's with him and refers to Satã as Josefa. He also calls Satã using adjectives and nouns in the feminine form only, which perhaps allows himself to ignore his desire towards a man. Satã, however, seems very comfortable as he can "be" a woman or a man, depending on the performance he chooses.

Another moment in the film that shows Satã's domination over the male is when he has sex with Renatinho. Their sexual intercourse echoes that of a straight couple, which is portrayed in the positions they are shot in. Renatinho, who would expect to be the active one during intercourse, takes a passive role. Sexuality in the film is quite explicit as in the *femmes fatales* more recent films, which, according to Stables's (1998) observations insert new elements that approximate the mainstream productions to pornographic films.

Language is also an important element of the film as it challenges patriarchal rule. The characters openly talk about sex using words intimating at pornography. The language used by the new *femme fatale* appropriates that of the forbidden, challenging what is perceived as acceptable and breaking imposed rules. The *femme fatale* becomes the symbol of the forbidden yet is simultaneously venerated for this as 'she offers up obscenities like sweets;

[44] Butler, J. (1990a), p.180.

the terms gain an additional friction and pornographic quality from their context (since these are lower-class words enunciated by elegant upper-class females).'[45] The word "fuck" becomes a prop internalized in the characters' lines as it did in the *femmes fatales* films of and from the 1990s. The word is frequently used as part of their seductions so it is also part of their performance. In Butler's (1990a) understanding, 'speech itself is a bodily act with specific linguistic consequences […] for language as a condition of both bodily seduction and the threat of injury' (p. xxvii).

The language used by the 1990s' *femmes fatales* also helps to highlight the sexual practices they adopt along with the new sexual arrangements they make. Sexual practices inserted in the films include sadomasochism, drug taking whilst having sex and lesbian practices. In *Madame Satã,* the drug use is explicit. For instance, when Renatinho is snorting cocaine in the toilet and he talks to him for the first time, João tells him: 'No man who surrenders to this sinful drug, Satan's dust, can ever satisfy a woman.' The use of the word "woman" is significant yet intriguing as it leaves a question mark about whether Satã is referring to himself as a woman or not. In the sequence, the spectator sees them through a hole in the door in a voyeuristic wherein the looker is observing something forbidden. Satã's approach towards Renatinho's is rather aggressive, instead of in the form of a "passive *bicha*" who wants to be possessed by an "active *bofe*".

In terms of female sexuality, more recent *femme fatale* films have had a new arrangement for the *femme fatale*: the same-sex couplings. As this poses a potential threat to social order, an attempt is made to convert the transgressive woman back to a heterosexual relationship by domesticating her and putting the male back in control. According to Butler, 'policing gender is sometimes used as a way of securing heterosexuality' (1990a: xii). In the context of *Madame Satã*, near the end of the film Laurita reveals to João (Satã) that Renatinho really loved him and that he wanted to live with him. However, in the same sequence she tells him that Renatinho was killed while Satã was in prison. He was the only one that fell in love with Satã, which could make a long-term relationship between the two possible. However, Renatinho is destroyed before this is actualized, thus avoiding such a same-sex relationship. This relates to Butler's point about the heterosexualization of desire, which:

> requires and institutes the production of discrete and asymmetrical oppositions between "feminine" and "masculine", where these are understood as expressive attributes of "male" and "female". The cultural matrix through which gender identity has become intelligible requires that certain kinds of "identities" cannot "exist" – that is, those in which gender does not follow from sex and those in which the practices of desire do not "follow" from either sex or gender (Butler 1990a: 24).

Although João throughout the film is given opportunities for redemption and to form the traditional family with Laurita and bringing her daughter up, he refuses it. What is intriguing about him is how easily he changes his gender roles and how his performance of gender is mutable and dual. For instance, Laurita asks him: where is that man who gave me a home? Also, the question from the drunkard previously mentioned about whether Satã was playing a man or a woman sums up his gender performance, which tempts the question: which gender

[45] Stables (1998) 'The Postmodern Always Rings Twice: Constructing the Femme Fatale in 90s Cinema', in E. A. Kaplan (ed.), *Women in Film Noir* (new-edition), London: BFI Publishing, (164-182), p.177.

are you now? However, João does not convert and ends up in prison. This is a punishment for his deviation from acceptable social norms.

CONCLUSIONS

By reading Madame Satã as an example of *femme fatale*, another possible approach to the analysis of the "deadly woman" has opened up—one based on performance rather than biological gender. As Butler argues, 'the action of gender, as in other ritual social dramas, requires a performance that is *repeated*. This repetition is at once a re-enactment and re-experiencing of a set of meanings already socially established; and it is the mundane and ritualized form of their legitimation.'[46] Thus, the *femme fatale* performance is a repetition of actions that go against what is established as socially acceptable. Satã resembles the *femme fatale* by also challenging established social norms and many similarities exist between Satã, other gay characters and the *femmes fatales* in other films.

Both the *femmes fatales* and the gays are domineering characters when it comes to seduction. They use similar devices and the visual style and iconography of the images are important to show the power they have, even if such power is temporary. They are both removed from their position of power and punished or destroyed often by death or imprisonment. Their counterparts who can't control them nor resist their fatality also receive similar punishment. Performativity is important, as is the language they use— more than the biological body. Language and sex become nearly an imitation of features present in pornographic films.

Femmes fatales often dwell in the underworld and so do gay characters. Both also display unacceptable sexual behavior for the society in which they live and threaten reproduction as neither of them have children. In recent films, fatale characters, especially the *femme fatale*, tend to be presented as dangerous, murderers, addicted to drugs and uncontrollable in many ways. Another common feature in films that portray both is the presence of sadism and masochism, the latter mainly by their counterparts. Hence, it is important that gay characters' fatale features are considered. This provides important insights to understand gay sexuality and contributes to understanding the portrayal of gays by cinema as well as the construction of gay sexuality by society. Therefore, it demystifies and deconstructs the understanding of active and passive roles that dominate popular culture as well as scholarship in queer studies, particularly in relation to Latin America.

REFERENCES

Bade, P. (1979) *Femme Fatale: Images of Evil and Fascinating Women,* London: Ash & Grant.

Bakhtin, M.M. (1984) *Rabelais and His World,* trans. H. Iswolsky, Bloomington: Indiana University Press.

Barry, P. (2002) *Beginning Theory: An Introduction to Literary and Cultural Theory*, 2nd ed., Manchester and New York: Manchester University Press.

[46] Butler, J. (1990a), p.191.

Beauvoir, S. (1973) *The Second Sex,* trans. E. M. Parshley, New York: Vintage.

Butler, J. (1990a) *Gender Trouble: Feminism and the Subversion of Identity,* New York and London: Routledge.

Butler, J. (1990b) 'Performative Acts and Gender Constitution: An Essay on Phenomenology and Feminist Theory', in Sue-Ellen Case (ed.), *Performing Feminisms: Feminist Critical Theory and Theatre,* Baltimore: Johns Hopkins University Press, pp.154-165.

Cantú, L. (2000) 'Entre Hombres/Between Men: Latino Masculinities and Homosexualities', in P.M. Nardi (ed.), *Gay Masculinities,* Thousand Oaks: Sage Publications, pp.224-246.

Green, J. N. (2003) O Pasquim e Madame Satã, a "Rainha" Negra da Boemia Brasileira, *TOPOI,* v. 4, n.7, Jul- Dez, pp.201-221.

Gutmann, M.C. & M.V. Vigoya (2005) 'Masculinities in Latin America', in M. S. Kimmel, J. Hearn and R.W. Connell (eds.), *Handbook of Studies on Men & Masculinities*, London: Sage Publications, pp.114-128.

Hart, L. (1994) *Fatal Women: Lesbian Sexuality and the Mark of Aggression,* Princeton, NJ: Princeton University Press.

Kulick, D. (1998) *Travesti: Sex, Gender and Culture among Brazilian Transgendered Prostitutes,* Chicago and London: The University of Chicago Press.

Morris, G. (2003) *Fists and Feathers: Madame Satã Reviewed.* Available online at www.brightlightsfilm.com/41/madame.htm. Accessed 24/07/2006.

Parker, R.G. (1991) *Bodies, Pleasures and Passions: Sexual Culture in Contemporary Brazil,* Boston: Beacon Press.

Place, J. (1978) 'Women in Film Noir', in E. A. Kaplan (ed.), *Women in Film Noir,* London: BFI Publishing, pp.35-54.

Shaw, D. (2000) Men in High Heels: The Feminine Man and Performances of Femininity in Tacones Lejanos by Pedro Almodovar, *Journal of Iberian and Latin American Studies,* 6:1, pp.55-62.

Stables, K. (1998) 'The Postmodern Always Rings Twice: Constructing the Femme Fatale in 90s Cinema', in E. A. Kaplan (ed.), *Women in Film Noir* (new-edition), London: BFI Publishing, pp.164-182.

Stam, R. (1989) *Subversive Pleasures: Bakhtin, Cultural Criticism, and Film*, Baltimore and London: The Hopkins University Press.

Straayer, C. (1998) 'Femme Fatale or Lesbian Femme: Bound in Sexual Difference', in E. A. Kaplan (ed.), *Women in Film Noir* (new-edition), London: BFI Publishing, pp.151-163.

White, P. (1998) 'Female Spectator, Lesbian Spectre: "The Haunting"', in E. A. Kaplan (ed.), *Women in Film Noir* (new-edition), London: BFI Publishing, pp.130-150.

In: Latin American Issues and Challenges
Editors: L. Naciamento and G. Sousa
ISBN 978-1-60692-349-8

Chapter 5

The Evolution and Contributions of Las Madres de Plaza de Mayo

Lisa Wagner and Madalena Sánchez
Dept. of Classical and Modern Languages, University of Louisville, KY USA

Abstract

In 1977, a small group of Argentine mothers formed La Asociación Madres de Plaza de Mayo to collectively seek information on the disappearance of their children during the Dirty War (1976-1983) and to bring the accused perpetrators to justice. Over the years, this organization has expanded its original mission to promote and protect the rights of all of society's oppressed. Members of Las Madres de Plaza de Mayo, Buenos Aires are currently participating in a number of community-based activities to help the "present-day-disappeared", or those individuals society labels as the unemployed, the poor, and the defenseless (children and seniors). For example, Las Madres have established a university with both degree programs and public course offerings to educate citizens against the ignorance that allowed them to fall victims to the Dirty War of the 1970s and 1980s. They also support a local group of workers who became jobless after the owners of the factory where they worked abandoned the establishment. With the support of Las Madres, the workers have re-opened their factory and once again have begun production. These are but two examples of Las Madres' social commitment to improving conditions in the communities of Buenos Aires. In the present project, we propose to investigate how the ideology, mission and role of Las Madres de Plaza de Mayo has evolved since its establishment as an organization in 1977. Specifically, we critically examine the types of social activities in which Las Madres currently participate through their humanitarian and civil activism, and to explore the types of support and opposition they routinely experience in Argentine society.

INTRODUCTION

During its thirty years of existence, La Asociación Madres de Plaza de Mayo has evolved from a small group of Argentine mothers who sought information on their disappeared children and justice for those responsible, into an internationally recognized human and civil rights organization with a global mission of promoting and protecting the rights of the oppressed around the world. Members of Las Madres de Plaza de Mayo, Buenos Aires are currently participating in a number of community-based activities to help the "present-day-disappeared", or those individuals society categorizes as the unemployed, the poor, and the defenseless (youth and seniors). For example, Las Madres recently purchased land, animals and seeds for a rural community in Buenos Aires so that its members could grow their own food and have regular employment. They also support a local group of workers who re-opened their factory and once again have begun production after the owners of the factory abandoned the establishment with no prior warning. In the present project, we propose to investigate how has the ideology, mission and role of Las Madres de Plaza de Mayo has evolved since its establishment as an organization in 1977. Specifically, we wish to identify and to document the types of daily activities in which Las Madres currently participate to further humanitarian and civil activism and to explore the types of support and opposition they routinely experience in Argentine society.

HISTORICAL BACKGROUND AND ESTABLISHMENT OF LAS MADRES DE PLAZA DE MAYO

Under Argentina's military dictatorship (1976-1983), tens of thousands of Argentine citizens mysteriously "disappeared"- kidnapped, tortured and murdered by their own government. While the disappeared ones comprised a heterogeneous group of Argentine citizens, a large percentage were students and young professionals who were kidnapped from the streets, their places of work or school, and from their own homes. When the first disappearances occurred, the Mothers of the victims went to local police stations to report crimes of kidnapping. Although their inquiries for information and accusations of governmental involvement were met with denial, these persistent office visits were not in vain. By sharing their personal stories with one another, the Mothers of the Disappeared[1] discovered that their families had not been the mere victims of isolated tragedies, but rather were part of a much larger series of heinous crimes against humanity. In April of 1977, fourteen Mothers organized and participated in their first public protest in La Plaza de Mayo, the most important square in Buenos Aires, and the group *Asociación Madres de Plaza de Mayo* was born [Brysk, 1994]. Next, Las Madres established weekly vigils in this prominent square. When the police told Las Madres that it was a breech of security for them to sit on benches in front of government buildings and that they must "keep moving" ("circular" in Spanish) the Mothers began to march around the Plaza [Madres de Plaza de Mayo, 1999]. During these vigils, Las Madres wore white embroidered handkerchiefs bearing the names of their disappeared children. Originally, Las Madres had chosen to wear these white cloths in a

[1] In Spanish, these women are called "Las Madres de los Desaparecidos", or "Las Madres", as they are most commonly known.

previous march, so that they could more easily identify one another within large crowds of participants. However, shortly afterwards, Las Madres attached a special significance to these white cloths: they would symbolize the diapers of their disappeared children and all innocent victims of the mass disappearances. In addition to the white embroidered cloths that Las Madres wore when marching, they also began to carry poster-sized photographs of their missing loved ones, hoping that someone would come forward with information as to their whereabouts.

By 1978, the number of members of the Asociación Madres de Plaza de Mayo had grown to the hundreds [Bosquet, 1983; Bennett & Simpson, 1985; Bonafini, 1985], and Las Madres began to use additional mediums to further their crusade: They published newspaper announcements, circulated petitions, went door-to-door in Buenos Aires to talk to neighbors about their plight, and sent delegates to international venues such as the Catholic Church's Puebla Conference, and the United Nations. In 1980, Las Madres de Plaza de Mayo was nominated for the Nobel Peace Prize, and by 1981 the group was leading mass demonstrations with tens of thousands of participants. In the decade of the '80s, Las Madres traveled to the U.S and to many countries throughout Europe and Latin America. Because Argentine authorities were largely ignoring their pleas, Las Madres attempted to appeal to the international community for justice. Over the course of their travels, Las Madres spoke at conferences, participated in radio and television interviews, and received numerous honors and distinctions for their recognized crusade.[2] These trips were successful, for international organizations began to investigate human rights violations in Argentina: The Argentine government could deny these reports of genocide no longer. However, while some members of the government began to acknowledge these occurrences, they justified their involvement by stating that unconventional techniques were necessary to maintain state order, and that "they were involved in something [against the government]" [Bosquet, 1983; Bonafini, 1985; Brysk, 1994]. In essence, this justification played upon both the principles and philosophies of powerful right-wing governments and religious institutions (e.g., the United States Government and the Roman Catholic Church), upon their quest to defeat communism and other leftist practices, and upon the fear of the average citizen that the government would dissolve and Argentina would be thrown into a state of total anarchy.

In 1983, the Argentine military dictatorship collapsed and human rights became a principal campaign issue. President Raúl Alfonsín assumed office in December 1983, and subsequently created CONADEP,[3] a national blue-ribbon investigatory commission on the disappeared. The President appointed ten well-known public figures to serve on the Commission, five of whom were prominent figures in the human rights movement. Members of the human rights movement also comprised most of CONADEP's staff. Nevertheless, many members of Las Madres de Plaza de Mayo and other human rights activist groups refused to participate in CONADEP, citing that its composition as an unicameral commission made it unaccountable to the people [Brysk, 1994].

The establishment of CONADEP marked a separation between those human rights activists willing to operate within systematic gubernatorial parameters, and those who chose

[2] "Premio a las Madres" [1983], Madrid; *Cambio* 16 "Homenaje de los estudiantes latinoamericanos a las Madres" [1986], Cordoba; *70 aniversario de la reforma universitaria y 60 años del nacimiento del Comandante Che Guevara;* "Reconocimiento de la Asociación de Vecinos de Nov. Barris" [1990], Barcelona), and "Premio León Felipe" [1990], Sevilla, *Ayuntamiento de Marinaleda;* [*http:// www.madres.org*]

[3] Comisión Nacional sobre la Desaparición de Personas

to continue to operate within their own sociopolitical spaces. Las Madres, themselves, experienced internal unrest along these two conflicting approaches to handling justice: One group of Madres believed in following CONADEP in the hopes of finding justice for their disappeared loved ones, while another group of Madres did not trust this commission and had little or no faith in its achieving its goals. The two sides could not reconcile their differences on this issue and others, and the original group of Las Madres split into two independent factions: Las Madres de Plaza de Mayo (Línea Fundadora), which supported CONADEP, and Asociación Madres de Plaza de Mayo, which did not. Over the years, marked differences in beliefs and practices have emerged between these two groups. Las Madres were originally an apolitical group. However, some members began to adopt a human rights stance that posits a direct relationship between capitalism, imperialism and repression. They also stood in opposition to the radical government in power. This political orientation was partially responsible for the spilt between Las Madres and Las Madres-Línea Fundadora in 1986 [Brysk, 1994]. La Asociación Madres de Plaza de Mayo and Las Madres-Línea Fundadora differed in several principal ways: 1) Las Madres-Línea Fundadora recognized CONADEP as a legitimate commission and were willing to work within the existing political system. Las Madres de Plaza de Mayo did not recognize CONADEP as an unbiased commission, and refused to work with the political system in place at the time; 2) The Government offered families settlements for the death of their loved ones if they would drop their cases against the government. While many of Las Madres de Plaza de Mayo-Línea Fundadora accepted these settlements, members of Las Madres de Plaza de Mayo did not; 3) Las Madres de Plaza de Mayo did not except exhumations of bodies which the government claimed were their missing loved ones, whereas many members of la Línea Fundadora felt these bodies would help them to achieve closure; 4) Las Madres de Plaza de Mayo believed their organization should be open to mother's outside of the city of Buenos Aires who had disappeared children. Las Madres-Línea Fundadora believed that the organization's membership should be limited to residents of Buenos Aires and mothers outside of the city of Buenos Aires should form their own groups.

CONADEP worked together for a period of nine months and documented nearly 9,000 cases of unresolved disappearances. The Commission identified 340 clandestine detention centers and catalogued patterns of disappearances among adolescents, conscripts, members of the clergy and missing babies born to detainees [Brysk, 1994]. The investigation included the collection of more than 1,400 depositions, visits to sites of former secret detention centers, morgues, hospitals, police stations, and prisons to investigate records. CONADEP filed an additional 1,300 requests for further information [Brysk 1994]. Although CONADEP also contacted the military requesting records and permission to conduct site visits, their requests were never answered. CONADEP issued a two-volume report on its findings entitled *Nunca más*, and brought a total of 1,097 cases to the federal appeals courts [Brysk, 1994]. However, many results of CONADEP's work were controversial. Many groups felt that CONADEP knowingly underrepresented the true number of disappeared and feared that the number of cases they documented would be recognized as the final figure of disappearances and would seriously downplay the magnitude of these practices on society. Furthermore, the Commission had documented a list of 1,500 persons who had been implicated in the disappearances from the collected testimonies. This list was not made public. However, portions of it were leaked to the weekly news publication *El Periodista*, and included the name of the papal nuncio. President Alfonsín intervened and denied the legitimacy of the entire list of implicated persons [Brysk, 1994]. Finally, the investigation by CONADEP concluded that there was no evidence that any of the disappeared who had not returned were still alive. This claim contradicted isolated cases of supposed contact between disappeared persons and their families before President Alfonsín assumed office.

Ultimately, CONADEP did not prove to be an adequate answer to the Argentine human rights violations that occurred in the 1970s and 1980s. The trials of the juntas took place between April and December 1985, with nine military officials standing trial. The Buenos Aires Federal Appeals Court heard 78 days of testimony from 833 witnesses. Witnesses included victims, activists, the accused, three pre-Proceso presidents, high-ranking Church and labor officials and a range of international experts and policymakers. The trial was open to the press and the general public. The defense argued that the officers lacked knowledge of the "excesses" that occurred under their command, and that repression had been pursued under a government issued mandate ordering the "annihilation of subversion" [Ciancaglini & Granovsky, 1986]. Five of the nine defendants were acquitted, two received life sentences, and three others received varying lengths of prison sentences. However, as evidence mounted more persons were brought to trial and by mid 1986 there were at least 3,000 cases being tried [Brysk, 1994]. The courts could not handle the surge of cases, and President Alfonsín enacted the *Punto Final* legislation in December 1986 to limit future claims and reduce military tension. The *Punto Final* legislation specified that no future charges could be brought against an accused that were not processed within sixty days. Although CONADEP vehemently opposed this measure, the law was enacted. However, while the *Punto Final* limited future claims of human rights violations, the military officials who had been accused and these claims processed by the deadline were still being called to court. Thus, President Alfonsín created another law called "Obedencia Debida",[4] which legitimized many of the accused claims that they were just following orders, and excused all but a few very high ranking officers of wrongdoing. One human right's publication estimates that 450 pending cases were reduced to 50 by the immediate application of this law [Brysk, 1994]. While legislation could not be applied retroactively, it could be applied to all cases, which at that time were under appeal, so dozens of convicted human rights violators were released. In October 1988, only 17 cases remained active, with several cases yet to have their status determined. In 1989, when Carlos Menem became President of Argentina, he pardoned all military officers with human rights prosecutions pending. In December of 1990, these pardons were extended to the former rulers convicted of human rights violations.

Despite the setbacks and lack of support Las Madres and other human rights groups received from Presidents Alfonsín and Menem, they did not abandon their cause. Upon taking office, President Néstor Kirchner consistently supported the pursuit of justice for the crimes of humanity committed during the years of the "Dirty War", and in August 2005, the Argentine Congress abolished both the "Obedencia Debida" and the "Punto Final", once again allowing accusations to be filed. However, the process is slow and risky for the accused and witnesses alike. Since 2005, only four human rights cases have gone to trial in Argentina, two involving police chiefs, one involving a former police chaplain and one involving a former member of the Naval Prefecture[5] [Valente, 2007]. These four cases have resulted in two convictions, the death of one of the defendants by poisoning, and the disappearance of a

---

[4] Translated as "Due Obedience"

[5] The Argentine Coast Guard

key witness in one of the convictions. Many believe that this defendant may have been killed to silence him because he could have provided information on the fate of the victims and stolen babies [Valente, 2007]. Witnesses have received threatening phone calls in which they have been asked to reveal their location, been asked to meet with families of the accused and have been played audio recordings of torture. While some witnesses have been intimidated by these threats, others refuse to be silent. Currently approximately 400 members of the military and police are awaiting trial, although a large portion of them are being held under house arrest as they are over the age of 70 [Valente, 2007]. To this day, however, many cases remain closed and unanswered.

Research Question

Las Madres de Plaza de Mayo is a dynamic group of predominantly female social actors whose crusade for justice and human rights embodies the complex intersection of peoples, culture, history, politics and society. While there are several texts that discuss the Argentine dictatorship of (1976-1983) and the phenomenon of "the disappeared",[6] none to date directly examines the evolution of Las Madres' contemporary humanitarian contributions to aid society's oppressed. La Asociación Madres de Plaza de Mayo is a unique group of social reformers who have redefined themselves both in terms of membership and in their mission in accordance with current social needs. The following sections of this chapter address several of the most notable social activities and projects Las Madres have initiated since extending their notion of the disappeared to include not only their own kidnapped family members, but marginal, oppressed groups that many wish would "disappear".

Methodology and Data Collection Techniques

The current discussion includes a synthesis of historical events and data collected from narrative texts, historical accounts, official documents and original publications from Las Madres de Plaza de Mayo. While there are many texts that document the events of Argentina's Dirty War from a political perspective, few focus on social response to the national situation and even fewer on the central role of Las Madres de Plaza de Mayo in bringing this question to a salient level. In the present work, we present the reader with a historical background of the events surrounding the creation of the Asociación Madres de Plaza de Mayo and their growth into a powerful human rights activist group. Finally, we show how Las Madres are not resigned to living in the past, but to using their power to define the present and the future.

[6] Bosquet, 1983; Bennett & Simpson, 1985; Bonafini, 1985; Bouvard, 1994; Brysk, 1994; among others

SOCIAL ACTIVISM: LAS MADRES' CONTRIBUTIONS (1990-2008) (R)EVOLUTIONALIZING LAS MADRES DE PLAZA DE MAYO: AN EXTENDED VISION OF THE DISAPPEARED

La Asociación Madres de Plaza de Mayo originated as a group with very specific demands: They wanted information about their disappeared children, they wanted them returned alive, and they wanted those responsible for their kidnappings and their perpetrators to be punished for these acts in a court of law. If one were to ask most of Las Madres when they began to focus on society's problems as a whole instead of their own personal problems, most would not be able to identify a defining moment, and would instead talk about the natural development of their mission. There are two important points in history which may help to understand the evolution of Las Madres' mission: 1) When Las Madres first began to inquire as to the whereabouts of their disappeared children, they did not recognize that their children had been involved in any political affairs. However, it slowly became clear that many of their children were extremely dissatisfied with life under the Argentine government and had begun a process of rebellion against the social injustices and oppression they experienced. Las Madres viewed their disappeared sons and daughters as voices for the people and crusaders for change. Thus, they made a conscious decision to continue the work of their children against social injustice; 2) The establishment of CONADEP further alienated Las Madres from the Argentine judicial system. They felt that this commission was but another by-product of the corrupt political system. When Alfonsín and Menem enacted legislation that freed the few individuals who were convicted of the disappearances, Las Madres felt they were fighting a losing battle against a flawed system.

LA UNIVERSIDAD POPULAR, MADRES DE PLAZA DE MAYO

Even before the creation of La Universidad Popular, Madres de Plaza de Mayo, Las Madres regarded education as the key to a better future. According to Las Madres' beliefs, part of the problem with the state of Argentine society is that the citizens are not prepared to be active participants in its workings. During the Dirty War, this ignorance prohibited them from recognizing many signs and events as dangerous for their civil liberties, and they did not question dubious practices until the situation had reached the level of a crisis. Las Madres believe that the only way to avoid a repetition of government oppression to the extreme of that which characterized the 'Dirty War', is to educate the Argentine people to become informed citizens and to become active contributors to society.

Students at La Universidad Popular, Madres de Plaza de Mayo, can choose from various fields of study including History, Documentary Film, Cooperativism, Political Economics, Human Rights, Journalism, Popular Education, Psychodrama, Social Psychology, Law, and Social Work. Each major allows for students to study a field that affects Argentine society and is expected to use his or her knowledge in order to better the society in some way. All students must take courses in political training as well as the history of Las Madres de Plaza de Mayo. La Universidad Popular also offers classes to the public, such as History of the Workers' Movement in Argentina, Social Conflicts and the Worker's Struggle, and History of Women: Women in History [Universidad Popular].

In the field of Social Work, students receive hands-on experience that leads to a better understanding of Las Madres' mission. All students, especially those studying Social Work, are able to use their skills within the community. Many are given a project which reflects the work involved in courses at La Universidad, as well as theoretical knowledge and methodology. In the 2006 academic year, eight new centers, including two cultural centers and one self-managed community in the Hospital Borda, were added, in which Social Work students allowed to take part in community projects relating to their professional field [Pérez, Chillemi, Bulich, Utrera, Bertón, 2007]. Students put their knowledge into practice in order to gain insight into the career and apply their skills to further aid Argentine society.

As part of a project called Sueños Compartidos (Shared Dreams), the members of the Social Work Department of La Universidad Popular went to a neighborhood, Villa 15, in order to construct new homes in an abandoned hospital from the 1950s [Minghetti, 2007]. Juan Carlos Minghetti, one of the major hands in the project, remembers that every day more people showed up to help. Many had never done any kind of construction, but they were working to build their future homes. First, a kitchen and dining area were built, which is still in use today and feeds people daily. Following the motto "El que sabe enseña y él que no sabe aprende",[7] the project organizers began to teach classes in productivity, safety, and human rights to the residents. Many of the residents also became electricians and plumbers or chose another specialization that would benefit the community. Minghetti claims that the main goal was to construct a functional and productive neighborhood that is able to contribute positively to society [2007].

Besides the construction of new homes, a day care, Jardín Materno Infantíl, was also built in the neighborhood. The female caretakers are also residents of the neighborhood. Other activities and facilities available to the community of Villa 15 include a Literacy Workshop for adults, T'ai Chi Chuan and salsa classes, cinema for children,[8] a political formation course for young people, a youth theater, courses in ceramic installations electrical work, and a literary café, a gymnasium and youth soccer [Minghetti, J.C., 2007].

Community-based activities in which students of Social Work participate include a radio station and a social work magazine. Many students working at the radio station and partake in the Cátedra Libre program, which promotes events related to the Social Work program, while offering a way of communication for related organizations and institutions [Pérez, et. al, 2007]. The magazine related to the field was created as a forum about the program, as well as a way of exchanging information with other similar programs, both locally and internationally.

In creating projects such as those mentioned, the Department of Social Work at La Universidad Popular allows students to practice the knowledge learned in the classroom. Nadia Minghetti notes that the formation of professionals that are capable of bringing about change is crucial in Argentine society. Thus, La Universidad Popular strives to employ intervention as a means of social control [2007].

Las Madres publicly became involved in Argentine society as a result of their "disappeared" children. They began to look at the way laws were made and realized that they were capable of bringing about social change. Thus, the idea of justice from the perspective of a mother whose child "disappeared," rapidly changed to that of justice for all those who

[7] Translated as "He who knows, teaches and he who doesn't know, learns"

[8] The cinema for children program is organized by film students from La Universidad Popular.

suffer from a corrupt government. Today, law students at La Universidad Popular form a part of the future of the judicial system in Argentina. They study in order to practice law so that justice might be brought to all who suffer, and to guarantee a system in which those who judge are not blind [Gallardo, 2007].

The school of law at La Universidad also encourages its students to strive for positive social change. The common thread that ties the students and faculty together is that the people's lawyer rebels against injustices, fighting to ensure that the legal system ensures dignity and life for Argentine society. They call themselves the people's soldiers, carrying out a process of liberation—locally, regionally, nationally, and eventually, hoping to bring about change in South America. The law school intends to help those that are not economically able to go to school by giving them scholarships. Like the students of Social Work, law students at La Universidad Popular continuously try to read, study, and understand the law so as to utilize it as an instrument of change [Universidad Popular Madres de Plaza de Mayo, 2008].

The Zanón Factory: A Case of Unfair Working Conditions

One of the beliefs of Las Madres de Plaza de Mayo is that everyone deserves the dignity of holding a job under decent working conditions and for a livable wage. In fact, Las Madres have established several mottos that have served as their guiding principles throughout most of their existence. One of these mottos is "La falta de trabajo es un crimen".[9]

The Zanón factory is the largest maker of ceramics in Latin America. In the 1990s, documentation surfaced of unfair working conditions and treatment. In 1995, workers were hired only on short-term contracts, were required to work long hours, and were fired for illnesses and for their inability to work long hours. Workers worked an average of 16-hour days, seven days a week. Working conditions were dangerous, with an accident occurring every three days [Equipo de Educación Popular, 2005]. When cited for firing workers, bosses at Zanón stopped firing workers directly, and instead began to morally break down workers and force them to retire voluntarily. For example, one manager showed photos of himself with guns, threatened workers and their families and made racist comments towards them [Equipo de Educación Popular, 2005]. In 2000, a 21-year-old worker died after being attacked upon entering the plant. The factory did not have adequate medical facilities or staff on the premises. Workers began a strike, but the government supported the ownership of the factory. The owners declared a state of preventative crisis and received a loan for 20 million pesos and justification for firing workers. In 2002, the workers once again went on strike, after the owners failed to pay them their Christmas bonuses and were two months behind in paying them their salaries. Zanón proposed to reopen the factory by contracting only 60 workers and reducing their salaries. Finally, the owners of Zanón closed the factory. The workers were left without a job and the owners owed them back wages.

What role did Las Madres de Plaza de Mayo play is helping the workers of Zanón take back their factory? First, they provided the workers with a forum in which to speak in La Plaza de Mayo and a banner with the motto "La única lucha que se pierde es la que se abandona".[10] In addition, first-year students at La Universidad Madres de Plaza de Mayo

---

[9] Translated as "Lack of work is a crime"

[10] Translated as "The only fight that is lost is the one that is abandoned"

chronicled the workers of Zanón's historical struggle in a timeline, which was included in a collection of essays in "Obreros sin patron: Sistematización de la experiencia de los obreros y obreras de Zanón" and published by Ediciones Madres de Plaza de Mayo [2005]. Lastly, Las Madres de Plaza de Mayo provided the workers of Zanón with legal representation and help in restructuring the factory's operations. Upon assuming full responsibility for the administration and production of Zanón, the workers increased their workforce by 50%, and the factory now employs 470 workers. All workers earn the same salary, and they decide everything related to the workings of the factory at general assemblies [FASINPAT].

TRANSFORMING THE EXESCUELA DE MECÁNICA DE LA ARMADA (ESMA): FROM TORTURE CHAMBER TO CULTURAL CENTER

Las Madres de Plaza de Mayo are longtime supporters of the arts and the freedom of expression this medium of creation perpetuates. During the dictatorship, citizens were discouraged from expressing their views, and expression which did not conform to governmental ideals was a dangerous undertaking. Many intellectuals and artists were no longer free to create, felt physically threatened, and were exiled. Las Madres are aware that culture and the arts are often associated with society's middle and upper classes, for many working people can't afford the lessons and materials to study and practice them. Therefore, Las Madres hope to make culture and the arts accessible to the general public.

The Escuela de Mecanica de la Armada (ESMA) in Buenos Aires, a former naval training center, housed a major torture center just off one of the main boulevards in the downtown section of the city. It also contained a warehouse where property looted from the homes of the disappeared was stored. The favored form of torture here as elsewhere was electroshock. The victim would be stretched out naked on a steel bed and tethered accordingly. A special electronic metal probe would be wielded and the victim shocked into revealing the names and whereabouts of close friends and associates with whom they supposedly conspired against the government. Some of the more creative tortures used included having the electric current pass through the body of a mother so that she could experience the pain the current brought to her teenage child who she could see and hear writhing and screaming in agony. At ESMA there was even a maternity ward where pregnant women were taken, beaten and tortured, but allowed to give birth to their children before being murdered. In turn, these children were given to military personnel who had expressed the desire to undertake such adoptions. Subsequent to their tortures, the surviving victim would be hauled out of the detention facility, and loaded onto a navy plane. They were then flown over the seaway behind the ESMA complex and dropped to their doom. Their broken bodies were weighted down with heavy objects to prevent floatation, and their bodies would sink to the bottom of the ocean. The location of the proposed cultural center is especially significant for Las Madres de Plaza de Mayo. Not only was ESMA a mass torture center for thousands of the disappeared, it was the detention site for three of Las Madres de Plaza de Mayo. In July 2005, forensic anthropologists, backed by a Federal Court and human rights organizations, finally recovered the remains of Azucena Villaflor, the founder of the Mothers of Plaza de Mayo, along with two other Madres, Esther Ballestrino de Careaga and María Ponce de Bianco. They were kidnapped December 8-10, 1977 while they looking for their 'disappeared' children and were later taken to ESMA before being flung to the ocean from a military aircraft. This was the first scientific proof of the 'death flights' – most of which took off from ESMA [Bril Mascarenhas, 2005].

Las Madres de Plaza de Mayo, was one of several groups to take possession of the buildings and grounds which were part of ESMA. They commemorated this event by painting and decorating the walls with colorful flowers and suns, designed to represent new life. This activity was followed by a short speech by the Director of the Cultural Center, Claudia Parodi. In explaining their objective, Parodi said, "I'm here because I have accepted this enormous undertaking of changing hate to love, tears to happiness, death to life. We will sing songs within these walls, talk about poetry… we will be teachers, students, musicians, actors, craftsmen, poets, honest dreamers, hopeful inhabitants of a better world that we believe in because we believe in ourselves"[11] [http://www.pagina12.com.ar/diario/elpais/1-98322-2008-02-01.html]. The center will be inaugurated in April 2008. In the future, the center hopes to create a "widespread publication so that people know we do at the center".

"Construyendo Sueños" ("Constructing Dreams"): Housing for the Poor

For Las Madres, one of the largest groups of the contemporary disappeared is the poor. Las Madres believe that everyone deserves to live a life with dignity, and a big step towards achieving this feat is having decent housing, clean water, and other sanitary conditions. Las Madres submitted bids to the government to build several autonomous communities in several areas within greater Buenos Aires. Much to the surprise of many, Las Madres were awarded the building contracts over much more experienced construction companies. Las Madres submitted proposals that were financially and socially superior to those of their competitors. First, the building costs they submitted were lower. Las Madres proposed a new type of pre-fabricated construction that they would manufacture. They also decided to employ a practice similar in nature to habitat for humanity: Residents of the area, both men and women, are helping with the construction. Workers are receiving on the spot training, and are attending special classes to train them in trades such as plumbing, electrical wiring and ceramics. Second, by involving residents in the construction of their own homes and community buildings, Las Madres is providing them with valuable job training and skills. Because of the stigma of living in a slum, those involved in the project generally have a very difficult time finding work. Half of the people building the new homes are women who have received training in an area that is traditionally dominated by men. There are obvious differences between the working methods of a human rights group and those of a private company. "We are doing the building, but we don't care about making profits under the capitalist logic of paying less wages for more hours of work," engineer Juan Enrique Reale, projects director in the Asociación Madres de Plaza de Mayo, told IPS. "This is a way to carry out small revolutions in the barrios by building decent housing and generating real work" [Peker, 2007].

The first project was launched on October 16, 2007 in Villa 15, better known as Ciudad Oculta,[12] is located in the southern Buenos Aires neighborhood of Villa Lugano. Nearly three

---

[11] Translation ours

[12] Translated as "Hidden City"

hundred workers are building two complexes of 36 housing units each. The three-bedroom units are 62 square meters in size, and are fully equipped with a bathroom, kitchen, hot water and central heating. These homes will replace the make-shift dwellings and dirt roads of the slum, where proper sanitation does not exist. The workers involved in the project wear coveralls with the phrase "decent housing" and a drawing of the trademark white scarf of the Madres de Plaza de Mayo, which the activists have traditionally worn on their heads since they began to hold silent walking vigils every Thursday in the plaza outside of the seat of government in Buenos Aires since the 1970s. The construction method used by the project comes from an Italian firm, M2 Emmedue, and uses structural panels of reinforced galvanized steel and expanded corrugated polystyrene, with a fast-drying concrete. The rapid concrete construction system, which has been used in more than 40 countries, is economical, and the homes are cool in the summertime and warm in the winter. The cost of each complex is around two million Argentine pesos,[13] which is financed by the Ministry of Human Rights of the government of the city of Buenos Aires. The participants/beneficiaries were selected from among the residents of Ciudad Oculta, many of whose residents were made homeless by a fire and who have since been living in unstable shacks constructed of sheet metal and cardboard.

Félix Narváez, 38, who has three children --10-year-old Yamil, eight-year-old Félix and two-year-old Kevin -- is one of the local residents whose house was destroyed by the fire over a year ago. Now he is not only the project's chief electrician but also a future owner of one of the modern new homes. "I am building this with love," he commented to IPS. "I'm very proud, because I feel respected here, not exploited, and I like the fact that people listen to me. The day of the fire, my son Félix asked me 'Now where are we going to sleep?' That was the most painful question I have ever been asked. But today I am building the answer, to give him a roof over his head." [Peker, 2007]. Jessica Reta, a 26-year-old mother of three, is an example of how the project is opening up new horizons. "I thought that my only purpose in life was to attend to my husband, children and home," Reta told IPS, as she helped build her new house. "I graduated from high school, but when I saw I couldn't move ahead and that no one would give me a job because I lived in a miserable neighborhood, my ambitions and hopes faded," she said. "We have courses in electricity, plumbing and laying tiles. The men who were our unemployed neighbors are now our teachers," she explained [Peker, 2007].

The number of mothers who are now showing up to work in coveralls and hard hats made it necessary to open up a new child care centre in the neighborhood to tend to the children while their mothers are working. In fact, Las Madres have a whole self-sustaining community planned. In addition to housing and a day care center, Las Madres de Plaza de Mayo plan to construct schools, a community center and a hospital for the residents. Hebe de Bonafini, the president of the Asociación Madres de Plaza de Mayo, said "Our housing project initiatives are making good on a debt that we owe the barrios and the homeless and marginalized." On Jan. 22, 2008, the Madres also began to build a new housing complex in Los Piletones, in Villa Soldati, another slum neighborhood in Buenos Aires. They plan to construct 432 housing units, a childcare center, two schools, a community centre and a hospital, while providing vocational training and decent working conditions for the local residents.

[13] 650,000 dollars

SUPPORT, THREATS AND OPPRESSION

During their early years, the Argentine government considered Las Madres de Plaza de Mayo a dangerous foe and did everything it could to avoid meetings with them.

Las Madres were not able to secure face to face meetings with elected officials, and even when they were granted entrance, the meetings were futile. During his term as President of Argentina,[14] Néstor Kirchner repealed the Due Obedience Law and the Final Stop evoked by Carlos Menem. For the first time since their existence, Las Madres were able to gain easy access to meetings with the President, and they have continued to maintain an ongoing dialogue with the Casa Rosada. In 2007, Cristina Fernández de Kirchner, wife of former President Nestor Kirchner was elected President of Argentina. President Cristina Kirchner has continued her husband's policy of contact with Las Madres de Plaza de Mayo and has been present at many of Las Madres' activities and achievements in the Argentine community.

Although there have been many different leaders in Argentina since the time of the Dirty War, a large number of the corrupt officials still hold positions of power in contemporary society. While one would like to believe that the state of terror is a thing of the past, many incidents continue to happen which indicate that the problem is far from over. One of the problems which Las Madres have identified is police brutality. When Las Madres protested during the Dirty War, they were often attacked by police dogs, sprayed with forceful hoses and beaten with batons. In recent years, there have been a number of alleged cases where police have attacked picketers on strike, demonstrators, and homeless individuals with undue force. As a human rights response to these cases, Las Madres have sent lawyers to represent the detained persons and have lobbied for the people's right to assemble and demonstrate peacefully.

Las Madres continue to receive death threats regarding their involvement in social and political activities. Since establishing their house and the university building complex, Las Madres have been the victims of several break-ins and robberies. Robbers have stolen many items of sentimental value to Las Madres, as well as photographs, audiovisual equipment and important intelligence documents and dossiers on their children's alleged oppressors. In addition, on one occasion, Hebe de Bonafini, President of Las Madres de Plaza de Mayo was almost run over by a car as she walked on the sidewalk. Advancements in technology have enabled Las Madres easier access in communicating with the community at large. However, recently, their website has served as yet another medium through which threats of death and violence have surfaced. Furthermore, hackers have hacked into the website[15] on numerous occasions causing the site to crash. Threats and violence have not been limited to Las Madres. Their family members and associates have been targeted as well. In 2001, María Alejandra Bonafini, the daughter of the President of the *Asociación Madres de Plaza de Mayo*,[16] Hebe de Bonafini, was attacked and tortured, in the house she shares with her mother in La Plata, Buenos Aires Province. On May 25, two men, who had identified themselves as telephone repairmen, forced their way past her into the house. They put a plastic bag over her head and beat her with an object that a doctor, who later examined her, indicated may have been a chain covered by a hose-pipe. They also burned her arms and back with cigarettes [Amnesty

[14] May 2003 to December 2007

[15] www.madres.org

[16] Mothers of Plaza de Mayo Association

International]. María Alejandra Bonafini had previously received death threats in connection with her mother's work as a high-profile human rights leader. Some months before this attack, Hebe de Bonafini is also reported to have received a telephone death threat in which she was told they were going to hit her "where it hurts the most" [Amnesty International]. It is believed that the threats to María Alejandra Bonafini are related to her mother's outspoken condemnation of the human rights situation in Argentina.

Conclusion

Since its establishment in 1977, La Asociación Madres de Plaza de Mayo has evolved from a small group of Argentine mothers who sought information on their disappeared children and justice for those responsible, into an internationally recognized human and civil rights organization with a global mission of promoting and protecting the rights of the oppressed around the world. In this article, we have explored many of the community-based activities in which members of Las Madres de Plaza de Mayo, Buenos Aires are currently participating to help the "present-day-disappeared", or those individuals society categorizes as the unemployed, the poor, and the defenseless (youth and seniors), and have described their role in present Argentine society. Although many of the founding members of Las Madres de Plaza de Mayo have passed away, and others are their 80s and 90s, Las Madres de Plaza de Mayo is an organization which now includes men and women, young and old. Through strong community ties and the establishment of La Universidad Popular, Madres de Plaza de Mayo, Las Madres have laid the foundation for future generations to continue their activism.

References

Amnesty International. (2001). Attack against daughter of president of Asociación Madres de Plaza de Mayo. *On the front line*. Retrieved 18 March 2008 from http://ara.controlarms.org/library/Index/ENGAMR010072001?open&of=ENG-NIC

Asociación Madres de Plaza de Mayo (Ed). (2001). *Locas: Cultura y utopias, 4*, October / November.

Asociación Madres de Plaza de Mayo (Ed). (2004). *Argentina: Una herida abierta-La dictadura militar contada a los más chicos*. Buenos Aires: Ediciones Madres de Plaza de Mayo.

Asociación Madres de Plaza de Mayo (Ed). (2002). *No olvidaremos: Proyecto contra la impunidad.* Buenos Aires: Ediciones Madres de Plaza de Mayo.

Asociación Madres de Plaza de Mayo (Ed). (2004). *Periódico Mensual: Las Luchas del Pueblo junto a Las Madres, 2.12*. Buenos Aires: Ediciones Madres de Plaza de Mayo. Bauducco, G. (2004). *Hebe: La otra mujer*. Buenos Aires: Ediciones Madres de Plaza de Mayo.

Bennett, J. and Simpson, J. (1985). *The Disappeared and the Mothers of the Plaza.* New York: St. Martin's Press.

Bielsa, R., Bonasso, M. et al. (2002). *¿Qué son las asembleas populares*? Buenos Aires: Ediciones Continente.

Bonafini, H. de. (1985). *Historias de vida*. Buenos Aires: El Cronista Comercial.

Bousquet, J.P. (1983). *Las Locas de la Plaza de Mayo*. Buenos Aires: El Cid.

Bouvard, M.G. (1994). *Revolutionizing Motherhood: The Mothers of the Plaza de Mayo*. New York: St. Martin's Press.

Brysk, A. (1994). *The Politics of Human Rights in Argentina: Protest, Change, and Democratization*. Stanford: Stanford University Press. 46-47, 71.

Buletín del 1er. (2002). Congreso Internacional de Salud Mental y Derechos Humanos. Buenos Aires: Universidad Popular Madres de Plaza de Mayo.

Bril Mascarenhas, Tomás. (2005). House of horror. *NewInternationalist, 385*. Retrieved 15 January 2008 from http://www.newint.org/features/2005/12/01/memorials/

Ciancaglini, S. and Granovsky, M. (1986). *Crónicas del apocalipsis*. Buenos Aires: Contrapunto, 204.

Comisión Nacional sobre la Desaparición de Personas (CONADEP). (1983). *Nunca más*. Buenos Aires: Editorial Universitaria de Buenos Aires.

FASINPAT. Zanón bajo control obrero. Wikimapia. Retrieved 18 March 2008 from http://wikimapia.org/6171195/es/FASINPAT_Zanon_bajo_control_obrero

Gallardo, Roberto Andrés. (2007). Las Madres, el poder judicial y la construcción de la justicia. *30.000 Revoluciones, 1*, 13-18.

Kohan, A. (2002). *¡A las calles!* Buenos Aires: Ediciones Colihue S.R.L.

Madres de Plaza de Mayo. (1997). *El corazón de la escritura, 3*. Buenos Aires: A.B.R.N. Producciones gráficas S.R.L.

Madres de Plaza de Mayo. (1999). *Historia de Las Madres de Plaza de Mayo, 1*. Buenos Aires: A.B.R.N. Producciones gráficas S.R.L.

Madres de Plaza de Mayo. (1987). *Nuestros Hijos*. Buenos Aires: Editorial Contrapunto S.R.L.

Marchak, P. (1999). *God's Assassins*. Montreal: McGill-Queen's University Press.

Mignone, E. F. (1988). *Organizaciones de derechos humanos en la Argentina*. Buenos Aires: Centro de Estudios Legales y Sociales, n.d.

Mignone, E. F. (1986). *Iglesia y dictadura*. Buenos Aires: Ediciones del Pensamiento Nacional.

Minghetti, J.C. (2007). Prácticas sociales y profesionales: Sueños compartidos. Experiencia de Villa 15. *Visión crítica: Etica y política, 1*, 35-39.

Minghetti, N. (2007). Conocimiento, intelectuales y construcción de una nueva sociedad. *Visión crítica: Etica y política, 1*, 56-57.

Pañuelos en Rebeldía Equipo de Educación Popular. (2005). OBREROS SIN PATRÓN Sistematización de la experiencia de los obreros y obreras de Zanón.

Peker, Luciana. (2007). Madres de Plaza de Mayo bring housing hope to slums. *IPS News*. Retrieved 18 March 2008 from http://ipsnews.net/news.asp?idnews=36444

Pérez, S.S., Chillemi, A.B., Bulich, M.A., Utrera, M. de las M., & Bertón, D. (2007). La formación de trabajadores sociales en la Universidad Popular Madres de Plaza de Mayo. *Visión crítica: Etica y política, 1*, 17-23.

Universidad Popular Madres de Plaza de Mayo. (2008). [Electronic website]. Retrieved 28 April 2008 from http://www.madres.org/univupmpm/univumpm.asp

Valente, Marcela. (2007). Survivors, activists disappointed over human rights trial. *IPS News*. Retrieved 15 March 2008 from http://ipsnews.net/news.asp?idnews=39714

Vázquez, I. (Ed.) (1994). *Historia de Las Madres de Plaza de Mayo.* Buenos Aires: Ediciones Madres de Plaza de Mayo. Verbitsky, H. (2003). *Civiles y militares: Memoria secreta de la transición*. Buenos Aires: Editorial Sudamericana.

In: Latin American Issues and Challenges
Editors: L. Naciamento and G. Sousa
ISBN 978-1-60692-349-8

Chapter 6

BANKS' RESPONSES TO THE ENTRY OF BANCO SANTANDER IN LATIN AMERICA

Eric Rodríguez*

Business School. Universidad de los Andes. Bogotá, Colombia. Cra 1 Este # 18A-70.
Universidad de los Andes Facultad de Administración, Bogotá, Colombia

ABSTRACT

This chapter is a revised version of Chapter II of my doctoral dissertation at Tulane University. I thank the members of my dissertation committee: Thomas Noe, Paul Spindt, and Venkat Subramaniam for their comments. All remaining errors are mine.

Foreign market entry strategy involves choices about which markets to enter and how to enter them. In most of the Foreign Direct Investment (FDI) literature it was always of the interest to determine what are the decisions of the foreign investing firm choice of ownership structure and from the point of view of the local firms, what are the characteristics that define the way they may react to this new entry. The main objective of the current study is to analyze the role of conglomerate groups in emerging economies when firms face the entrance of new aggressive competitors on the market.

Following the research idea by Khanna and Tice (2000), this chapter focused on addressing how specific characteristics of incumbent firms in the Latin American retail banking market may affect their responses to these new competitors. Specifically, we concentrated on Banco Santander's entry, which was the most aggressive competitor buying majority stakes in its acquisitions and putting its brand name on them.

To solve the above question, we selected financial statements data from banks in three different countries – Colombia, Chile, and Mexico -- where Banco Santander followed the same investment strategy. As the part of our study, we run a regression model with different

* PhD. Associated professor. Tel: (571) 339 4949 Ext 3960; Fax: (571) 332 4560; E-mail: efr@adm.uniandes.edu.co

banks characteristic and, following Campello (2002) research study, we used growth in loan market share as a proxy for performance and the dependent variable.

First results are related to existing literature that studies the role financial conglomerates (FC) play on supporting their firms to exogenous shocks. We found that banks may better fight the entrance of Banco Santander if they belong to a Financial Conglomerate (FC). This is consistent with previous findings related to internal capital markets, Gertner, Scharfstein, and Stein (1994). However we get contrary results to Khanna and Tice (2000), with respect to the effect that has firm size on the incumbent reaction. Even if size characteristic appeared significant, its sign is negative.

On the second part of the study, we divided the sample into three groups according to a cluster analysis based on the dependent variable and the two significant variables found above. These three groups can be described as: Large banks in Financial Conglomerates, Medium banks in Financial Conglomerates and Small Stand-alone banks. When we ran the same regression model for the second and third groups, we found a change in the sign of the bank size coefficient. This positive sign may be explained by the fact that large banks were the ones that lost their loan market share. Medium and small banks could gain loan market share, consistent with Khanna and Tice (2000).

In line with the empirical work of Kasyap and Stein (2000), we also found that the impact of Banco Santander's entry is stronger for banks with lower ratios of securities to assets, within the group of small banks.

The chapter is organized as follows. Section 1 describes the entry strategy of Spanish banks in Latin America. Section 2 describes the data sample and research design. Section 3 examines the results for the first model regression (All banks in the sample). Section 4 looks for different results in subgroup samples (Medium and small banks). Section 5 concludes.

1. Spanish Direct Investments in the Latin American Retail Banking Market

Retail banking is a mature industry and no reason exists to expect foreign banks to have any particular advantage over domestic banks familiar with their local environment as found by Tschoelgl (1987). Historically, only Citibank (or Citigroup) has pursued a global retail strategy, though it has focused on credit card and banking services for an urban professional class without attempting to enter the mass retail market as the Spanish banks have done lately.

Since 1995, three Spanish banks—Banco Santander (Santander), Banco Bilbao Vizcaya (BBV), and Banco Central Hispano (BCH)—have become the largest foreign banks in Latin America. These banks have spent over US$4 billion to acquire large stakes in almost 30 major banks in more than ten different countries (Table 1). What is novel about this expansion is that the Spanish banks are acquiring some of the largest domestic banks in their target countries and entering the general commercial and mass retail market.

By the late 1980s, competition for market share within the local Spanish market has intensified, Intermediation margins fell, and the banks worried about their long-term profitability. Besides entering new product markets—stock brokerage, pension funds, and value-added services—several of the big banks began to view international expansion as a way to enhance profitability by exploiting their skills more fully.

Banco Santander, then the largest bank in Spain , grew via acquisition, but remained a mid-sized institution until the late 1980s. Between 1989 and 1992, Santander seized the moment to revolutionize Spain's retail banking by introducing mutual funds, high-yield checking and savings accounts, and low-interest mortgages. The market quickly became too competitive for any major bank to gain significant market share, so in 1994, Santander bought Banco Español de Crédito (Banesto). This catapulted Santander into first place among Spanish banks.

Santander built its current assault on Latin America around Santander Investment, its investment-banking arm, and many of its acquisitions are banks with a strong local investment banking franchise. Santander has generally bought majority stakes in its acquisitions and has put its brand name on them. Its Latin American operations accounted for almost 50% of foreign assets and for 48% of net attributable profits in 1997.

Table 1. Acquisitions of Banks in Latin America by Spanish Banks since 1990

Acquisition Year	Acquirer	Bank Acquired	Country	% Stake	Purchase Price US$mn
1990	Santander	Caguas Central Federal Savings Bank	Puerto Rico	100	51
1991	BBV	Probursa	Mexico	70	480
1992	BCH	GFBital	Mexico	8	105
1995	Santander	Banco Interandino & Intervalores	Peru	100	45
	Santander	Banco Mercantil	Peru	100	44
1996	BBV	Banco Francés del Río de la Plata	Argentina	52	300
	BBV	Banco Ganadero	Colombia	59	328
	BBV	Banco Oriente & Banco Cremi	Mexico	100	21
	BBV	Banco Continental	Peru	60	256
	BBV	Banco Provincial	Venezuela	40	300
	Santander	Banco Osorno y La Unión	Chile	51	496
	Santander	Banco Central Hispano Puerto Rico	Puerto Rico	99	289
	Santander	Banco de Venezuela	Venezuela	93	351
1997	BBV	Banco de Crédito Argentino	Argentina	100	466
	Santander	Banco Río de la Plata	Argentina	64	1,068
	Santander	Banco Noroeste	Brazil	80	500
	Santander	Banco Geral do Comercio	Brazil	50	202
	Santander	Banco Comercial Antioqueño	Colombia	55	146
	Santander	Grupo Financiero InverMéxico	Mexico	61	502
1998	BBV	Banco Excel Economico	Brazil	55	450
	BBV	Banco Hipotecario de Fomento	Chile	55	352
	BBV	Banco Ponce	Puerto Rico	100	166
	BCH	Banco de Galicia y Buenos Aires	Argentina	10	200
1999	Santander	Banco de Río Tercero	Argentina		6
	BBV	CorpBanca	Argentina	100	84

Source: Annual Reports and new reports.

Given that the Spanish banks wished to expand internationally to overcome competitive saturation in their home market, the issue of where to go was relatively straightforward. Western Europe was already well-served by domestic institutions. With Europe being of only limited interest, that left the emerging markets of Asia, Eastern Europe, and Latin America. Before the recent crisis, most Asian countries did not permit foreigners to acquire local commercial banks. Also, the Spanish banks had no particular advantage vis-à-vis other foreign banks in either Eastern Europe or Asia.

Conversely, the commonality of language and familiarity with the region, has made Latin America comfortable. The Spanish banks have bought large stakes in large banks, automatically; they have chosen to compete in the mass market, rather than in a niche. They are competing in the lower and middle-income markets where they come into competition with the largest domestic banks. The only foreign bank that had previously made foray into Latin America comparable in its geographic scope was Citibank. In contrast to the Spanish banks, Citibank focused on the upper income market. If the entrant wishes to compete in retail banking by introducing new products, it must gain market share in significant chunks as opposed to growing organically from scratch. The inability to patent innovations necessitates having an extensive branch network over which to deliver the product, matters. Thus, the entry strategy of the Spanish banks is in sharp contrast to the strategies of Bank of Boston and Citibank, which have traditionally focused on a smaller clientele, and hence, have been content to grow more organically.

Santander has been most aggressive in seeking majority stakes with full managerial control and brand-image coordination, whereas BBV initially preferred minority stakes. In contrast to these two strategies, BCH has opted for joint ventures with local partners without promoting its own.

Santander was the most assertive in its Latin American expansion, primarily because of its strong capital base, prior investment banking experience in the region, and the strong personality and leadership of its chairman.

Relative to domestic banks in Latin America, the Spanish banks are better managed and have more experience with a competitive market. Therefore, the Spanish banks in Latin America provide an interesting example of a situation where the foreign direct investors have no advantage vis-à-vis each other, but do vis-à-vis their host-country competitors.

The Spanish banks have transferred knowledge from Spain to Latin America. One obvious parent contribution has been the introduction of an aggressive posture built on the introduction of new products. Generally, wherever local regulations have permitted, the Spanish banks have introduced the lottery-linked deposit accounts they offer in Spain (Guillén & Tschoegl 1998). These deposits accounts have been an innovation everywhere the Spanish banks have introduced them.

These banks have also improved the issuing, pricing and term of mortgages relative to all the banks targeting the mass market; introduced mini-branches in supermarkets, gas stations, and other non-traditional venues; and improved the assessment of credit risk and other banking processes in the banks they have acquired.

2. Data and Research Methodology

The entry of Banco Santander in Latin American following the chunk strategy puts pressure on the mass retailing bank market where incumbent banks reacted. Their responses were influenced by their specific characteristics, size, profitability, leverage, and ownership structure. Here arises the main question of our research: What are the incumbent banks' specific characteristics that helped them fight Santander's aggressive threat?

To answer this question we chose three different countries where Santander followed the same strategy. The countries of Colombia, Chile, and Mexico, all have banks of different sizes, owned by local or foreign firms and belonging or not to a financial conglomerate (Table 2).

From 1995 to 1998, Banco Santander entered many Latin American Financial Markets, but we selected the above three countries because of their information availability. They have well developed system information for their financial sector and government institutions where all Banks must report financial statements quarterly: Superintendencias Bancarias. We have a total of 83 banks, 32 for Colombia, 28 for Chile and 23 for Mexico.

Table 2. Banks frequency distribution by country

Country	Financial Conglomerate		*Country*	Local or Foreign	
	In FC	Stand Alone		Local	Foreign
Colombia	18	14	Colombia	21	11
Chile	15	13	Chile	11	17
Mexico	10	13	Mexico	14	9
	43	40		46	37

2.1. Research Design

Incumbent banks' responses to Santander's entry varied depending on their specific characteristics. Some responded aggressively and fought for their market share, others just tried to maintain their participation, while others just gave up part of their market.

This paper is then an empirical study that follows the idea of Khanna and Tice (2000), and analyzes the reaction of incumbent banks in three Latin American countries, Colombia, Chile, and Mexico, where the entry strategy of Banco Santander was the same: buy a large share market through the acquisition of local banks.

The study takes places in a 2 year window frame. Time 1 being December of the year before the entry of Banco Santander and time 3 being December of one year after the entry. We measured the banks' characteristics at the beginning of the fiscal year 1 and banks reaction at the end of the fiscal year 2.

Colombian data comes from the Superintendencia Bancaria de Colombia, and the year of entry of Banco Santander was 1997 when it decided to buy Banco Industrial Colombiano (BIC), the bank that belonged to the economic group Bavaria. Chilean data comes from Superintendencia de bancos e Instituciones financieras (SBIF) and the year of entry of Banco Santander was 1996 when it bought Banco Santiago and Banco Osorno y la Union. Mexican data comes from the Comision Nacional Bancaria y de Valores in Mexico and the year of entry of Banco Santander was 1997 when it bought Grupo Financiero InverMexico.

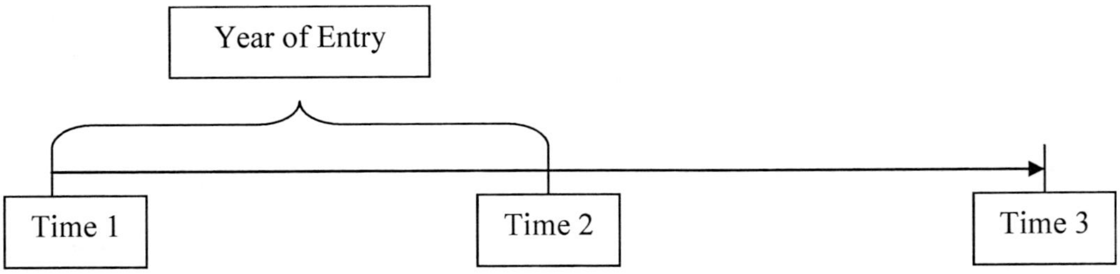

Figure 1. Two year window frame of the study.

Because of the many mergers and acquisitions on the banking industry within the time window analysis, banks that disappeared are not on the sample and banks that merged are represented in the sample by only one bank with consolidated financial statements. Information about mergers and acquisitions were checked on the financial news reports of the *ISI Emerging Markets* database.

2.2. Bank Characteristics Variables

To describe incumbent characteristics, we selected the following variables. All of them are measured for each incumbent bank the year -1, one year before the entrance of Banco Santander.

Independent Variables

ECONOG Dummy: 1 if the bank is part of a Financial Conglomerate, 0 otherwise
PASSE: Total assets of bank i divided by Total assets for all banks in the country as a proxy of size
LIASSE: Total liabilities of bank i divided by total assets of bank i as a proxy of leverage
INVTOT: Total security investments divided by total assets as a proxy of liquidity
NPLTOT: Non Performing loans divided by total loans as a proxy of risky loans
FINMAR: The difference between Interest income and Interest expenses divided by Interest income.

Dependent Variable

As the dependent variable to represent the way incumbent banks react to the threat of Banco Santander, we will use the variation on the loan market share. In the line of Campello (2002), we use variation of market share in loans as a proxy of the incumbent bank reaction to the entrance of Banco Santander.

VARLOAN: Is defined as loan market share the year +1 (One year after the entrance of Banco Santander) minus loan market share the year -1 (One year before the entrance of Banco Santander).

3. Incumbent Banks' Responses

To explain how incumbent banks react to the entry of Banco Santander, we ran the following regression model that involves all the above defined variables.

$$\Delta(\textit{Loan}\text{ market share}) = \eta + \alpha_1 ECONG_{-1} + \alpha_2 PASSE_{-1} + \alpha_3 LIASSE_{-1} + \alpha_4 INVTOT_{-1} + \alpha_5 NPLTOT_{-1} + \alpha_6 FINMAR_{-1} + \xi$$

Where $\Delta(\textit{Loan}\text{ market share}) = \textit{Loan}\text{ market share}_{\text{year }+1} - \textit{Loan}\text{ market share}_{\text{year -1}}$

Summary statistic for 83 incumbent banks in 3 countries where Banco Santander followed the same entry strategy.

Two characteristics are significant at less than 1%: The dummy variable for financial conglomerate, where the coefficient is positive. This implies that financial conglomerates support incumbent banks to fight the new competition attack. This is consistent with the hypothesis of internal capital market presented by Khanna and Palepu (2000) and Campello (2002), where they found that internal capital markets relieve the impact of external financial constrains on investment

The other significant characteristic is asset size and, in that case, the coefficient is negative as opposed to Chen and Hambrick (1995) and Khanna and Tice (2000). This implies that the larger the bank, the more loan market share they lose. This result may be explained by the fact that main large banks in each country consistently lost loan market share.

One of the strategies of Banco Santander to enter Latin American markets was the reduction of financial margins. To see which incumbent banks followed the strategy, this is, which banks also reduced their financial margins; we ran the same regression model with a new dependent variable defined as follows:

Table 3. Summary Statistics. Incumbent banks

	Mean	Minimun	Maximun	Std. Dev.
Independent VAR				
PASSE	0.0350	0.0001	0.2909	0.0546
LIASSE	0.8535	0.1350	1.0419	0.1297
INVTOT	0.1726	0.0000	0.6853	0.1454
NPLTOT	0.0311	0.0000	0.2206	0.0368
FINMAR	0.3096	-0.3886	0.9759	0.2060
Dependent VAR				
VARLOAN	0.0001	-0.0297	0.0280	0.0069

VARMAR: Financial margin of bank i the year +1 (One year after the entrance of Banco Santander) minus financial margin of bank i the year -1 (One year before the entrance of Banco Santander).

Table 4. Regression coefficients for all banks. Dependent Variable VARLOAN

Variables	Beta	P Value	
PASSE	**-0.6088**	**0.0000**	***
LIASSE	0.0850	0.5539	
INVTOT	0.0805	0.4365	
NPLTOT	-0.0691	0.5056	
FINMAR	0.1596	0.2446	
ECONOG	**0.3297**	**0.0061**	***
Sig. Level	*0.0001*		
Num Observations	*83*		

*,**,*** denote statistical significance at the 10%, 5%, 1% levels, respectively. Significant coefficients and their p-values a shown underlined.

Two characteristics are significant with a negative coefficient. The percentage of risky loans is significant at less than 5%. This implies that banks are affected by their non-performing loans, the greater the percentage of risky loans, the less they are able to increase their financial margin. The other characteristic with a negative coefficient is the financial margin one year before the entry of Santander and it is significant at less than 10%. This implies that banks with less financial margin before the entry of Banco Santander may not followed the margin reduction strategy.

Another significant characteristic at less than 10%, is asset size and, in that case, the coefficient is positive. This implies that the larger the bank, the more he is able to reduce its margin.

Table 5. Regression coefficients for all banks. Dependent Variable VARMAR

Variables	Beta	P Value	
PASSE	**0.5242**	**0.0710**	*
LIASSE	0.0765	0.6160	
INVTOT	-0.0295	0.7634	
NPLTOT	**-0.8101**	**0.0395**	**
FINMAR	**-0.1776**	**0.0549**	*
ECONOG	-0.0098	0.7606	
Sig. Level	*0.0099*		
Num Observations	*83*		

*,**,*** denote statistical significance at the 10%, 5%, 1% levels, respectively. Significant coefficients and their p-values a shown underlined.

4. Reactions of Medium and Small Banks

The next step is to identify different types of reactions among banks related to their size and their ownership structure. We then raise the following question: Do all banks respond the same way or are there different kind of reactions according to their size?

To answer the question, we divided data in groups according to the size of assets and the fact that the bank is a stand-alone firm or belongs to a financial conglomerate. We used a two way cluster analysis based on the dependent variable (VARLOAN) and the two significant variables found in the previous section, PASSE (assets size) and ECONOG (Financial conglomerate). This cluster analysis divided data into groups.

Figure 2 shows confident intervals at a 95% level for three different groups. Variables depicted are: Change in loan market share (VARLOAN) and asset size (PASSET). Additionally, we calculated mean and standard deviation for these two characteristics in each group. (Table 6)

Confidence intervals at the 95% for groups 1,2, and 3. PASSE represents asset size. VARLOAN represents loan market share variation.

Table 6. Summary statistics for each group as a result of the cluster analysis

Group	**Data**	*PASSE*		*VARLOAN*		*ECONOG*
		Mean	**Std. Dev**	**Mean**	**Std. Dev**	
1	10	*0.1590*	*0.0681*	*-0.0118*	*0.0073*	YES
2	33	*0.0307*	*0.0209*	*0.0041*	*0.0065*	YES
3	40	*0.0075*	*0.0103*	*-0.0002*	*0.0019*	NO

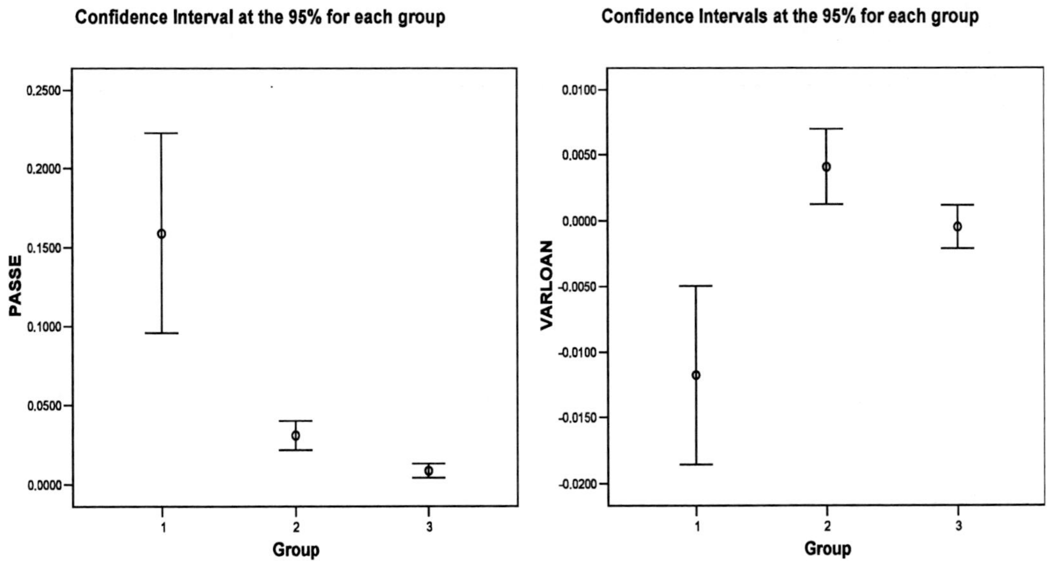

Figure 2. Confidence intervals at the 95% for each bank group.

According to these results, we defined the groups as follow:

Group 1: Large banks that belong to a financial conglomerate. (Large in FC)
Group 2: Medium banks that belong to a financial conglomerate (Medium in FC)
Group 3: Small stand-alone banks. (Small stand-alone)

All large banks variation on loan market share are negative, so they lost their loan market. This same effect is unclear for group 2 and 3.

Table 7. Summary statistics for banks characteristics in each group

	Large in FC		Medium	in FC	Small Stand-alone	
	Mean	**Std. Dev.**	**Mean**	**Std. Dev.**	**Mean**	**Std. Dev.**
Independent						
PASSE	*0.1590*	*0.0681*	*0.0307*	*0.0209*	*0.0075*	*0.0103*
LIASSE	0.9007	0.0504	0.8935	0.0636	0.8086	0.1657
INVTOT	0.1901	0.0811	0.1456	0.1323	0.1904	0.1660
NPLTOT	0.0502	0.0287	0.0306	0.0324	0.0267	0.0410
FINMAR	0.3077	0.1247	0.3112	0.1289	0.3087	0.2683
Dependent						
VARLOAN	*-0.0118*	*0.0073*	*0.0041*	*0.0065*	*-0.0002*	*0.0019*

There are 10 banks in the first group, 33 banks in the second group and 40 banks in the third group.

To analyze what incumbent banks' characteristics explain their reactions, we ran another regression model for groups 2 and 3. We did not ran the regression on group 1 due to the size of the sample (10 Banks).

The regression model used with these two groups is:

$$\Delta(Loan \text{ market share}) = \eta + \alpha_1 PASSE_{-1} + \alpha_2 LIASSE_{-1} + \alpha_3 INVTOT_{-1} + \alpha_4 NPLTOT_{-1} + \alpha_5 FINMAR_{-1} + \xi$$

Results for group 2 are shown in table 8. In this case, asset size is significant at less than 1%, but now the sign is positive. This implies that, within the group of medium banks the larger the bank, the more it can grow in market share. This is consistent with the findings of Chen and Hambrick (1995) and Khanna and Tice (2000). Group 3 presents the same result with a positive coefficient and is significant at less than 5%.

Additionally, and more interesting, we found on group 3 new characteristics that appear significant now. The percentage of risky loans is significant at less than 1% and it has a negative sign. This implies that Small stand-alone banks are affected by their non-performing loans. The greater the percentage of risky loans, the less they are able to grow.

The other two variables that appeared significant are the proxy of liquidity (INVTOT) and financial margin (FINMAR). Both are significant at less than 10% with positive coefficients. This suggests within Small stand-alone banks, the ones with a better position of liquidity and financial margin, may fight for a higher loan market share against the new entrant.

The above is consistent with the Kasyap and Stein (2000) paper, where they found that small banks, facing constraints in their sources of external finance due to contractive monetary polices, may react by drawing down his stock of securities.

In the case of group 3, the existence of new explanatory variables can be related to the fact that they are not supported by a financial conglomerate and these other characteristics play an important role on the impact that has the new entry.

Table 8. Regression coefficients banks in groups 2 and 3. Dependent Variable VARLOAN

Variables	Group # 2			Group # 3		
	Beta	P Value		Beta	P Value	
PASSE	**0.5934**	**0.0039**	***	**0.5030**	**0.0479**	**
LIASSE	-0.3209	0.1978		-0.0718	0.7566	
INVTOT	0.2927	0.1175		**0.3131**	**0.0621**	*
NPLTOT	-0.0042	0.9822		**-0.7104**	**0.0047**	***
FINMAR	-0.0689	0.7499		**0.3907**	**0.0911**	*
Sig. Level	*0.0397*			*0.0141*		
Num Observations	*33*			*40*		

*,**,*** denote statistical significance at the 10%, 5%, 1% levels, respectively. Significant coefficients and their p-values a shown underlined.

5. Summary and Conclusions

This chapter wants to contribute to the understanding of the effect of the Spanish banks' expanding strategy in the Latin American banking systems. Some argued that foreign bank entry has benefited the Latin America banking system by lowering loan and deposit volatility and increasing efficiency, Barajas *et. al.* (2000), however not all banking systems are well developed in Latin America and the consequences may lead to a contrary effect: Industry bank concentration just on few actors, the ones that are able to face the aggressive threat.

The principal conclusion can be simply stated: size matters. The impact on loan market share caused by the entry of Banco Santander is more severe on Large banks than Medium and Small banks. In the case of Medium and Small banks, the larger their asset size the better they faced new competitors.

Additionally, if the bank is part of a financial conglomerate, its internal capital markets may compensate possible financial constraints due to spread reductions forced by new entrant's competitive strategies. This is consistent with previous empirical works that found reasons why internal capital markets may be desirable. Gertner, Scharfstein, and Stein (1994) argued that internal capital markets provide headquarters with valuable flexibility to move funds from less desirable investments to more desirables ones. This is especially true if the desirable division is the bank which is, in many cases, the head-manager of this internal capital market and faces the entry of a new foreign competitor.

We also found empirical evidence related to the role that security investments play in the case of small banks. Consistent with Kasyap and Stein (2000), we found that extreme changes in competitive conditions matter more for the lending of those banks with the least liquid balance sheets.

Finally, we recommended for future research to extend the sample analysis to all banking systems in Latin America where Banco Santander followed the same investing strategy to verify if the above results hold. Also, future research, should analyze incumbent banks strategies two or three years after the entry of Banco Santander because the aggressive entrant strategy of the Spanish bank seems unsustainable in the long run.

REFERENCES

Barajas, A., R. Steiner, and N. Salazar, 2000, "Foreign Investment in Colombia's Financial Sector," in Claessens, S. and Marion Jansen, (eds.) *The Internationalization of Financial Services: Issues and Lessons for Developing Countries*, Boston, Mass.: Kluwer Academic Press.

Berger Philip G., and Eli Ofek., 1995, "Diversification's effect on firm value", *Journal of Financial Economics,* 37, 39-65.

Bradley, D. 1977. "Managing Against Expropriation" *Harvard Business Review* 17-83.

Burton, F. N. and Inoui, H. 1984. "A country risk appraisal model of foreign asset expropriation in developing countries", *Applied Economics,* 19: 1009-1048

Chen M. and D. Hambrick, 1995, "Speed, Stealth, and Selective Attack: How Small Firms differ from Large Firms in Competitive Behavior", *Academy of Management Journal,* 38, 423-487.

Deyoung Robert Nolle Daniel, 1996. "Foreign owned banks en USA. Earning market or buying it?". *Journal of money, Credit and banking*, 28 (4), 622-636.

Fowler J. 2002. "A Dynamic Model of Expropriation" Working paper, Government department Harvard University.

Froot, K. 1993. Introduction, in K. Froot, (ed.), *Foreign Direct Investment,* University of Chicago Press, Chicago.

Gatignon, H. and Anderson E. 1986. "Modes of foreign Entry: A Transaction Cost Analysis and Propositions", *Journal of International Business Studies*, 17 (3): 1-26.

_____ . 1988. "The Multinational corporation degree of control over foreign subsidiaries: An empirical test of transaction cost explanation", *Journal of Law, Economics, and Organizations*, 4: 305-336.

Gertner, Robert H., David S. Scharfstein, and Jeremy C. Stein, 1994, "Internal versus external capital markets", *Quarterly Journal of Economics,* 109, 1211-1230.

Guillén Mauro, Tschoegl Adrian E., 1999. "At Last the Internationalization of Retail Banking? The Case of the Spanish Banks in Latin America". *The Wharton Financial Institutions center. Working paper series.*

Henisz W. J. and Williamson O. E. 1999. "Comparative Economic Organizations -- Within and Between Countries", *Business and Politics*, 1 (3):261-276.

_____ . 2000. "The Institutional Environment for Multinational Investment ", *Journal of Law, Economics and Organizations*, 4: 305-336.

_____ , and Delios A. 2003. "Political Hazards, Experience and Sequential Entry Strategies: The International Expansion of Japanese Firms, 1980-1998", *Strategic Management Journal,* 24. (12): 1153-1164.

Hennart, J. F. 1988. "A Transaction Cost Theory of Equity Joint Ventures", *Strategic Management Journal* 9: 361-374.

_____ . 1991. "The Transaction Costs Theory of Joint Ventures: An Empirical Study of Japanese Subsidiaries in the United States", *Management Science*, 37 (4): 483-497.

Houston, J. Christopher James, and David Marcus, 1997. "Capital markets frictions and the role of internal capital markets in banking", *Journal of Financial Economics,* 46 (2), 135-164.

_____ . 1998 "Do Bank Internal Capital Markets Promote Lending?", *Journal of Banking and Finance* 22, 899-918.

Houston, J., and Christopher James, 2001, "Do Relationships have limits? Banking Relationships, Financial Constraints, and Investments", *Journal of Business,* 74 (4), 347-374.

Kashyap, Anil, and Jeremy C. Stein, 1995. "The impact of monetary policy on bank balance sheet", *Carnegie-Rochester Series on Public Policy,* 42, 151-195.

_____ . 2000, "What do a million observation of banks say about the transmission of monetary policy", *American Economic Review*, 90, 407-428.

Khanna, Naveen, and Sheri Tice, 2000, "Strategic responses of incumbents to new entry: effect of ownership structure, capital structure and focus". *Review of financial studies,* 13, 749-779.

_____ . 2001. "The bright side of internal capital markets", *Journal of Finance.* 52, 1489-1531.

Khanna, T. and Palepu K. 1997. "Why Focused Strategies may be wrong for Emerging Markets" *Harvard Business Review* 41-51.

_____ . 1998. "Emerging Market Business Groups, Foreign Investors and Corporate Governance", *NBER Volume on Concentrated Ownership*, 265-294, University of Chicago Press.

_____ . 2000, "Is Group Affiliation Profitable in Emerging Markets? An Analysis of Diversified Indian Business Groups". *Journal of Finance*. 55 (2), 867-891.

Kobrin, S. J. 1980. "Foreign Enterprise and Forced Divestment in LDCs," *International Organization,* 34 (1): 65-88.

_____ . 1984. "Expropriation as an Attempt to Control Foreign Firms in LDCs:Trends from 1960 to1979", *International Studies Quarterly* 3: 329-48.

Kogut, B. 1988, "Joint Venture: Theoretical and empirical perspectives", *Strategic Management Journal* 9: 319-332.

_____ , and Singh, H. 1988, "The effect on national culture on the choice of entry mode", *Journal of International Business Studies* 19: 411-432.

Linda Goldberg, B. Gerard Dages, Daniel Kinney, 2000. "Foreign and domestic bank participation in emerging markets: Lessons from Mexico and Argentina". *Economic Policy Review,* Vol 6. No 3, 17-36.

Lamont, Owen, 1997, "Cash f low and investment: Evidence from internal capital markets", *Journal of Finance,* 52, 83-110.

Murillo Campello, 2002 "Internal Capital Markets in financial conglomerates: Evidence from small bank responses to monetary policy". *Journal of Finance,* 57 (6), 2773-2805.

Noe T., Rebello M., Shrikhande M. 2002, "Structuring International Cooperative Venture", *The Review of Financial Studies,* 15 (4): 1251-1282.

Oxley, J. E. 1997. "Appropriability Hazards and Governance in Strategic Alliances: A Transaction Cost Approach", *Journal of Law, Economics and Organization*, 13 (2): 387-409.

_____ . 1999. "Institutional Environment and the Mechanisms of Governance: The Impact of Intellectual Property Protection on the Structure of Inter-firm Alliances," *Journal of Economic Behavior and Organization*, 38 (3): 283-309.

Scharfstein, David S., and Jeremy C. Stein, 2000, "The dark side of internal capital markets: Divisional rent seeking and inefficient investment", *Journal of Finance,* 55, 2537-2564.

Schnitzer, M. 1999 "Expropriation and Control Rights: A Dynamic Model of Foreign Direct Investment", *International Journal of Industrial Organization* 17 (8): 1113-1137.

_____ . 2002. "Debt vs. Foreign Direct Investment: The Impact of Sovereign Risk on the Structure of International Capital Flows", Economica 69: 41-67

Shane, S. A. 1992. "The Effect of Cultural Differences in Perceptions of Transaction Costs on National Differences in the Preference for Licensing", *Management International Review*, 32 (4): 295-311.

Shin, Hyuan-Han, and Reé M. Stulz, 1998, "Are internal capital markets efficient?", *Quaterly journal of economics,* 113, 531-552.

Teece, D. 1977. "Technology transfer by multinational firms", *Economic Journal* 87: 242-261.

Thomas J. and Worrall T. 1994. "Foreign Direct Investment and Risk of Expropriation", *Review of Economic Studies*, 61: 81-108.

Tschoegl Adrian E., 1987. "International Retail Banking as a Strategy: An Assessment". *Journal of International Business studies,* 19 (2): 67-88.

United Nations,1996. *World Investment Report 1996*, New York: United Nations.

Wheelock, David C., and Paul W. Wilson, 2000. "Why do banks disappear? The determinants of U.S. bank failures and acquisitions". *Review of Economics and Statistics,* 82, 127-138.

Williamson, O. E. 1985. *The Economic institutions of Capitalism,* New York: The Free Press

_____ . 1996. *The Mechanisms of Governance*, New York: Oxford University Press.

In: Latin American Issues and Challenges
Editors: L. Naciamento and G. Sousa

ISBN 978-1-60692-349-8

Chapter 7

ANALYST ORIGIN AND THEIR FORECASTING QUALITY ON THE LATIN AMERICAN STOCK MARKETS*

Jean-François Bacmann†
RMF Investment Management, Quantitative Analysis, Huobstrasse 16, CH-8808 Pfäffikon SZ.
Guido Bolliger‡
Olympia Capital Management, 21-25 Rue Balzac, F-75008 Paris, France

ABSTRACT

This paper investigates the relative performance of local, foreign, and expatriate financial analysts on Latin American emerging markets. We measure analysts' relative performance with three dimensions: (1) forecast timeliness, (2) forecast accuracy and (3) impact of forecast revisions on security prices. Our main findings can be summarized as follows. Firstly, there is a strong evidence that foreign analysts supply timelier forecasts than their peers. Secondly, analyst working for foreign brokerage houses (i.e. expatriate and foreign ones) produce less biased forecasts than local analysts. Finally, after controlling for analysts' timeliness, we find that foreign financial analysts' upward revisions have a greater impact on stock returns than both followers and local lead analysts forecast revisions. Overall, our results suggest that investors should better rely on the research produced by analysts working for foreign brokerage houses when they invest in Latin American emerging markets.

---

* The first version of this article was entitled "Who are the best? Local versus foreign analysts on Latin American stock markets". It was written at a time when Bacmann was affiliated to the University of Neuchâtel and Bolliger to the University of Neuchâtel as well as the International Center FAME. The views expressed in this article are individual views of the authors and do not necessarily reflect their employers' opinions.

† Phone: ++4155 417 77 10 . Fax: ++4155 417 77 11. Email: Jean-Francois.Bacmann@rmf.ch

‡ Phone: ++331 4953 7426. Fax: ++331 4256 7009. Email: guidobolliger@olympiagroup.com

Keywords: analysts' forecasts, home bias, international diversification, emerging markets, herding behaviour.
JEL Classification: G14, G15, G24

1. INTRODUCTION

Past research suggests that geographic proximity is related to information flow. However, the empirical evidence on the impact of geographic proximity on the quality of investors' information is mixed. Brennan and Cao (1997) report that US investors are less informed about foreign markets conditions than are local investors. Kang and Stulz (1997) find no evidence that foreign investors outperform in Japan. Using US mutual fund holdings, Coval and Moskowitz (2001) show that investors located near potential investments have significant informational advantages relative to the rest of the market. According to Choe et al. (2000), foreign investors on the Korean market are disadvantaged relative to domestic individual investors. Inversely, Seasholes (2000) reports that foreigners act like informed traders in emerging markets. He finds that foreign investors profits come from trading stocks of large firms with low leverage and liquid shares. Similarly, Grinblatt and Keloharju (2000) exihibit evidence that foreign investors on the Finnish stock market generate superior performance than local investors. It is likely that the previous mixed findings are driven by the information available to the investors. This is why our research does not focus on the relative performance of investors but on the relative performance of analysts located at the upstream side of them.

Research devoted to financial analyst forecast accuracy documents that some groups of analysts display a better forecasting ability than others. Stickel (1992) finds that Institutional Investor All-American analysts provide more accurate earnings forecasts and tend to revise their forecasts more frequently than other analysts. Clement (1999) investigates the origin of financial analysts differential accuracy. He documents a negative relationship between financial analysts relative accuracy and the complexity of their stock portfolio. On the other hand, he shows that analysts' performance improves with their age and that analysts working for big research houses with more resources available, outperform their peers. Agency problems such as corporate financing business conflicts, have also an impact on financial analysts' performance. Lin and McNichols (1999) and Michaely and Womack (1999) show that analysts whose employer is affiliated with a company through an underwriting relationship issue more optimistic forecasts than unaffiliated analysts.

The present paper is directly related to these two streams of research. The objective is to investigate the relative performance of local, expatriate, and foreign analysts on Latin American emerging markets. Local analysts are those who work for local research firms. Expatriate analysts work for foreign brokerage houses but are located in the country. Finally, foreign analysts work for foreign research firms with no local presence. Ex-ante, three main reasons may be at the origin of differential performance across the three groups of analysts: geographical distance, agency problems, and available resources.

Residence may give local and expatriate analysts several advantages compared to foreign ones. First, they may have a better knowledge of the local economy. Local economy has been shown to have a significant impact on emerging stock markets ;see Harvey (1995). Second, they may be more familiar with the institutional context in which the companies evolve. Institutional factors have a significant influence on the properties of financial analyst forecasts ; see Hope (2003). Third, they may have a better knowledge of the local culture. Finally, they may have a better human network in the country. This network may give them access to relevant private information. On the other hand, being closer from the analyzed firms, they may be more subject to agency problems such as conflict of interests. Foreign and expatriate analysts usually work for important international research firms. These big research firms have more resources available, they have the financial capacity to attract the best analysts, and their international expertise may help them to better anticipate international macro-economic fluctuations. Overall, if geographic proximity improves the quality of the information available to analysts, local and expatriate analysts should outperform their foreign counterparts. On the other hand, if the quantity of resources available to the analysts, their reputations as well as their expertise are the key determinant of their performance, foreign and expatriate analysts should outperform local ones. Finally, if conflict of interests, caused by tighter investment banking relationships between firms and banks having a local representation, have an important influence on the quality of financial analysts' output in these markets, foreign analysts should outperform both local and expatriate ones.

We conduct our investigation on Latin American markets for two reasons. First, due to geographical considerations, Latin American markets have always presented a great interest for US institutional investors. As a consequence, they create an important demand for financial analysts services on these markets. Second, as underlined by Choe et al. (2002), private information is likely to be more important on emerging stock markets than on developed ones.

We measure analysts' relative performance with three dimensions: (1) forecast timeliness, (2) forecast accuracy and (3) impact of forecast revisions on security prices. Our main findings can be summarized as follows. Firstly, there is a strong evidence that foreign analysts supply timelier forecasts than their peers. In particular, we detect a greater number of leaders among foreign analysts than among analysts with local residence. This finding suggests that both local and expatriate analysts have a tendency to revise their earnings forecasts in order to accommodate the opinions of foreign analysts. Secondly, analyst working for foreign brokerage houses (i.e. expatriate and foreign ones) produce less biased forecasts than local analysts. Lead foreign and expatriate analysts produce much more accurate forecasts than other analysts suggesting that leaders have an important informational advantage over other analysts. Finally, after controlling for analysts' timeliness, we find that foreign financial analysts' upward revisions have a greater impact on stock returns than both followers and local lead analysts forecast revisions. This suggests that the market considers forecast revisions provided by foreign leader analysts as being more informative than the revisions provided by their local counterparts.

Our research has important practical implication: investors should better rely on the research produced by analysts working for foreign brokerage houses when they invest in Latin American emerging markets. Moreover, our paper complements previous research in three ways. Firstly, we contribute to the literature on the importance of geography in economics by showing that location has an impact on the quality of the information provided by analysts. If foreign (local) investors rely mostly on foreign and expatriate (local) analysts' research in order to take their investment decisions, our results may explain the superior performance of foreign investors on some markets; see Seasholes (2000) and Grinblatt and Keloharju (2000). Secondly, by showing that analysts' location/affiliation has a significant impact on their forecast accuracy, we contribute to the large amount of literature which investigates the origins of financial analysts forecasts' bias. Thirdly, we complement, and somehow contradict, the recent research which also investigate the impact of analysts' location on forecast accuracy. Malloy (2003), Chang (2003), and Orpurt (2002) document that analysts located closer to the companies they follow make more accurate forecasts than their more distant counterparts. As underlined by Kini et al. (2003), the almost opposite conclusion drawn from our investigation may be due to differences in the industrial structure of the countries examined in these different papers. If, in Latin America, a good understanding of the sectors is a major determinant of forecast accuracy, a foreign (and to some extent an expatriate) analyst who focuses on a sector in multiple countries may have an advantage over a local analyst who focuses on multiple local firms across multiple sectors. Of course, the reverse may be true for other markets. This shows that the conclusions drawn from these studies may not be generalized to all countries.

The paper proceeds as follows. Section 2 presents the data used in this study. Section 3 investigates the relative timeliness of financial analysts. Section 4 tests for differences in forecast accuracy. Section 5 examines the impact of forecast revisions on security prices; and Section 6 concludes.

2. Data and Overview Statistics

The analysts' forecasts[1] are provided by Institutional Broker Estimate System (I/B/E/S) for 7 Latin American emerging markets: Argentina, Brazil, Chile, Colombia, Mexico, Peru and Venezuela. One year earning per share (EPS) forecasts are used from 1993 to 1999. We use the Nelson Directory of Investment Research to classify financial analysts. The Nelson Directory of Investment Research provides the name and the coordinates of each analyst that follows a particular company. Financial analysts who work for local brokerage houses are classified as local, those who work for foreign brokerage houses with residence in the country as classified as expatriate, and those who work for foreign brokerage houses without residence in the country are classified as foreign. Stock prices are extracted from Datastream. To be included in the sample, a forecast should meet the following conditions:

1. Realized EPS has to figure in the I/B/E/S Actual File.
2. The forecast must be issued between the end of previous fiscal year and current year earning reporting date.
3. The forecast must be issued by an analyst listed in the Nelson Directory of Investment Research.
4. The company for which the forecast is issued must be followed by at least 3 analysts of each group during a given year.

The last condition restricts the sample to big and medium-sized companies. The final sample includes 61'209 EPS forecasts. Table 1 shows that local analysts have produced 59% more forecasts than their foreign counterparts and more than twice much forecasts than expatriate analysts. The number of analysts and brokerage houses active on Latin American markets has sensibly increased between 1993 and 1999. This is due to the increasing coverage

[1] Note that we make no distinction between individual analysts and team of analysts.

of the I/B/E/S database but also to the increasing attractiveness of these markets for foreign investors.

Table 1. Summary statistics by year

Year	No. Forecasts			No. Analysts			No. Brokers			No. Stocks
	Local	Foreign	Expatriate	Local	Foreign	Expatriate	Local	Foreign	Expatriate	
1993	1670	783	432	74	56	41	35	18	10	84
1994	4937	2345	2263	114	84	87	49	36	16	208
1995	4999	2526	1989	236	123	122	51	32	20	200
1996	4764	2864	1899	257	163	147	57	37	17	180
1997	5229	3888	2056	245	238	170	56	33	16	212
1998	4508	3694	2141	244	232	175	50	24	15	205
1999	3674	2624	1924	182	176	148	41	19	11	170
Total	29781	18724	12704	719	584	365	93	61	27	351

This table reports yearly statistics for the data. No. Forecasts represents the number of annual earnings forecasts made each year. No. Analyst represents the number of analysts who produced a forecast during the fiscal year t. The total number of analysts who produced an earning forecast during the entire period is indicated in the last row. No. Brokers represents the number of banks (or brokerage companies) for which analysts work each year. The total number of brokers identified during the entire period is indicated in the last row. No. Stocks is the number of firms in the sample. The total number of firms for which forecasts were produced during the period is indicated in the last row.

Table 2. Summary statistics by country

Country	No. Forecasts			No. Analysts			No. Brokers			No. Stocks
	Local	Foreign	Expatriate	Local	Foreign	Expatriate	Local	Foreign	Expatriate	
Argentina	5114	2685	1835	135	215	86	22	36	9	45
Brazil	11897	7238	6349	293	244	191	30	31	19	160
Chile	2224	1530	697	67	150	39	11	25	4	29
Colombia	160	364	174	6	43	15	2	17	2	11
Mexico	12905	7700	3753	242	286	128	21	35	12	82
Peru	651	927	226	27	111	27	7	32	3	17
Venezuela	110	279	97	1	66	15	1	18	2	7

This table reports statistics by country and by industry. *No. Forecasts* represents the number of annual earnings forecasts made each year. *No. Analyst* represents the number of analysts who produced a forecast during the fiscal year *t*. *No. Brokers* represents the number of banks (or brokerage companies) for which analysts work in each country. *No. Stocks* is the number of firms in the sample.

Table 2 shows that most of the forecasts (81%) are concentrated on Brazil and Mexico. In addition, in each country excepting Brazil, foreign analysts tend to be more numerous than local and expatriate ones. However, from Table 1, we see that this finding is reversed at the aggregated level: local analysts are more numerous than foreign ones and the difference between foreign and expatriate is smaller. Thus, foreign analysts tend to follow several different markets while local and expatriate analysts are more focused on specific markets.

Non-tabulated results indicate that the average number of analysts employed by foreign brokerage houses amounts to 7.9 while it amounts to 5.5 for local ones suggesting that, on average, foreign brokerage houses are bigger than local ones. Our sample contains 91 companies out of 351 that have quoted American Depositary Receipts (ADR). Lang et al. (2002) show that non-U.S. companies listed on U.S. exchanges have richer informational environment than other non-U.S. firms. Therefore, we will control for ADR listing in the subsequent analysis.

Table 3 shows that expatriate analysts are the less active ones. On average, they produce a forecast every 77 day while their foreign and local peers do it every 73, respectively 71 day. Similarly, expatriate analysts revise less frequently than their counterparts: on average 1.33 times per firm each year against 1.92 times for foreigners and 2.45 for locals. Although the frequency of forecast revisions gives an insight on the activity of financial analysts, this does not indicate that more active analysts have advantages in collecting and processing information. They may simply change their mind several times to accommodate the opinions of others. Therefore, in the subsequent section, we propose to measure analysts' relative activity with their timeliness.

Table 3. Frequency of forecast issuance and revision

	Panel A: number of calendar days elapsed between forecasts			
	Mean	Min	Median	Max
Local analysts	70.63	1.00	59.00	344.00
Foreign analysts	73.00	1.00	59.75	372.00
Expatriate analysts	77.29	1.00	65.75	362.00
	Panel B: number of revisions per analyst			
	Mean	Min	Median	Max
Local analysts	2.45	0.00	1.00	50.00
Foreign analysts	1.92	0.00	1.00	19.00
Expatriate analysts	1.33	0.00	1.00	11.00

This table reports summary statistics on financial analysts' activity. Panel A presents statistics about the number of calendar days that separate two consecutive forecasts by analyst for a particular company in a given year. Panel B reports statistics on the number of revisions by analyst for a particular company in a given year.

3. Analysts' Timeliness

3.1. Empirical Design

Cooper, Day and Lewis (2001, thereafter CDL) show that timely analysts' (leaders) forecast revisions provide greater value to investors than other analysts' (followers) forecasts. They argue that timeliness is an important and necessary indicator of financial analysts' relative performance. Using forecast accuracy alone to assess the relative performance of financial analysts can lead to misclassification errors because less informed analysts can improve the accuracy of their forecasts by simply mimicking timely skilled analysts.

The leader to follower ratio (*LFR*) developed by CDL is used to distinguish leaders from followers.[2] This ratio is computed for each analyst/firm/year unit. It is distributed as $F_{(2KH,2KH)}$,[3] where *H* is the number of other analysts following a particular firm in a given year and *K* is the total number of forecasts provided by the analyst during the year for that firm. Similar to CDL, analysts having *LFR* significantly greater than 1 at the 10% level are considered as leaders. Moreover, each analyst is required to produce at least 3 forecasts per year for the firm under consideration. As mentioned CDL, this restriction minimizes the possibility for an analyst to be classified as leader thanks to a single lucky forecast.

In order to test whether a group (local or foreign) tends to lead the other one, we compare the number of local leaders to the foreign ones. However, since the total number of analysts is different between the 2 groups, such a comparison is not directly possible. Thus, the proportion of leaders in a given group g, L_g, is compared to the proportion of analysts in group g in the sample, P_g. In order to determine whether a group of analysts has significantly more (less) leaders than its proportion in the population suggests, we test the following hypothesis:

$$H_0 : L_g = P_g \ vs \ H_1 : L_g \neq P_g .$$

Consequently, the following normally distributed statistic is computed:

$$Time_g = \frac{\left(L_g - P_g\right)}{\sqrt{P_g \cdot \left(1 - P_g\right)}} \cdot \sqrt{N} ,$$

where:

$$L_g = \frac{Number\ of\ leaders\ in\ group\ g}{Total\ number\ of\ leaders} ,$$

$$P_g = \frac{Number\ of\ analysts\ from\ group\ g}{N} ,$$

$$N = Total\ number\ of\ analysts .$$

---

[2] A precise description of the *LFR* computation methodology is given in the Appendix.

[3] CDL derive the distribution of the *LFR* by assuming that the time elapsed between the arrival of two subsequent revisions follows an exponential distribution.

Table 4. Financial analysts' timeliness

Panel A: LFR for Latin America						
	Analysts' origin	No. observations	No. leaders	% leaders	% observations	Difference
		N		L_g	P_g	
Latin America	Local	5599	621	47.7	49.6	-1.9***
	Foreign	3457	444	34.1	30.6	3.5***
	Expatriate	2226	236	18.1	19.7	-1.6***
Panel B: LFR by country						
Country	Analysts' origin	No. observations	No. leaders	% leaders	% observations	Difference
		N		L_g	P_g	
Argentina	Local	938	90	45.9	53.6	-7.7***
	Foreign	476	62	31.6	27.2	4.4***
	Expatriate	337	44	22.4	19.2	3.2***
Brazil	Local	1948	231	44.6	46.5	-1.9***
	Foreign	1247	176	34.0	29.7	4.2***
	Expatriate	998	111	21.4	23.8	-2.4***
Chile	Local	315	26	43.3	48.1	-4.8***
	Foreign	246	29	48.3	37.6	10.8***
	Expatriate	94	5	8.3	14.4	-6.0***
Colombia	Local	4	0	0.0	20.0	-20.0***
	Foreign	12	3	100.0	60.0	40.0***
	Expatriate	4	0	0.0	20.0	-20.0***
Mexico	Local	2323	264	52.6	52.0	0.6
	Foreign	1388	163	32.5	31.0	1.4***
	Expatriate	760	75	14.9	17.0	-2.1***
Peru	Local	65	10	58.8	44.8	14.0***
	Foreign	58	6	35.3	40.0	-4.7
	Expatriate	22	1	5.9	15.2	-9.3***
Venezuela	Local	6	0	0.0	12.8	-12.8***
	Foreign	30	5	100.0	63.8	36.2***
	Expatriate	11	0	0.0	23.4	-23.4***

This table reports the number of analysts identified as leaders as well as the test of the null hypothesis, which is stating that the proportion of leaders in a given group equals the proportion of analysts from the given group in the total sample. The last column represents the difference between the percentage of leaders in a given group, L_g, and the percentage of analysts from the given group, P_g. The significance of this difference is determined by the following normally distributed statistic: $Time_g = \frac{(L_g - P_g)}{\sqrt{P_g \cdot (1-P_g)}} \cdot \sqrt{N}$. Panel A reports results for all Latin American markets. Panel B reports results by country

***, **, * denote significance at the 1%, 5%, and 10% levels, respectively.

3.2. Results for Analysts' Timeliness

According to the LFR statistic, 1301 leaders out of 11282 observations are detected. Table 4 shows the breakdown of the leaders according to their origin. The proportions of local and expatriate analysts within the leaders are significantly smaller than their proportions within the full sample.[4] On the other hand, there are more leaders among foreign analysts than their proportion in the sample would suggest. These results indicate that, on average, foreign analysts lead while local and expatriate analysts herd. Analysts with local residence have a tendency to issue their forecasts shortly after foreign analysts and their revisions do not induce other analysts to revise their own forecasts.

Panel B of Table 4 shows the breakdown of the leaders across the different countries. The individual country results are consistent with those obtained for Latin America. The exceptions are Brazil and Peru. In Brazil, the proportion of expatriate analysts identified as leaders is significantly more important than their proportion in the population. The same is true for local analysts in Peru.

In summary, the above results indicate that foreign analysts have a greater tendency to lead than analysts with local residence. This holds at the aggregated level as well as for most of the individual stock markets. The implications of these findings in terms of forecast accuracy and earnings forecasts' informativeness are investigated in the following two sections.

4. Forecast Accuracy

4.1. Empirical Design

Forecast accuracy is the most widely used measure of the quality of an analyst's research. Indeed, the more accurate earnings forecast is, the more accurate the price extracted from any valuation model will be. Forecast accuracy is measured using the average percentage forecast error adjusted for the horizon bias.[5] Analyst i 's percentage forecast error at date t is,

$$FE_{ijt} = \frac{FEPS_{it} - EPS}{|EPS|},$$

where:

$FEPS_{it} =$ analyst i 's EPS forecast for company j at date t,

$EPS =$ reported earning per share at the end of the forecast horizon.

In order to correct for the horizon bias, CDL forecast accuracy regression is used. Compared to the matching forecasts methodology used by Stickel (1992), this operation is

4 The inverse is automatically true for foreign leaders.

5 Prior studies such as Kang, O'Brien and Sivaramkarishnan (1994) show that forecast bias increases with forecast horizon.

much less data-consuming and better suited for our study. Each FE_{ijt} is regressed on the length of time from forecast release to earning announcement date. The residuals from this regression are used to measure forecast accuracy. Formally,

$$FE_{ijt} = \alpha + \beta \cdot T + \varepsilon_{ijt}, \tag{1}$$

where:

$T =$ number of days until the earnings announcement date,

$\varepsilon_{ijt} =$ residual forecast error for analyst i on firm j at date t.

The relative accuracy of each group of analysts is computed in three successive steps. First, for a given firm, the average residual forecast error is computed for each analyst,

$$MFE_{ij} = \sum_{t=1}^{K} \left| \varepsilon_{ijt} \right| / K,$$

where:

$MFE_{ij} =$ mean forecast error by analyst i for firm j,

$K =$ number of forecasts issued by analyst i for firm j during a given year.

Second, for each firm/year, individual analysts' mean forecast errors are averaged over all analysts of a given group g,

$$MGFE_{gj} = \sum_{i \in g} MFE_{ij} / N_j^g,$$

where:

$MGFE_{gj} =$ mean group forecast error for firm j,

$N =$ number of analysts from group g following firm j during a given year.

Finally, the mean difference forecast error between 2 groups is computed as

$$MDFE = \sum_{j=1}^{J} \left[MGFE_{Aj} - MGFE_{Bj} \right] / J$$

where J is the number of company/year units. In order to assess whether one group of analysts produces more (less) accurate forecasts than the other, the following hypothesis is tested:

$$H_0 : MDFE = 0 \ vs \ H_1 : MDFE \neq 0 .$$

A parametric mean test, a Wilcoxon sign rank test of equality of medians as well as a non-parametric binomial sign test are performed to test the hypothesis.

4.2. Results for Forecast Accuracy

The slope coefficient of equation (1) equals 0.01 and is significantly different from zero.[6] Emerging market analysts' bias decreases significantly with the distance between forecast release date and earnings announcement date. The intercept is not statistically different from zero.

Hypothesis tests and descriptive statistics for the mean difference forecast errors ($MDFE$) are reported in Table 5. Panels A through C report the difference across each category of analysts for all Latin American countries, for individual countries as well as for different security categories. The distribution of the MDFEs appears to be highly skewed by the presence of some extreme observations. As this may bias the results of the parametric tests, we will only consider the non-parametric results of column 7 and 8 for our analysis and conclusions.

Panel A shows that the median MDFE is positive for the whole sample and each individual countries indicating that local analysts' average forecast error is greater than foreign analysts' one. The Wilcoxon sign rank test and the binomial test reject the null hypothesis of equal forecasting skills at the aggregate level as well as for five of the individual countries. The superior ability of foreign analysts to predict firms earnings does not depend on size. Surprisingly, this superior ability disappears for American Depositary Receipts, which have a richer information environment and are the least distant firms for foreign analysts. Conflicts of interest due to increased investment and commercial banking relationship with foreign banks following U.S. exchange listing may explain this finding.

The results in panel B indicate that, excepting for Venezuela, the average error is greater for local analysts forecasts than for expatriate ones. The difference between both groups of analysts is statistically significant at the Latin American level but only weakly or not significant at the country and security category levels.

As indicated by the results in panel C, no difference between the forecasting skills of expatriate and foreign analysts can be found. As reported, in panel D, there is a strong evidence that leaders produce more accurate forecasts than follower analysts. Their mean forecast error appears to be much smaller than that of follower analysts. This is particularly true for local and foreign leaders for which the null hypothesis is rejected at the 1% level. The leader-follower criterion appears more important than the geographical one. However, no comparison is performed across leaders from each analyst group as the number of firm/year units for which leaders of both types are simultaneously identified is very low. Two important conclusions can be drawn about the behavior of financial analysts on Latin American markets. First, contrary to what has been documented by CDL, leader analysts do not "trade accuracy for timeliness". Indeed, foreign analysts are able to release timelier and more accurate forecasts. Second, follower analysts do not exactly reproduce the earnings per share

[6] Results are not shown. They are available on request by the authors.

forecasts issued by leader analysts. Even if their forecast releases closely follow leader analysts' ones, they avoid to reproduce exactly the information released by leader analysts.

Table 5. Financial analysts relative forecast accuracy

Distribution of the Mean Difference Forecast Errors (*MDFE*)									Sign of *MDFE*	
Panel A: Difference in forecast accuracy between local and foreign analysts										
Sample	N	Mean		Stdev	Min	Median		Max	% Local > Foreign	
Latin America	1263	-0.16		7.98	-238.88	0.02	***	62.10	54.95	***
Argentina	191	-0.01		0.88	-9.22	0.02	**	4.59	58.64	***
Brazil	557	-0.55		11.68	-238.88	0.02		47.11	53.68	**
Mexico	332	0.22		3.52	-4.97	0.02		62.10	53.31	
Chili	112	0.11	**	0.50	-1.96	0.03	**	3.31	55.36	
Peru	38	0.23		0.98	-0.42	0.05		5.46	60.53	*
Colombia	21	0.32	*	0.83	-0.38	0.10	**	3.54	71.43	**
Venezuela	12	-0.06		0.43	-1.13	0.02		0.36	50.00	
High Market Value	493	-0.01		6.54	-121.27	0.02	**	62.10	54.56	**
Small Market Value	323	0.16		2.25	-9.22	0.02	*	35.44	53.25	
ADR	277	0.04		0.88	-5.35	0.02		10.51	53.07	
Panel B: Difference in forecast accuracy between local and expatriate analysts										
Sample	N	Mean		Stdev	Min	Median		Max	% Local > Expatriate	
Latin America	1263	0.61	*	12.89	-20.69	0.01	**	402.14	52.26	*
Argentina	191	0.05		0.89	-4.24	0.02		10.27	53.40	
Brazil	557	1.04		18.48	-20.69	0.01		402.14	51.35	
Mexico	332	0.45		7.65	-13.31	0.01		136.34	52.41	
Chili	112	0.08	*	0.46	-0.76	0.00		3.03	50.89	
Peru	38	0.29	*	1.03	-0.65	0.08	*	5.59	60.53	*
Colombia	21	0.24		0.80	-0.36	0.02		3.20	61.90	*
Venezuela	12	-0.09		0.33	-0.75	-0.07		0.55	41.67	
High Market Value	493	0.63		9.60	-3.35	0.00		163.62	49.49	
Small Market Value	323	0.00		2.65	-20.69	0.02		35.23	52.94	
ADR	277	0.05		0.67	-3.61	0.01		6.81	52.71	
Panel C: Difference in forecast accuracy between expatriate and foreign analysts										
Sample	N	Mean		Stdev	Min	Median		Max	% Expatriate > Foreign	
Latin America	1263	-0.77		18.81	-641.02	0.00		19.46	50.75	
Argentina	191	-0.06		1.35	-12.48	0.01		4.41	52.88	
Brazil	557	-1.59		28.10	-641.02	-0.01		19.46	48.29	
Mexico	332	-0.23		4.45	-74.23	0.01		18.11	52.41	
Chili	112	0.03		0.38	-2.58	0.05	**	0.91	58.04	**
Peru	38	-0.06		0.22	-0.45	-0.08	**	0.53	34.21	**
Colombia	21	0.08		0.22	-0.25	0.04		0.50	52.38	
Venezuela	12	0.03		0.47	-1.28	0.10		0.52	66.67	*
High Market Value	493	-0.65	*	8.29	-120.94	0.01		3.71	52.54	

Table 5. Continued

Sample	N	Mean	Stdev	Min	Median		Max	% Expatriate > Foreign	
Small Market Value	323	0.16	1.97	-11.16	0.01		19.46	51.39	
ADR	277	-0.02	0.67	-4.70	0.01		3.71	52.71	
Panel D: Difference in forecast accuracy between leaders and followers									
Sample	N	Mean	Stdev	Min	Median		Max	% Leaders > Followers	
Local Leaders	426	-0.04	1.31	-11.04	-0.05	***	17.08	39.20	***
Foreign Leaders	350	-3.74	70.33	-1315.50	-0.58	***	12.09	40.57	***
Expatriate Leaders	198	0.07	6.13	-40.74	-0.02		73.38	44.95	*

This table presents descriptive statistics as well as hypothesis tests for the Mean Difference in Forecast Errors (*MDFE*). In Panel A, the third column reports the average difference between local analysts' forecast errors and foreign analysts' forecast errors. Column 6 reports the median difference between local analysts' forecast errors and foreign analysts' forecast errors. Column 8 reports the percentage of firm/year units for which the average forecast error of local analysts was greater than the average forecast error of foreign ones. In Panel B, the third column reports the average difference between local analysts' forecast errors and expatriate analysts' forecast errors. Column 6 reports the median difference between local analysts' forecast errors and expatriate analysts' forecast errors. Column 8 reports the percentage of firm/year units for which the average forecast error of local analysts was greater than the average forecast error of expatriate ones. In Panel C, the third column reports the average difference between expatriate analysts' forecast errors and foreign analysts' forecast errors. Column 6 reports the median difference between expatriate analysts' forecast errors and foreign analysts' forecast errors. Column 8 reports the percentage of firm/year units for which the average forecast error of expatriate analysts was greater than the average forecast error of foreign ones. In Panel D, the third column reports the average difference between lead analysts' forecast errors and follower analysts' forecast errors. Column 6 reports the median difference between lead analysts' forecast errors and follower analysts' forecast errors. Column 8 reports the percentage of firm/year units for which the average forecast error of lead analysts was greater than the average forecast error of follower ones. A parametric mean test is performed on column 3 numbers, a Wilcoxon signed rank test of equality of medians is performed on column 6 numbers, and a non-parametric sign test is performed on column 8 numbers. Note that in Panel D, the total number of firm/year units for each group of leader is lower than the number of leaders that has been identified. This is explained by the fact that there can be several leaders for a particular company in a given year.

***, **, * denote significance at the 1%, 5%, and 10% levels, respectively.

Overall, this section shows that foreign analysts foreign analysts have a better ability to analyze Latin American firms' earnings potential than their local peers. There is no significant difference between the performance of foreign and expatriate analysts and only a weak difference between expatriate and local analysts in the favor of expatriate ones. These finding indicate that analysts who work for foreign institutions may have greater resources, expertise and/or talent than their local peers. Finally, timely analysts are the most accurate ones. Consequently, lead analysts do not give up forecast accuracy when releasing more timely forecasts.

5. Impact of Forecast Revisions on Security Prices

5.1. Empirical Design

This section investigates whether one group of analysts' revisions provides more information to investors. The objective is to determine whether the stock price reaction following forecast revisions differs between the different groups of analysts. The reaction around forecast revisions for a given firm is proxied by the cumulative excess return during the forecast release period (days 0 and +1). This cumulative excess return is computed as the difference between the buy-and-hold returns for the firm's common stock and the value-weighted Datastream country index.

The incremental information content of each revision is measured by the scaled distance relative to the consensus forecast.[7] More precisely:

$$FSUR_{ijt} = \frac{FEPS_{ijt} - CF_{jt-1}}{\sigma(CF_{jt-1})}$$

where:

$FSUR_{ijt} =$ forecast surprise following analyst i's revision for firm j at date t,

$CF_{jt-1} =$ consensus EPS forecast for firm j at date $t-1$,

$\sigma(CF_{jt-1}) =$ standard deviation of the consensus forecast[8] at date $t-1$.

The consensus forecast is based on the average of the forecasts issued by analysts (excluding analyst i) during the 2 months preceding date t. Each analyst is required to provide at least 3 forecasts per year for the firm and each consensus forecast is required to contain at least 2 individual forecasts.

The impact of forecast revisions on security prices is measured by the following cross-sectional regression equations:

$$CAR_{jt} = \beta_0 + \beta_1 FSUR_{ijt} + \beta_2 LOC_i + \beta_3 FOR_i + \beta_4 LNSIZE_{jt} + \varepsilon_{jt} \quad (2)$$

$$CAR_{jt} = \beta_0 + \beta_1 LOC_i \times FSUR_{ijt} + \beta_2 FOR_i \times FSUR_{ijt} + \beta_3 EXPAT_i \times FSUR_{ijt} + \beta_4 LNSIZE_{jt} + \varepsilon_{jt} \quad (3)$$

$$CAR_{jt} = \beta_0 + \beta_1 FSUR_{ijt} + \beta_2 LOCLEAD_{ij} + \beta_3 FORLEAD_{ij} + \beta_4 EXPATLEAD_{ij} + \beta_5 LNSIZE_{jt} + \varepsilon_{jt} \quad (4)$$

[7] Our results are not sensitive to the choice of the scaling factor.

[8] Similar to Stickel (1992), a standard deviation less than 0.25 is arbitrarily set to 0.25 to mitigate small denominators. Our results are not affected by this operation.

$$CAR_{jt} = \beta_0 + \beta_1 LOCLEAD_{ij} \times FSUR_{ijt} + \beta_2 FORLEAD_{ij} \times FSUR_{ijt} + \beta_3 EXPATLEAD_{ij} \times FSUR_{ijt} + \beta_4 FOL_i \times FSUR_{ijt} + \beta_5 LNSIZE_{jt} + \varepsilon_{jt} \quad (5)$$

where:

CAR_{jt} = cumulative excess return for firm j during the forecast release period (days 0 and +1),

LOC_i = dummy variable set to 1 if analyst i is a local one and 0 otherwise,

FOR_i = dummy variable set to 1 if analyst i is foreign and 0 otherwise,

$LNSIZE_j$ = logarithm of the market value (in USD) of common stock at fiscal year end,

$EXPAT_i$ = dummy variable set to 1 if analyst i is an expatriate and 0 otherwise,

$LOCLEAD_{ij}$ = dummy variable set to 1 if analyst i is a local analyst that has been identified as leader for company *j* and 0 otherwise,

$FORLEAD_{ij}$ = dummy variable set to 1 if analyst i is a foreign analyst that has been identified as leader for company *j* and 0 otherwise,

$EXPATLEAD_{ij}$ = dummy variable set to 1 if analyst i is an expatriate analyst that has been identified as leader for company *j* and 0 otherwise,

FOL_{ij} = dummy variable set to 1 if analyst i has been identified as follower for company *j* and 0 otherwise,

Equations (2) and (4) measure the abnormal return associated with the different groups of analysts' forecast revisions. Equation (3) and (5) measures the proportion of abnormal return explained by each group of analysts' forecast revisions. The size variable is a proxy for the differences in firms' information environment[9] but also for foreign investors' ownership since they tend to concentrate their investments on high-capitalization liquid firms.

5.2. Results for the Impact of Forecast Revisions on Security Prices

Table 6 reports the mean cumulative abnormal return during the forecast release period. The price reaction depends on the size of the revision. The cumulative abnormal returns display important standard deviations and consequently only the stock returns associated with the bottom 50% sub-sample display statistically significant price reactions. Conversely, other revisions do not impact on prices. This is consistent with Stickel (1992, 1995) who documents a non-linear relation between forecast revisions and price reactions. Therefore, the regressions are restricted to revisions of a given magnitude.

Results for the cross-sectional regressions (2) and (3) are reported in table 7. First, panel A results indicate that, following downward revisions, there is no difference in the average

---

[9] Stickel (1995), among others, reports that buy and sell recommendations induces a greater price reaction for smaller companies than for larger ones.

size of the stock price reaction across groups. On the other hand, following large upward revisions (top 10%), the average cumulative abnormal return is significantly smaller for local analysts than for expatriate ones. The same is true for foreign analysts but the regression coefficient is only marginally significant. Second, results reported in panel B indicate that the stock price reaction following analysts forecast revisions is only significant for expatriate analysts large upward revisions. Unfortunately, the null hypothesis of equality across coefficients cannot be rejected by the F-tests presented in columns 7 through 9.

Table 6. Stock price reactions following forecast surprises

	All FSUR	Bottom 10%	Bottom 50%	Top 50%	Top 10%
Mean (%)	-0.07 **	-0.16	-0.12 **	-0.02	-0.17
Standard deviation (%)	4.39	4.73	4.52	4.27	4.42
N	16699	1670	8352	8347	1670

This table reports some descriptive statistics about the cumulative abnormal returns (CARs) following forecasts' revisions. Cumulative abnormal returns are computed as the difference between the buy-and-hold return for the firm's common stock and the value-weighted Datastream country index during the forecast release period (days 0 and 1). The column All FSUR reports statistics on CARs for all forecast surprise level. Bottom 10% reports CARs for forecast surprises located in the top 10% of the distribution. Bottom 50% reports statistics for CAR's located in the bottom 50% of the distribution. In the column Top 50%, statistics are reported for CAR's located in the top 50% of the distribution. Top 10% reports statistics for CAR's located in the top 10% of the distribution.
***, **, * denote significance at the 1%, 5%, and 10% levels, respectively.

Table 7. Stock price reactions following analyst forecast revisions

Panel A: $CAR_{jt} = \beta_0 + \beta_1 FSUR_{ijt} + \beta_2 LOC_i + \beta_3 FOR_i + \beta_4 LNSIZE_{jt} + \varepsilon_{jt}$

FSUR Cutoff	β_0	β_1	β_2	β_3	β_4	N
Bottom 10%	-0.46	0.09	-0.24	0.02	0.08	1670
	(-0.60)	(0.63)	(-0.77)	(0.05)	(0.88)	
Bottom 50%	-0.59 *	0.07	0.07	0.17	0.06	8352
	(-1.91)	(1.03)	(0.51)	(1.17)	(1.55)	
Top 50%	0.03	-0.04	-0.20	-0.27 **	0.02	8347
	(0.09)	(-0.56)	(-1.57)	(-1.97)	0.58	
Top 10%	1.07	0.20	-0.60 **	-0.52 *	-0.16 *	1670
	(1.35)	(1.42)	(-2.13)	(-1.68)	(-1.73)	

Table 7. Continued

Panel B: $CAR_{jt} = \beta_0 + \beta_1 LOC_i \times FSUR_{ijt} + \beta_2 FOR_i \times FSUR_{ijt} + \beta_3 EXPAT_i \times FSUR_{ijt} + \beta_4 LNSIZE_{jt} + \varepsilon_{jt}$

FSUR Cutoff	β_0	β_1	β_2	β_3	β_4	$\beta_1 = \beta_2$	$\beta_1 = \beta_3$	$\beta_2 = \beta_3$	N
Bottom 10%	-0.56	0.13	0.05	0.06	0.08	0.40	0.25	0.01	1670
	(-0.76)	(0.86)	(0.30)	(0.35)	(0.87)				
Bottom 50%	-0.50 *	0.13	0.13	0.03	0.06	0.99	0.56	0.02	8352
	(-1.73)	(1.52)	(1.52)	(0.25)	(1.55)				
Top 50%	-0.14	-0.11	-0.03	0.12	0.02	0.42	2.89 *	1.04	8347
	(-0.51)	(-1.25)	(-0.29)	(0.98)	(0.53)				
Top 10%	0.64	0.13	0.22	0.35 **	-0.16	0.46	2.24	0.65	1670
	(0.84)	(0.81)	(1.36)	(1.99)	(-1.74)				

This table presents the coefficients obtained by regressing the cumulative abnormal returns following forecast revisions on the magnitude of the revision, firm size, and dummy variables indicating analysts' status. Revisions are dated within the firm's current fiscal year over the 1993-1999 period. CAR_{jt} is the cumulative abnormal return to security i during the release period (days 0 and +1). $FSUR_{ijt}$ is the forecast surprise following analyst i's revision at date t. $LNSIZE_{jt}$ is the natural logarithm of the market value (in USD) of common stock at fiscal year end. LOC_i is a dummy variable that takes a value of 1 if analyst i is employed by a local brokerage house and 0 otherwise. FOR_i is a dummy variable that takes a value of 1 if analyst i is employed by a foreign brokerage house without local residence and 0 otherwise. $EXPAT_i$ is a dummy variable that takes a value of 1 if analyst i is employed by a foreign brokerage house with local residence and 0 otherwise. All coefficients are multiplied by 100. T-statistics are based on White (1980). For each regression the adjusted R^2 are less than 0.01.

***, **, * denote significance at the 1%, 5%, and 10% levels, respectively.

Table 8 reports the results for the cross-sectional regressions (4) and (5). First, as reported in panel A, the average cumulative return does not differ between leader and follower analysts. Second, as indicated by panel B results, there is a significant market reaction following foreign and expatriate leaders large upward revisions (top 10%). The F-tests indicate that the regression coefficients associated to foreign leaders' revisions are significantly higher than those associated to local leaders and followers' revisions.

Overall, this section shows that there are almost no significant differences in the incremental information contained in financial analysts forecasts revisions. However, the market seems to consider the forecasts issued by local and, to some extent, by expatriate leaders as being more informative than those issued by other analysts. This is consistent with the view that foreign leaders' revisions have a greater information content than other analysts' revisions.

6. CONCLUSIONS

Foreign financial analysts' EPS forecasts are more timely than expatriate and local analysts' forecasts. Building on CDL methodology, 1301 leader analysts are identified. Out of these leaders, 444 are foreign. This is significantly greater than the proportion of foreign analysts' forecasts in the sample. Conversely, analysts with local residence display a significant tendency to follow the "crowd".

In terms of forecast accuracy, analysts working for foreign brokerage houses are better at predicting firms' EPS than local analysts. Surprisingly, we detect no significant differences in forecast accuracy for companies with quoted ADRs. This may indicate that foreign and expatriate analysts' superior performance vanishes for companies with richer information environment.

Finally, stock prices react positively to upward forecast revisions released by foreign and expatriate leader analysts. The coefficient associated to foreign leaders forecast surprises is significantly greater than that associated to follower forecast surprises. It is also marginally greater than the coefficient associated to local leaders forecast surprises.

We see that foreign analysts outperform their local peers across all our performance measures. This suggests that residence does not give local financial analysts an advantage relative to their foreign counterparts. The difference between foreign and expatriate analysts' performance is less evident. Foreign analysts outperform their expatriate peers for one out of three performance measures. This suggests that agency problems, due to tighter investment banking relationships between resident analysts' firms and local companies, are not influencing financial analysts' objectivity on Latin American markets. Overall, our results are consistent with better information and greater sophistication on the part of analysts employed by foreign brokerage houses. This superiority may be linked to the superior resources available to analysts who work for important international brokerage houses, to the better international expertise of these analysts, or to their greater talent.

The present results are consistent with a better information on the part of foreign investors. Foreigners' portfolio profits on emerging markets, such as those documented by Seasholes (2000), may be driven by the better ability of foreign analysts at analyzing firms' situation for their clients. However, further research is needed to understand which category of investors (foreign or domestic) trade around foreign and local analysts' revisions. Finally, the practical implication of this investigation is that investors should rely more heavily on foreign financial analysts' forecasts than on local ones when they invest in Latin American markets.

Table 8. Stock price reactions following leaders and followers forecast revisions

Panel A: $CAR_{jt} = \beta_0 + \beta_1 FSUR_{ijt} + \beta_2 LOCLEAD_{ij} + \beta_3 FORLEAD_{ij} + \beta_4 EXPATLEAD_{ij} + \beta_5 LNSIZE_{jt} + \varepsilon_{jt}$

FSUR Cutoff	β_0	β_1	β_2	β_3	β_4	β_5	N
Bottom 10%	-0.56	0.09	-0.63	0.52	-0.61	0.09	1670
	(-0.76)	(0.64)	(-1.19)	(0.86)	(-0.59)	(0.92)	
Bottom 50%	-0.48	0.07	-0.24	-0.03	-0.30	0.06	8352
	(-1.66)	(1.05)	(-1.15)	(-0.10)	(-0.72)	(1.57)	
Top 50%	-0.17	-0.03	0.17	-0.33	0.22	0.02	8347
	(-0.62)	(-0.52)	(0.78)	(-1.17)	(0.64)	(0.64)	
Top 10%	0.60	0.20	-0.18	0.78	0.97	-0.16 *	1670
	(0.79)	(1.38)	(-0.40)	(1.24)	(1.23)	(-1.72)	

Panel B: $CAR_{jt} = \beta_0 + \beta_1 LOCLEAD_{ij} \times FSUR_{ijt} + \beta_2 FORLEAD_{ij} \times FSUR_{ijt} + \beta_3 EXPATLEAD_{ij} \times FSUR_{ijt} + \beta_4 FOL_{ij} \times FSUR_{ijt} + \beta_5 LNSIZE_{jt} + \varepsilon_{jt}$

FSUR Cutoff	β_0	β_1	β_2	β_3	β_4	β_5	$\beta_1 = \beta_2$	$\beta_1 = \beta_3$	$\beta_1 = \beta_4$	$\beta_2 = \beta_3$	$\beta_2 = \beta_4$	$\beta_3 = \beta_4$	N
Bottom 10%	-0.55	0.24	0.04	0.46	0.07	0.08	0.26	0.23	0.43	0.77	0.01	1.04	1670
	(-0.75)	(0.76)	(0.14)	(1.05)	(0.51)	(0.86)							
Bottom 50%	-0.50 *	0.26	0.12	0.42	0.05	0.06	0.19	0.14	0.93	0.50	0.07	1.19	8352
	(-1.73)	(1.03)	(0.46)	(1.04)	(0.68)	(1.56)							
Top 50%	-0.14	-0.11	0.33	0.34	-0.05	0.02	1.41	1.32	0.05	0.00	1.64	1.48	8347
	(-0.53)	(-0.45)	(1.11)	(1.26)	(-0.78)	(0.55)							
Top 10%	0.64	0.10	0.88 ***	0.60 **	0.17	-0.16 *	3.60 *	1.35	0.08	0.35	4.41 **	1.44	1670
	(0.85)	(0.37)	(2.80)	(1.96)	(1.18)	(-1.73)							

This table presents the coefficients obtained by regressing the cumulative abnormal returns following forecast revisions on the magnitude of the revision, firm size, and dummy variables indicating analysts' status. Revisions are dated within the firm's current fiscal year over the 1993-1999 period. CAR_{jt} is the cumulative abnormal return to security i during the release period (days 0 and +1). $FSUR_{ijt}$ is the forecast surprise following analyst i's revision at date t. $LNSIZE_{jt}$ is the natural logarithm of the market value (in USD) of common stock at fiscal year end. $LOCLEAD_{ij}$ is a dummy variable that takes a value of 1 if analyst i is a local leader and 0 otherwise. $FORLEAD_{ij}$ is a dummy variable that takes a value of 1 if analyst i is a foreign leader and 0 otherwise. $EXPATLEAD_{ij}$ is a dummy variable that takes a value of 1 if analyst i is an expatriate leader and 0 otherwise. FOL_{ij} is a dummy variable that takes a value of 1 if analyst i is a follower and 0 otherwise. All coefficients are multiplied by 100. T-statistics are based on White (1980). For each regression the adjusted R^2 are less than 0.01.

***, **, * denote significance at the 1%, 5%, and 10% levels, respectively.

APPENDIX

Leader-to-Follower Ratio

The Leader-to-Follower Ratio (LFR) for a particular analyst a who provides forecasts for firm j is expressed a follows:

$$LFR_a^j = \frac{T_{0,a}^j}{T_{1,a}^j}, \tag{6}$$

where T_0 and T_1 are respectively the cumulative lead- and follow time for the K forecasts made by analyst a on firm j during a particular fiscal year. They are defined as follows:

$$T_{0,a}^j = \sum_{k=1}^{K} \sum_{h=1}^{H} t_{jhk}^0 \tag{7}$$

$$T_{1,a}^j = \sum_{k=1}^{K} \sum_{h=1}^{H} t_{jhk}^1 \tag{8}$$

t_{jmk}^0 (t_{jmk}^1) denotes the number of days by which forecast h precedes (follows) the k-th forecast may by analyst a for firm j. H is the number of forecasts made by other analysts that precede and follow the release of the k-th forecast of analyst a. The above figure provides an illustration of the idea underlying the LFR ratio. The forecast issued by analyst a for firm j at date t is denoted as $F_{a,t}^j$.

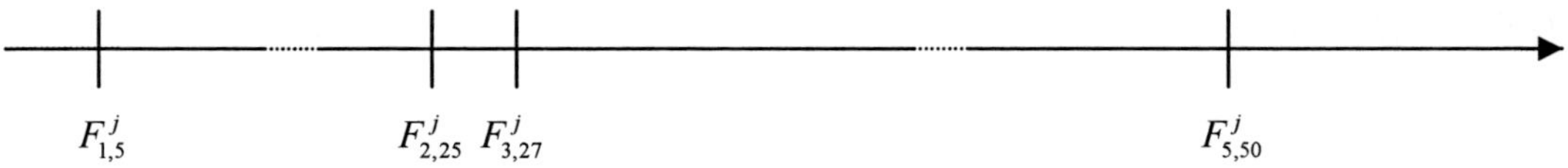

From this example, we see that analyst 2 issues a forecast on day 25. The preceding forecast was issued 20 days before on day 5. The following forecast is released soon afterward, on day 27. Taking into account only these one preceding and one following forecasts, analyst 2's LFR ratio is $\frac{20}{2} = 10$. Analyst 2 would therefore classified as a leader. To the same extent, analyst 3 is a follower analyst. He issues a forecast right after analysts 2 and no one free-rides on its forecast since the next to issue a forecast is analyst 4, only 23 days later. Its LFR would then be $\frac{1}{23} \cong 0.04$.

Acknowledgements

The authors thanks Michel Dubois, Christophe Pérignon, René Stulz, Ernst-Ludvig Von Thadden, and participants at FAME doctoral workshop, 5th Conference of the Swiss Society for Financial Market Research, 2002 FMA European meeting, 2002 EFMA meeting, and 2002 FMA US meeting for their helpful comments.

The authors acknowledge the contribution of Thomson Financial for providing earnings per share forecast data, available through the Institutional Brokers Estimate System. This data has been provided as part of a broad academic program to encourage earnings expectations research.

The authors aknowledge the financial support of the Swiss National Science Fondation (grant nr. 1214-065220).

References

Brennan, M.J. and H.H. Cao, 1997, International portfolio investment flows, *Journal of Finance* 52, 1851-1880.

Brown, L.D., 1997, Analyst forecasting errors: Additional evidence, *Financial Analysts Journal,* November/December, 81-88.

Chang, C., 2002, *Information footholds: Expatriate analysts in an emerging market,* Working Paper, Haas School of Business, U.C. Berkeley.

Choe, H., Kho, B.C. and R.M. Stulz, 2000, *Do domestic investors have more valuable information about individual stocks than foreign investors?,* Working paper, Seoul National University and Ohio State University.

Cooper, R.A., Day, T.E. and C.M. Lewis, 2001, Following the leader: A study of individual analysts' earnings forecasts, *Journal of Financial Economics* 61, 383-416.

Coval, J.D. and T.J. Moskowitz, 2001, The geography of investment: Informed trading and asset prices, *Journal of Political Economy* 109, 811-841.

Grinblatt, M. and M. Keloharju, 2000, The investment behaviour and performance of various investor types: A study of Finland's unique data set, *Journal of Financial Economics* 55, 43-67.

Harvey, C.R., 1995, Predictable risk and returns in emerging markets, *Review of Financial Studies* 8, 773-816.

Hope, O., 2003, *Accounting policy disclosures and analysts' forecasts,* Contemporary Accounting Research, Forthcoming.

Kang, S., O'Brien, J. and K. Sivaramakrishnan, 1994, Analysts' interim earnings forecasts: Evidence on the forecasting process, *Journal of Accounting Research* 32, 103-112.

Kang, J. and R.M. Stulz, 1997, Why is there a home bias? An analysis of foreign portfolio equity ownership in Japan, *Journal of Financial Economics* 46, 2-28.

Kini, O., Shehzad, M., Rebello, M. and A. Venkateswaran, 2003, *On the determinants of international analyst research coverage,* Working Paper, Robinson College of Business, Georgia State University.

Lang, M.H., Lins, K.V. and D. Miller, 2003, ADRs, analysts, and accuracy: Does cross listing in the U.S. improve a firm's information environment and increase market value, *Journal of Accounting Research,* Forthcoming.

Lin, H. and M.F. McNichols, 1998, Underwriting relationships, analysts' earnings forecasts and investment recommendations, *Journal of Accounting and Economics* 25, 101-127.

Malloy, C.J., 2003, The geography of equity analysis, Journal of Finance, Forthcoming.

Michealy, R. and K.L. Womack, 1999, Conflict of interest and the credibility of underwriter analyst recommendations, *Review of Financial Studies* 12, 653-686.

Orpurt, S.F., 2003, *Local asymmetric information advantages: International evidence from analysts' European firm earnings forecasts,* Working Paper, Graduate School of Business, University of Chicago.

Seasholes, M., 2000, *Smart foreign traders in emerging markets,* Working paper, Harvard Business School, Cambridge, M.A.

Stickel, S., 1992, Reputation and performance among security analysts, Journal of Finance 47, 1811-1836.

Stickel, S., 1995, The anatomy of the performance of buy and sell recommendations, *Financial Analysts Journal,* September/October, 25-39.

White, H., 1980, A heteroscedasticity-consistent covariance matrix estimator and a direct test for heteroscedasticity, *Econometrica* 48, 817-838.

In: Latin American Issues and Challenges
Editors: L. Naciamento and G. Sousa

ISBN 978-1-60692-349-8

Chapter 8

INCOME MOBILITY IN LATIN AMERICA: A PSEUDO-PANEL APPROACH*

José Cuesta, Hugo Ñopo and Georgina Pizzolitto*
Inter-American Development Bank, World Bank

ABSTRACT

This paper presents a comparative overview of income mobility patterns in Latin America. We construct a pseudo-panel for 14 Latin American countries between 1992 and 2003, unprecedented in the Region for its length and breadth. Estimates of time-dependence unconditional income mobility show that this is rather limited, as previously found in the scarce existing literature. However, after introducing personal, socioeconomic, demographic and geographical controls, conditional income mobility rises substantively for the Region. Also, unconditional and conditional income mobility show large variations across countries.

Keywords: Income Mobility, Poverty, Pseudo-Panels, Latin America

1. INTRODUCTION

Latin America is the most unequal region in the world. The discussion behind this salient feature has agreed on some of its causes: pervasive levels of macro-economic vulnerability,

* A version of this chapter was also published in World Poverty Issues, edited by Marilyn M. Watkins published by Nova Science Publishers, Inc. It was submitted for appropriate modifications in an effort to encourage wider dissemination of research.

* Cuesta and Ñopo: Inter-American Development Bank; Pizzolitto: World Bank. The results and conclusions expressed in this research document are those of the authors and do not compromise the views of neither Bank nor their Boards of Directors.

inequality in political voice and problems of social exclusion that are rooted in history (Vos et al. (2006), World Bank (2003) and IADB (1998) among others). The role of mobility on the analysis of inequality has been emphasized only recently, however (see Fields (2005), Galiani (2006) for recent reviews). The static measures of inequality are not enough to picture the well being of individuals in a society, and so they need to be complemented by the dynamics of mobility. For example, societies with prevailing exclusion (that is, individuals or groups neglected of access to services, consumption goods and assets) should expectedly have low upward mobility. Instead, societies that have actively combated exclusion should reflect high upward mobility (as reported for Chile by Scott 2000). In societies vulnerable to macro-economic shocks and ineffective social protection mechanisms, individuals may face high levels of downward income mobility (as reported for Argentina by Corbacho et al 2003).

This study is a contribution to the limited literature on income mobility in Latin America.[1] The lack of analysis has been the result of data requirements that the Region has been unable to provide fully yet, that is, panel data. By constructing, alternatively, a pseudo-panel for 14 countries between 1992 and 2003, this regional study applies the new methodological developments on the analysis of mobility in an unprecedented number of countries and years. There are several reasons for choosing a regional focus, but the most important one, from a policy-making stance, is that it allows for country-specific effects to be compared with sub-regional and region-wide effects. Of course, the analysis of regional mobility has shortcomings on its own, such as the need to exclude countries and periods from the analysis due to data limitations –as explained below. After this introduction, Section 2 defines mobility along the lines of the categorization in Fields (2005) and discusses the methodology used to estimate *unconditional* income mobility and *conditional* mobility (after controlling for personal, socioeconomic demographic and geographical features). Section 3 describes the construction of the pseudo-panel used in this study and explores mobility trends for the Region. Section 4 discusses the main results of the analysis: one, unconditional mobility is very low but rises significantly when controls are introduced; two, country-specific income mobility varies largely. Section 5 provides concluding remarks.

2. The Estimation of Mobility

The measurement of income mobility started with Lillard and Willis (1978). It basically involves the establishment of a relationship between past and present income:

$$y_{i,t} = \beta y_{i,t-1} + \mu_{i,t} \qquad (1)$$

Where $y_{i,t}$ is the total labor income for household i at time t, μ_{it} is a disturbance term and the parameter β, the coefficient of the slope in a regression of the income over its lagged value, is the measure of mobility. Fields (2005) refers to it as *time-dependence* mobility and it

[1] However, this literature is recently growing with the use of several methods to analyze mobility from transition matrices to econometric techniques or by estimating measures of permanent incomes. These techniques may refer to panel data, pseudo-panel or longitudinal data. The unit of observation can also vary, from individuals to workers, districts within a city or cities and regions in a country. For a detailed description see Fields et al (2006).

will be the focus of our paper. A value of β equal to 1 represents a situation with no income convergence; a value of β below 1 corresponds to a situation in which there is convergence, while zero represents an extreme case in which mobility would be total (as there would be no relationship between past and present incomes). Although there are no ex-ante restrictions about the range of values that β should take, they are regularly within the [0,1] interval. Additionally, the mobility estimator obtained from (1) is called *unconditional* in the sense that it does not take into account the presence of covariates (other than past income) that may explain present income. When the estimation is performed with additional controls, we have the time-dependence conditional estimation of mobility:

$$y_{i,t} = \beta y_{i,t-1} + \delta X_{i,t} + \mu_{i,t} \qquad (2)$$

Provided that an analysis of mobility of this sort implies to follow individuals (or households) over time, the quintessential data tool has been panel data. Unfortunately the development of this kind of tool has been only recent in Latin America and the few panels of data available as of today cover only short periods.[2] This has constituted an important barrier to the analysis of mobility in the Region. The development of pseudo-panel techniques that was initiated by Deaton (1985) has been an interesting alternative to overcome this data limitation. A pseudo-panel is formed creating synthetic observations obtained from averaging real observations with similar characteristics (regularly, birth year) in a sequence of repeated cross sectional data sets. In this way, the synthetic units of observations can be thought as being "followed" over time. The model then requires an appropriate modification:

$$\overline{y}_{c(t),t} = \beta_c \overline{y}_{c(t-1),t-1} + \delta_c \overline{X}_{c(t),t} + \mu_{c(t),t} \qquad (3)$$

Where the individual index, i, has been replaced by a cohort index, $c_{(t)}$, that is time-dependent. Analogously to Equation (1), the slope β_c is the parameter of interest. The literature has then focused on exploring the conditions under which such parameter can be consistently estimated in a context of repeated cross-section (instead of real panel data). The works of Browning et al. (1985), Moffit (1993), Collado (1997), Mckenzie (2004), Verbeek and Vella (2005) and Antman and Mckenzie (2005), among others, have provided set of conditions that the interested reader can explore.

Not surprisingly, there are pros and cons about the use of pseudo-panels for the analysis of mobility. Among arguments in favor of it we can cite at least three. The first is that they suffer less from problems related to sample attrition (because the samples are renewed at every period). Other is that, being constructed averaging groups of individual observations, they also suffer less from problems related to measurement error (at least the individual-level one). A third argument in favor, more practical, is that because of the wide availability of cross-sectional data it is possible to construct pseudo-panels that are appropriately

[2] This is the case of a two-period Chilean panel available in the CASEN survey of 1996-1998 or a two-period panel in El Salvador, for rural areas. A panel can also be constructed for Mexico, using the Encuesta Nacional de Empleo Urbano (ENEU), that have a rotating panel, with household followed for five consecutive quarters. Also in Argentina (1988 to date), Brazil (1980 to date), Peru (1991-1997), and Venezuela (1994-1999) have household survey with the same design. See Fields et al (2006) for more details.

representative covering long periods back in time, substantially more than what can be covered by real panels. The main argument against its use has to do with the fact that the decision about the clustering of observations in cohorts depends on a trade off (number of cohorts vs. number of observations in each cohort) for which the literature has not been conclusive yet. The larger the number of cohorts, the smaller is the number of individuals per cohort. One the one hand, one would like to have a large number of cohort observations such that the regressions performed with the resulting pseudo panels suffer less from small sample problems. However, on the other hand, if the number of observations per cohort were not large enough, the average characteristics per cohort would fail to be good estimates for the population cohort means (McKenzie 2004). In addition, Antman and McKenzie (2005) note two caveats from the use of pseudo-panels. They may introduce biases if the average cohort household fails to account for changing trends in household dissolution and creation (such as migration, for instance). Also, intra-cohort mobility is utterly ignored.

The pseudo-panel approach has been recently undertaken in the region to estimate mobility as defined above, at least by Navarro (2006) for Argentina, Antman and Mckenzie (2005) for Mexico and by Calónico (2006) for a set of 8 countries (Argentina, Brazil, Chile, Colombia, Costa Rica, Mexico, Uruguay and Venezuela). The latter found low patterns of mobility for all these countries during the 1992-2002 period. When trying to compare the results from both papers for Argentina we still found some differences. First, they use different time spans. Navarro computed mobility for the period (1985-2004), while Calónico did it for (1992-2003). Second, the studies differ in the concept of income that is used. While Calónico uses monthly labor incomes, Navarro based her analysis in hourly wages received by individual in their main occupation. Third, Navarro narrows her estimations to the conglomerate of Gran Buenos Aires in Argentina in order to construct a much larger pseudo panel. All in all, Navarro (2006) presents a higher degree of income mobility than Calónico (2006), a result supported by Albornoz and Menendez (2004) and Fields and Sanchez-Puerta (2005) using panel data for Argentina. Likewise, Antman and McKenzie (2005) report for specific age-education cohorts in Mexico between 1987 and 2001 little mobility between the earnings of rich and poor households but rapid convergence in the average household's earnings, suggesting higher levels of conditional mobility.

Our study complements the previous three both in scale and scope as it explores 14 countries during the period 1992 to 2003. On top of obtaining the cohort-mobility estimators - (both unconditional and conditional β and β_c in Equations (2) and (3), respectively), we also explore the role of the initial level of income on the change magnitude observed in the incomes of the pseudo-individuals as well as other controls. This new estimator will tell the impact that the changes, rather levels, of initial income has on the variation of that income to be expected in the next period.

$$\Delta\overline{y}_{c(t),t} = \beta_c \overline{y}_{c(t-1),t-1} + \delta_c \Delta\overline{X}_{c(t),t} + \mu_{c(t),t} \tag{4}$$

3. DATA

The raw data for this study comes from national household surveys of 14 Latin American countries in the region. These surveys have been harmonized to ensure a comparable definition of household incomes across countries. Countries included in the pseudo-panel share the same sources of labor incomes: labor –approximately 75% of the Region's average household incomes– and non-labor incomes –accounting for the remaining 25%. Countries that fail to report non-labor incomes in their household surveys were excluded of the pseudo-panel. That was the case of Dominican Republic, Guatemala, Nicaragua and Ecuador. Due to problems in the income variables, we also excluded from the analysis data from Brazil and Mexico for the year 1992.[3] All incomes were deflated using the Consumer Price Index of each country and year. We also adjusted the incomes using the Purchasing Power Parity – reported in the World Development Indicators – to make them comparable across countries.

We construct the pseudo-panel with data from these 14 countries using surveys between 1992 and 2003 and focusing on household heads aged 21 to 65. Birth cohorts include household heads born in seven-year spans, starting with those born between 1927 and 1933 and ending with those born between 1976 and 1982. Cohorts are constructed based on year of birth, country of residence and gender. Our pseudo-panel averages observations pertaining to the same cohort that appear in subsequent household surveys (each observation is appropriately weighted by the sample expansion factors). As a result, the constructed pseudo-panel follows eight birth cohorts over six periods. This comprises a total of 139,132 individual observations collapsed into 1,024 synthetic observations representing household heads. That number of observations is the result of collapsing the dataset by country (14 countries), gender (1 for men and 0 for women) and the eight birth cohorts (from 1927-33 to 1976-82), for the six periods of analysis. That would imply a total of 14x2x8x6=1,344 synthetic observations. However, some countries had missing household surveys for some years (especially the earlier ones subject to analysis) and some others were not usable due to the lack of a possibility to harmonize variables, as mentioned in the previous paragraph. As a result the number of synthetic observations was reduced to 1,024. Table 1 below reports cohorts' sizes (and annex 1 reports the information sources used to construct the cohorts in each country).

Table 1. Cohorts' sizes

Year	Period						Total
Birth Cohort	T1	T2	T3	T4	T5	T6	1993-2002
	1992-3	1994-5	1996-7	1998-9	2000-1	2002-3	
1927-33	2,055	1,284	851	303	...	...	4,493
1934-40	2,554	2,513	2,296	2,339	1,639	1,468	12,809
1941-47	3,084	3,098	2,845	2,879	2,768	3,121	17,795
1948-54	4,030	4,035	3,727	3,867	3,701	4,190	23,550
1955-61	4,516	4,585	4,171	4,519	4,570	5,166	27,527
1962-68	3,901	4,281	3,949	4,434	4,856	5,565	26,986
1969-75	9,34	2,319	2,411	3,182	3,968	4,858	17,672
1976-82	...	...	1,837	1,544	2,144	2,775	8,300
Total	21,074	22,115	22,087	23,067	23,646	27,143	139,132

Source: Own calculations based on IDB Research Department Harmonized Household Surveys.

[3] We observed that even after adjusting for consumer price index, incomes presented dramatic fluctuations. The high inflation rates (and currency changes in Brazil) explain these inconsistencies in the evolution of incomes variables.

Table 2. Data Descriptive Statistics

Variable	Number of observations (in pseudo panel)	Mean	Standard Deviation
Log Per Capita Household Incomes	1,024	5.36	0.68
% Female-headed households	1,024	0.50	0.50
Age	1,024	43.22	13.84
Years of Education	1,010	7.15	2.26
No Education	1,024	0.10	0.11
Primary incomplete	1,024	0.23	0.13
Primary complete	1,024	0.21	0.09
Secondary incomplete	1,024	0.19	0.10
Secondary complete	1,024	0.13	0.07
Tertiary complete	1,024	0.07	0.07
Tertiary incomplete	1,024	0.07	0.05
Number of Children aged 0 to 16 years	1,024	1.84	0.69
Number of other relatives living in the household	1,024	0.60	0.40
Dwelling Index	864	…	…
Southern Cone	1,024	0.38	0.49
Andean Region	1,024	0.38	0.46
Mexico and Central America	1,024	0.33	0.47

Source: Own calculations based on IDB Research Department Harmonized Household Surveys.

This pseudo-panel exceeds both the depth and breath other pseudo-panels for the Latin American region. Also, this pseudo-panel strikes a balance between a relevant number of cohorts and a meaningful size of the cohort. An insufficiently large number of cohorts cause pseudo-panel estimations to suffer from small sample problems. An insufficiently large cohort size causes its averages not to be good estimates for the population cohort characteristics.

Table 2 provides the basic descriptive statistics of the pseudo-panel: personal, socioeconomic, demographic and geographical characteristics of synthetic household heads of the constructed cohorts. The average household head in the pseudo-panel earns about US$ 456 dollars per month with a standard deviation of US$ 419 in PPP-adjusted real terms. The average household head is 43 years old and has seven years of education. Regarding attainment, 10% of the household heads have no education; 44% have primary education – either incomplete or complete–, while 33% have started or completed secondary education. The remaining 14% have college education. The average household has two children. We also construct an index of the dwelling characteristics to reflect the assets of the household. The index varies from zero to two and reflects the quality and availability of services in the dwelling.[4] The mean of the dwelling index is 1.27. Table 2 also reports the distribution of observations by sub-regions.[5]

Figure 1 below depicts regional and sub-regional trends of per capita monthly household incomes for selected birth cohorts (results do not change for the rest of cohorts). These trends confirm previous evidence based on individual labor incomes pointing to limited mobility in the region (see Calónico 2006). Even when trends differ among sub-regions, cohorts of young adults, prime-age and retirees follow similar patterns within each sub-region.[6]

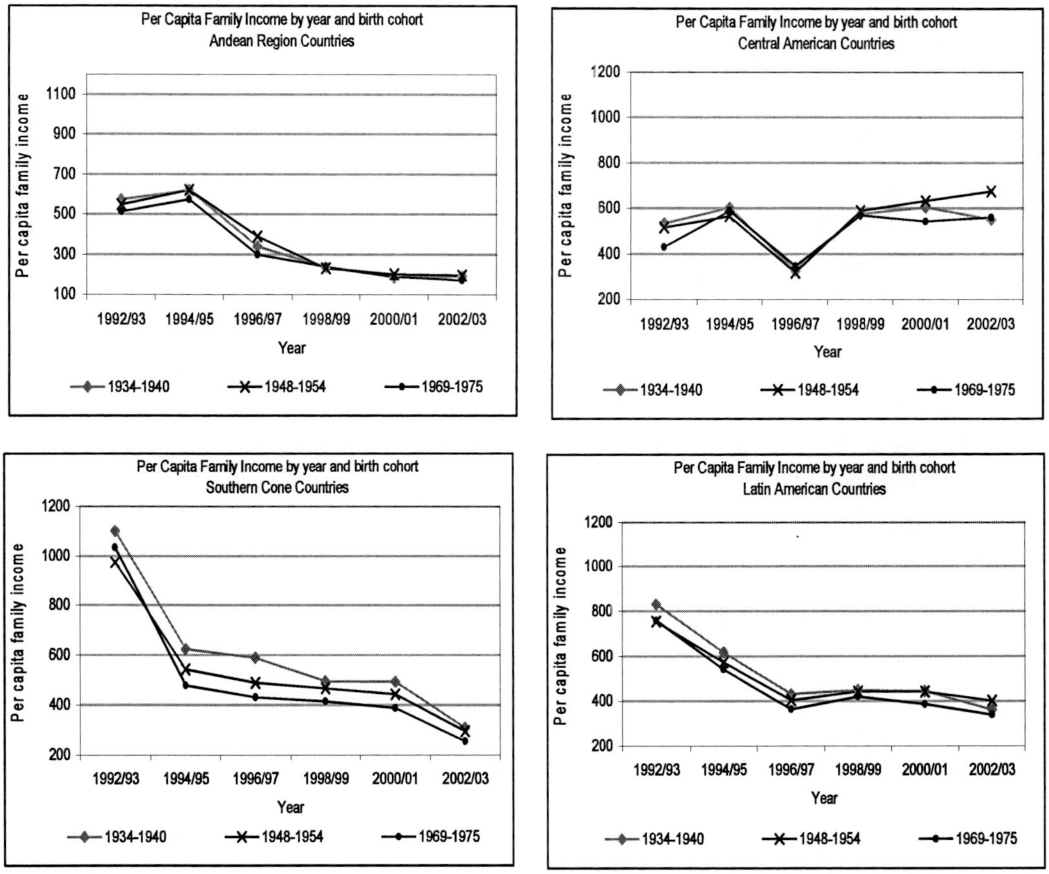

Source: Own calculations based on IDB Research Department Harmonized Household Surveys.

Figure 1. Income Trends by Sub-Region.

---

[4] The index takes into account the quality of the materials used for the walls, the number of rooms, if the household has a restroom with a toilet connected to a sewerage system or to a septic tank, the access to a source of safe water, and the possession of a phone, refrigerator and stove. The index is constructed taking the average of the selected dwelling characteristics.

[5] Southern Cone includes: Argentina, Brazil, Chile, Uruguay and Paraguay. Andean Region includes: Bolivia, Colombia, Perú and Venezuela. Central América includes: Costa Rica, El Salvador, Honduras, México and Panamá.

[6] Interestingly, these trends differ from nominal per capita household incomes and even PPP-adjusted national per capita GDP. It is worth noting that the former refers to the nominal purchasing power of each national currency in its respective country, while the latter to the international purchasing power of local currency based on estimated incomes from national accounts. The PPP-adjusted real trends that we report refer to the real purchasing power of local currencies in the international economy or, more specifically, how, for instance, the purchasing power of a Chilean peso or a Venezuelan Bolivar would fare in the US over time.

Table 3. Poverty Mobility

Period	Mobility around the US$1/day threshold (% of synthetic households)		Mobility around the US$2/day threshold (% of synthetic households)	
t+1 t	Poor	Non Poor	Poor	Non Poor
Poor	11.72%	4.86%	36.74%	8.09%
Non Poor	4.61%	78.8%	7.60%	47.57%
	Incidence with respect to US$1/day threshold (distribution of synthetic households in each category)		Incidence with respect to US$2/day threshold (distribution of synthetic household in each category)	
N	178	846	536	488
%	17.38%	82.62%	52.34%	47.66%

Source: Own calculations based on IDB Research Department Harmonized Household Surveys.

When we analyze mobility with respect to poverty lines (using the international thresholds of US$1/day and US$2/day/person for extreme and total poverty, respectively), we also conclude that mobility is limited. Before discussing these results, it is worth noting that the US$1 /day and US$2/day per person are widely used international poverty lines accepted to estimate global poverty. World Bank (1990) introduced its use. The construction of the US$1/day line is based on an average of six country specific extreme poverty lines (Bangladesh, Indonesia, Kenya, Morocco, Nepal and Tanzania) that are subsequently expressed in national 1985 PPP$ terms –and updated in 2000 to US$1.08 to reflect 1993 PPP$. Criticisms1 accuse this methodology of either consistently underestimating the number of the poor (Reddy and Pogge, 2003) or of having grossly overestimated them (Sala-i-Martin 2006). Others consider that these income or consumption-based lines overlook other dimensions of poverty (UNDP 2006), and recommend the inclusion of early death, adult illiteracy, child's malnutrition and population access to safe water in the calculation of poverty (which has, in effect, resulted in the construction of the Human Poverty Index). Notwithstanding the relevance of such criticisms, they are not the focus of the paper. We follow the vast tradition of considering the US$2/day international poverty line as an appropriate threshold for international comparisons across the typically middle-income economies in Latin America (and further compare them with estimates accruing from a US$1/day line)

Table 3 below reports that about 15% of the households (represented by their household heads) crossed the US$2/day/person threshold and less than 10% did so with respect to the US$ 1/day/person line. Interestingly, the numbers of households slipping into and moving out these thresholds are almost identical: 51% of these mobile households moved out of the threshold line; the remaining 49% slipped into poverty.

Further analysis reveals that households moving in and out of extreme poverty (threshold of US$1/day/person) share more characteristics than those moving around the US$2/day/person poverty line. Table 4 shows that households pertaining to the two cohorts defined between 1955 and 1968 represent two thirds of the 'mobile' households around the extreme poverty line. In contrast, those cohorts only explain 37% and 25% of the mobility out and into the US$2/day/person line, respectively. Households whose heads are aged 18 to 34 represent some 57% of those slipping into poverty but only 28% of those able to escape from poverty.

Table 5 confirms the existence of disparities between mobility around the US$1 and US$2/day/person lines. There are not statistically significant differences between households moving in and out of the US$1/day/person line in terms of gender and education of the household head, household size and dwelling characteristics. Only age plays a role, with poor households able to move out of extreme poverty being older, on average, than other 'mobile' households. In contrast, younger and more educated household heads in smaller households are more likely to slip into poverty than are such households to move out of poverty. This may simply reflect the different initial conditions of non-poor households before slipping into poverty rather than conditions that cause a household's slipping into poverty at any given time.

Table 4. Cohorts Mobility

Birth Cohort	Poor to Non Poor	Non Poor to Poor
US$1/day/person		
1927-1933	0.00	0.03
1934-1940	4.08	2.49
1941-1947	4.35	2.09
1948-1954	3.42	7.02
1955-1961	18.97	31.01
1962-1968	46.09	34.96
1969-1975	15.90	5.53
1976-1980	7.20	16.88
Total	100.0	100.0
US$2/day/ person		
1927-1933	1.80	0.55
1934-1940	7.43	5.56
1941-1947	10.01	2.74
1948-1954	15.19	9.92
1955-1961	23.91	9.98
1962-1968	13.50	14.31
1969-1975	26.05	36.61
1976-1980	2.10	20.33
Total	100.0	100.0

Source: Own calculations based on IDB Research Department Harmonized Household Surveys.

Table 5. Differences in Characteristics among Households

Characteristics	Poor to Non Poor	Non Poor to Poor	Remains Poor	Never Poor
US$1/day/ person				
Age	44.86	38.84	41.25	38.91
		[6.02]**	[3.61]	[5.95]***
Gender	0.23	0.25	0.41	0.48
		[-0.03]	[-0.18]**	[-0.25]***
Years of education	6.79	7.29	7.52	7.20
		[-0.50]	[-0.73]**	[-0.40]
Number of Children	2.01	2.10	2.42	1.83
		[-0.09]	[-0.40]***	[0.18]
Number of Other relatives	0.77	0.67	0.73	0.38
		[0.10]	[0.05]	[0.39]***
Dwelling Characteristics	1.18	1.13	1.22	1.35
		[0.05]	[-0.04]	[-0.17]***
US$2/day/ person				
Age	42.79	34.11	39.13	39.55
		[8.68]***	[3.66]**	[3.24]*
Gender	0.50	0.41	0.36	0.52
		[0.09]	[0.14]**	[-0.02]
Years of education	7.18	8.25	7.25	7.01
		[-1.08]***	[-0.07]	[0.17]
Number of Children	1.86	1.85	2.11	1.77
		[0.01]	[-0.24]***	[0.09]
Number of Other relatives	0.57	0.44	0.58	0.32
		[0.13]**	[0.00]	[0.25]***
Dwelling Characteristics	1.31	1.22	1.20	1.42
		[0.09]*	[0.11]***	[-0.11]***

Source: Own calculations based on IDB Research Department Harmonized Household Surveys.
*** statistical significance at 1%; (**) at 5%; (*) at 10%. T-statistics are presented in brackets.

4. Estimation Results

In this section we provide estimates of income mobility. Table 6 below reports estimates of time-dependence income mobility for Latin America as a region. Mobility is first reported as the elasticity of current incomes with respect to past incomes. As indicated in the Section 2, the inclusion of personal, socioeconomic, demographic and geographical controls determines several specifications of conditional mobility. In addition to specification I, the unconditional mobility model, specifications II to IX are constructed by introducing progressively such controls. The lower part of Table 6 reports the controls included in each specification. The sequential introduction of such controls allows us to better understand the marginal impact of socioeconomic and demographic factors versus geographical location. A second time-dependence mobility indicator is also reported as the elasticity of future income changes with respect to initial incomes. This indicator differs from the former most traditional measure of time-dependence mobility in that captures how the magnitude of changes rather than levels of incomes affect the expected income mobility of that pseudo-individual.

Results confirm a very low degree of income mobility for Latin America as a region, as previously found in literature. The estimate of the unconditional mobility indicator, β , is as high as 0.996 (see specification I in the upper panel in Table 6). This changes substantially after controls are introduced. Specifications II to IV gradually introduce personal and socioeconomic controls such as age, gender, education, number of children and housing conditions (that is, the dwelling index acting as a proxy for satisfaction of basic needs). The estimated mobility indicator falls from 0.99 to 0.70. Furthermore, specifications V to VIII introduce regional controls. A meager additional 0.5% of inter-temporal income variation is captured when these regional controls are added to previous specifications. When country dummies are introduced instead of regional dummies (specification IX), they capture an additional 10% of the inter-temporal income variation. This evidence suggests that a misleading attribution of demographic and socioeconomic impacts to past incomes may well generate a false sense of limited time-dependence income mobility.

Table 6. Estimates of Unconditional and Conditional Time-Dependence Income Mobility in Latin America[7]

	I	II	III	IV	V	VI	VII	VIII	IX
Estimated Income Mobility - Equation (3) $\overline{y}_{c(t),t} = \beta_c \overline{y}_{c(t-1),t-1} + \delta_c \overline{X}_{c(t),t} + \mu_{c(t),t}$									
B	0.966	0.744	0.707	0.704	0.949	0.723	0.69	0.693	0.588
	(645.45)**	(64.85)**	(55.59)**	(50.24)**	(199.03)**	(62.07)**	(55.40)**	(50.50)**	(46.91)**
R^2	0.998	0.997	0.998	0.999	0.999	0.997	0.999	0.999	0.999
N. observations	800	800	800	672	800	800	800	672	672
Estimated Income Mobility - Equation (4) $\Delta \overline{y}_{c(t),t} = \beta_c \overline{y}_{c(t-1),t-1} + \delta_c \Delta \overline{X}_{c(t),t} + \mu_{c(t),t}$									
B	-0.034	-0.196	-0.184	-0.182	-0.051	-0.203	-0.196	-0.196	-0.202
	(22.41)**	(16.25)**	(15.75)**	(13.64)**	(10.65)**	(17.94)**	(18.16)**	(15.85)**	(16.76)**
R^2	0.390	0.520	0.550	0.560	0.550	0.590	0.620	0.630	0.720
N. observations	800	800	800	672	800	800	800	672	672
Controlling By									
Age	No	Yes	Yes	Yes	No	Yes	Yes	Yes	Yes
Age^2	No	Yes	Yes	Yes	No	Yes	Yes	Yes	Yes
Gender	No	Yes	Yes	Yes	No	Yes	Yes	Yes	Yes
Years of Education	No	Yes	No	No	No	Yes	No	No	No
Number of Children	No	Yes	Yes	Yes	No	Yes	Yes	Yes	Yes
Number of Other relatives	No	Yes	Yes	Yes	No	Yes	Yes	Yes	Yes
Educational Dummies	No	No	Yes	Yes	No	No	Yes	Yes	Yes
Dwelling Characteristics	No	No	No	Yes	No	No	No	Yes	Yes
Regional Dummies	No	No	No	No	No	Yes	No	Yes	No
Country Dummies	No	No	No	No	Yes	No	Yes	No	Yes

Source: Own calculations based on IDB Research Department Harmonized Household Surveys.

7 For presentation reasons, complete estimates for all specifications in this table and Table 7 are not reported in this paper. They are available upon request to the authors.

Table 7. Country-specific Estimates of Unconditional and Conditional Time-Dependence Income Mobility in Latin America

Country	Estimated Income Mobility Equation (3) $\overline{y}_{c(t),t} = \beta_c \overline{y}_{c(t-1),t-1} + \delta_c \overline{X}_{c(t),t} + \mu_{c(t),t}$		Estimated Income Mobility Equation (4) $\Delta\overline{y}_{c(t),t} = \beta_c \overline{y}_{c(t-1),t-1} + \delta_c \overline{\Delta X}_{c(t),t} + \mu_{c(t),t}$		
	Specification I (*)	Specification IV(*)	Specification IV		N
	β	β_c	β_c	R2	
Argentina	0.975	0.74	0.035	0.37	70
	192.20**	2.70**	0.44		
Bolivia	0.973	0.37	-0.026	0.47	40
	125.66**	5.24**	0.35		
Brazil	0.982	0.85	-0.051	0.95	56
	840.59**	20.14**	3.87**		
Chile	0.995	0.68	-0.068	0.89	56
	333.34**	7.60**	2.70*		
Colombia	0.964	0.81	-0.136	0.96	70
	204.16**	20.66**	7.80**		
Costa Rica	0.973	0.53	-0.472	0.85	28
	238.98**	2.59*	2.31*		
Honduras	0.96	0.09	-0.118	0.9	44
	123.32**	1.71*	2.27*		
Mexico	0.945	0.42	-0.32	0.9	56
	133.95**	12.54**	7.44**		
Panama	0.999	---	---		
	281.24**	---	---		
Peru	0.945	0.15	-0.056	0.87	44
	133.95**	17.1*	1.45		
Paraguay	0.996	0.88	-0.069	0.95	42
	175.12**	10.00**	2.69*		
El Salvador	0.955	0.47	0.017	0.53	28
	257.19**	2.86*	0.17		
Uruguay	1.005	0.3	-0.465	0.87	70
	306.65**	8.68**	10.11**		
Venezuela	0.896	0.4	-0.342	0.98	54
	151.62**	16.27**	15.08**		

* R^2 for specification I in all countries revolves around 0.95 and for specification IV exceeds 0.99.
Source: Own calculations based on IDB Research Department Harmonized Household Surveys.

The impact of previous incomes on today's incomes is additionally explored by looking at how initial levels of income affect changes observed in the following period. See the middle panel in Table 6. This alternative set of specifications confirms that the level of previous incomes plays a significant role in explaining today's incomes. The higher is the starting level of income, the lower its variation should be expected in a subsequent period. Its magnitude, however, varies according to the selected specification. Unsurprisingly, those with higher incomes are more capable of sustaining them, either because they possess larger stocks of human capital or have better access to insurance against shocks. When controls are introduced (specifications II to IX), this result becomes stronger, turning sizeable variations even less likely.

If initial levels of income play a significant role in explaining mobility, a country-specific analysis of mobility should reveal the heterogeneity of existing income levels across the Region. Table 7 reports country-specific estimates of mobility for the specification IV, which includes all personal, socioeconomic and demographic controls.

The estimates of income mobility in Table 7 are expressed as elasticities, which allows for a meaningful comparison across countries with different starting income levels. Estimated elasticities vary widely across country, as predicted. High levels of time-dependence income immobility (β exceeding 0.8) are only found in Brazil, Colombia and Paraguay, while the rest of the Region shows much higher levels of mobility (lower β). Countries such as Chile or Argentina show a moderate immobility (β between 0.66 and 0.79) compared with other 'mobile' countries (β below 0.66). These results confirm that a higher mobility is found across countries when countries are considered separately than when countries are being pooled regionally (as it was the case with results for Argentina using Navarro (2006) and Calónico (2006). Also, our results are consistent with Contreras et al (2004)'s conclusion of restrained mobility in Chile. Even when this limited evidence does not allow for generalizations, it may be that region-pooled estimates average out different country-specific patterns of income mobility.

The above conclusion holds when country specific estimates of mobility are obtained using changes in income (equation 4) instead of levels of income (equation 3). The right hand side columns in Table 7 show that the level of past incomes may exert either a positive or negative impact in future incomes. Higher levels of past incomes are associated with larger increases in current incomes in Argentina, Chile and El Salvador, although it is only Chile (which managed to sustain growth during the last 20 years) where such an impact is statistically significant. In the remaining countries, higher levels of previous incomes are associated with lower variations of future incomes. Poorer countries exhibit larger time-dependence income mobility.

5. Conclusions

Difficulties in the construction of panel-data have prevented a comprehensive analysis of mobility in Latin America and elsewhere in the developing world. This paper sheds more light on the implications of mobility in the Region by constructing, alternatively, a pseudo-panel for 14 countries over 11 years and 8 birth cohorts. Our analysis focuses on the standard notion of income mobility and, in addition, explores a notion of mobility around poverty lines. We show that the Region as a whole is highly immobile in income terms. However, a sizeable part of this immobility results from failing to account from the effects that personal and socioeconomic controls have on mobility (over 30% of the unconditional time-dependence mobility). Country-specific differences are also substantive and tend to cancel out when grouped into traditional sub-regions (Andes, Southern Cone, Central America). Current levels of incomes not explained by past levels of incomes vary widely across countries, well exceeding in some cases 50% of estimated changes.

Household mobility around poverty lines was found symmetrical in size: as many as those households moving into poverty, moved out of poverty. The analysis of the characteristics of 'mobile' households shows interesting features, such that younger households being twice as likely to slip into poverty as to move out of it. Despite the limitations of the analysis (an econometric analysis of the effects of such controls on poverty mobility is also needed), we reject as simplistic and misleading the widely accepted notion of a dominating socioeconomic immobility throughout the Region. This is a first step towards uncovering the underlying dynamics of poverty mobility in a Region that for long has implemented one-size-fits-all economic reforms and poverty strategies.

ANNEX 1.

Table A.1. Household Surveys – and periods considered to construct the pseudo panels

Country	Survey	Period					
		T1	T2	T3	T4	T5	T6
		1992-1993	1994-1995	1996-1997	1998-1999	2000-2001	2002-2003
Argentina	Encuesta Permanente de Hogares (EPH)	x	x	x	x	x	x
Brasil	Pesquisa Nacional por Amostra de Domicilios (PNAD)		x	x	x	x	x
Bolivia	Encuesta de Hogares	x	x	x	x	x	x
Chile	Encuesta de Caracterización Socioeconómica Nacional (CASEN)	x	x	x	x	x	x
Colombia	Encuesta Continua de Hogares	x	x	x	x	x	
Costa Rica	Encuesta de Hogares de Propósitos Múltiples (EHPM)	x	x	x	x	x	x
Honduras	Encuesta Permanente de Hogares de Propósitos Múltiples			x	x	x	x
México	Encuesta Nacional de Ingreso y Gastos de los Hogares (ENIGH)		x	x	x	x	x
Panamá	Encuesta de Hogares		x	x	x	x	x
Paraguay	Encuesta Permanente de Hogares			x	x	x	x
Perú	Encuesta Nacional de			x	x	x	x

	Hogares sobre Medición de Niveles de Vida						
El Salvador	Encuesta de Hogares de Propósitos Múltiples (EHPM)				x	x	x
Uruguay	Encuesta Continua de Hogares	x	x	x	x	x	x
Venezuela	Encuesta de Hogares por Muestreo		x	x	x	x	x

Source: Own calculations based on IDB Research Department Harmonized Household Surveys.

REFERENCES

Albornoz, F. y Menéndez, M. (2004). *"Income dynamics in Argentina during the 1990s: 'Mobiles' did change over time".* World Bank, forthcoming.

Antman, F. and Mckenzie, D. (2005). *"Earnings Mobility and Measurement Error: A Pseudo-Panel Approach",* World Bank Policy Research Working Paper # 3745.

Bourguinon F. and Goh C. (2004). *"Estimating individual vulnerability to poverty with pseudo-panel data".* The World Bank, Washington DC.

Browning, M., Deaton, A. y Irish M. (1985). "A profitable approach to labor supply and commodity demand over the life-cycle". *Econometrica* 53, (3): 503-544.

Calónico S. (2006). *"Pseudo-Panel analysis of Earnings Dynamics and Mobility in Latin America".* Research Department, Inter-American Development Bank, Washington DC.

Collado, M.D. (1997). "Estimating dynamic models from time series of independent crosssections". *Journal of Econometrics* 82: 37–62.

Contreras, D., Cooper, R., Herman, J. and Neilson, C. (2004). *"Dinámica de la pobreza y movilidad social en Chile".*Universidad de Chile. Mimeo.

Corbacho, A., M. Garcia-Escribano, M. and G. Inchauste (2003) *"Argentina: Macroeconomic Crisis and Household Vulnerability",* IMF Working Paper.

Deaton, A. (1985). "Panel data from times series of cross-sections". *Journal of Econometrics* (30): 109–126.

Fields, G.F and Sánchez Puerta, M. (2005). "Earnings mobility in urban Argentina". *Background Paper Prepared for the World Bank.* World Bank, Washington DC.

Fields G., Duval R., Freije S. and Sánchez Puerta M. (2006). "Inter-generational income mobility in Latin America". Economia, forthcoming.

Galiani, Sebastián (2006). "Notes on Social Mobility." Mimeo. Universidad de San Andrés.

Inter-American Development Bank, IADB (1998).*Economic and Social Progress Report* 1998/9. IADB, Washington DC.

Lillard, L. y Willis, R. (1978). "Dynamics aspects of earnings mobility". *Econometrica 46* (5): 985-1012.

Mckenzie, D. (2004). "Asymptotic theory for heterogeneous dynamic pseudopanels". *Journal of Econometrics.* 120(2), 235-262.

Milanovic, B. (2006). "Global income inequality: What it is and Why it Matters?". World Bank Policy Research Working Paper 3865. World Bank, Washington DC.

Moffit, R. (1993). "Identification and estimation of dynamic models with a time series of repeated cross-sections". *Journal of Econometrics* 59: 99–124.

Navarro A. I. (2006). "Estimating income mobility in Argentina with pseudo-panel data". Department of Economics, Universidad de San Andres. Mimeo

Reddy, S. and Pogge T. (2003). "How not to count the poor". Available at www.socialanalysis.org

Sala-I-Martin, X. (2006)."The world distribution of incomes: falling poverty and convergence, period". *Quarterly Journal of Economics,* May 2006, 121 (2): 351-97.

Scott, C. (2000) "Mixed Fortunes: A Study of Poverty Mobility among Small Farm Household in Chile, 1968-86," *Journal of Development Studies*, 36, 155-180.

United Nations Development Programme, UNDP, 2006. *Human Development Report.* New York: Oxford University Press.

Verbeek, M. y Vella, F. (2002). *"Estimating dynamic models from repeated cross-sections". Mimeo,* K.U. Leuven Center for Economic Studies.

World Bank (2003) *Inequality in Latin America and the Caribbean. Breaking with History?* World Bank, Washington DC.

World Bank (1990). *World Development Report 1990.* World Bank, Washington DC.

In: Latin American Issues and Challenges
Editors: L. Naciamento and G. Sousa
ISBN 978-1-60692-349-8

Chapter 9

LATIN AMERICA: TERRORISM ISSUES[*]

Mark P. Sullivan

ABSTRACT

In the aftermath of the September 2001 terrorist attacks on New York and Washington D.C., U.S. attention to terrorism in Latin America intensified, with an increase in bilateral and regional cooperation. Latin American nations strongly condemned the attacks, and took action through the Organization of American States (OAS) to strengthen hemispheric cooperation. In June 2002, OAS members signed an Inter-American Convention Against Terrorism. President Bush submitted the convention to the Senate in November 2002; on October 7, 2005, the Senate agreed to the resolution of advice and consent on the convention. In its annual report on global terrorism, the State Department highlights threats in Colombia, Peru, and the tri-border area of Argentina, Brazil, and Paraguay. The State Department also has designated four terrorist groups (three in Colombia and one in Peru) as Foreign Terrorist Organizations, and Cuba has been listed as a state sponsor of terrorism since 1982. In the second session of the 1 09th Congress, issues of concern will likely include continued Latin American cooperation on terrorism and oversight related to the release of the State Department's annual report on global terrorism expected in April 2006.

TERRORISM IN LATIN AMERICA: U.S. CONCERNS

Over the years, the United States has been concerned about threats to Latin American and Caribbean nations from various terrorist or insurgent groups that have attempted to influence or overthrow elected governments. While Latin America has not been the focal point in the war on terrorism, countries in the region have struggled with domestic terrorism for decades

[*] This is an edited, reformatted and augmented version of a CRS Report RS21049 dated January 18, 2006.

and international terrorist groups have at times used the region as a battleground to advance their causes. The State Department's annual report on international terrorism, recently re-titled *Country Reports on Terrorism,* highlights U.S. concerns about terrorist threats around the world, including in Latin America. The 2004 report, issued in April 2005, notes that the international terrorist threat in the Western Hemisphere remained low in 2004, compared to other regions of the world, but also maintained that "terrorists may seek safe-haven, financing, recruiting, illegal travel documentation, or access to the United States from the area and pose serious threats." The report describes terrorist activities in the region in 2004, most notably in Colombia, Peru, and the tri-border area (TBA) of Argentina, Brazil, and Paraguay. The report also examines activity by Cuba, which has been designated by the State Department as a state-sponsor of terrorism since 1982.

In the aftermath of 9/11, U.S. attention focused on potential links in the region to the Al Qaeda terrorist network, but the State Department's 2002 report on terrorism maintained that "there was no confirmed credible information" of an Al Qaeda presence in Latin America. The 2003 State Department report on terrorism maintained that reports of an Al Qaeda presence in the TBA remained "uncorroborated by intelligence and law-enforcement officials," while the 2004 report asserted that there was no credible evidence of operational Islamic cells in the TBA countries. There were increased concerns in 2004 by some Central American officials about potential Al Qaeda threats in the region, although U.S. officials maintained that there was no evidence supporting such concerns.[1] The State Department's 2004 report maintains that there were "widespread, unfounded media reports alleging formal links between transnational criminal gangs and Islamic extremists" in Central America.

Colombia

Colombia remains of paramount concern to the United States because of the threat to democracy posed by three groups that have been designated by the Secretary of State as Foreign Terrorist Organizations (FTOs): two leftist guerrilla groups, the Revolutionary Armed Forces of Colombia (FARC) and the National Liberation Army (ELN), and a rightist paramilitary group, the United Self-Defense Forces of Colombia (AUC). According to the 2004 terrorism report, the three groups continued to conduct car bombings, political murders, and indiscriminate use of land mines, and also targeted critical infrastructure, public recreational areas, and modes of transportation. Colombia has the highest kidnapping rate in the world, with over 1,500 in 2004. Nevertheless, the Colombian government has made significant progress in regaining control of national territory, promoting desertion and reintegration of former illegal armed militants, and demobilizing the AUC. In 2004, acts of terrorism dropped by 42.5%, murders by 13.2%, massacres by 42.4%, and kidnappings by 42.4%. The FARC and AUC have been heavily involved in drug trafficking, which has been the key to their growth over past decade. In February 2003, a U.S. civilian contractor and a Colombian national were murdered by the FARC after their plane crashed. The FARC continues to hold hostage three U.S. contractors from that plane crash. All three Colombian FTOs reportedly exploit the Venezuelan side of the border with Colombia as a safe area to

[1] "U.S. Officials Dispute Al Qaeda Role in Hemisphere," *Homeland Security Monitor* (Intellibridge), September 30, 2004; Jerry Seper, "Al Qaeda Seeks Tie to Local Gangs." *Washington Times,* September 28, 2004.

transship arms and drugs, rest, secure logistical supplies, and commit kidnappings. The State Department report indicates that "it is unclear to what extent and at what level the Venezuelan government approves of or condones material support to Colombian terrorists." (For more on Colombia, see CRS Report RL32250, *Colombia: Issues for Congress.)*

Peru

Peru is another country of concern. The brutal Shining Path (Sendero Luminoso or SL) insurgency, which the Department of State has designated an FTO, was significantly weakened in the 1 990s with the capture of its leader Abimael Guzman. In 2001-2003, terrorist acts committed by the group increased from previous years, but in 2004 annual terrorist incidents dropped to 40 from 100 in 2003. According to the State Department terrorism report, SL has a few hundred armed members concentrated in the coca-growing valleys where they are reportedly increasing their involvement in the drug trade; the group also reportedly is trying to rebuild support in the universities where it had considerable influence in the 1 980s.

Tri-Border Area

In recent years, U.S. concerns have increased over activities of the radical Lebanon-based Islamic group Hizballah (Party of God) and the Sunni Muslim Palestinian group Hamas (Islamic Resistance Movement) in the tri-border area of Argentina, Brazil, and Paraguay, which has a large Muslim population. According to the 2003 terrorism report, the TBA "has long been characterized as a regional hub for Hizballah and Hamas fundraising activities, but it is also used for arms and drug trafficking, contraband smuggling, document and currency fraud, money laundering, and the manufacture and movement of pirated goods." The 2004 report asserts that was no credible evidence that operational Islamic terrorist cells exist in the TBA countries.

Allegations have linked Hizballah to two bombings in Argentina: the 1992 bombing of the Israeli Embassy in Buenos Aires that killed 30 people and the 1994 bombing of the Argentine-Israeli Mutual Association (AMIA) in Buenos Aires that killed 86 people. As noted in the 2004 terrorism report, all 22 Argentine defendants charged in the 1994 bombing were acquitted by a three-judge panel that faulted the investigation of the original judge and prosecutors. The acquittal prompted protests by Argentina's large Jewish community. (For additional information on Argentina, see CRS Report RS2 1113, *Argentina: Political Conditions and U.S. Relations.)*

Cuba

The Department of State includes Cuba among its list of six states sponsoring terrorism (the other five states are Iran, Libya, North Korea, Sudan, and Syria). Cuba was added to the list in 1982. The Communist government led by Fidel Castro had a history of supporting revolutionary movements and governments in Latin America and Africa, but in 1992, Castro said that his country's support for insurgents abroad was a thing of the past. Most analysts accept that Cuba's policy generally did change, largely because the breakup of the Soviet Union resulted in the loss of billions in subsidies.

The State Department's 2004 terrorism report maintains that Cuba continues to actively oppose the global war on terrorism. The report asserts that Cuba's "actions and public statements run contrary to the spirit of the UN conventions on terrorism that it has signed." (Cuba has ratified all 12 international conventions on terrorism.) The report also maintained that Cuba continued to provide limited support to FTOs as well as safe haven for terrorists. It asserted that Cuba provides safe haven to various Basque ETA members from Spain despite a November 2003 request from the Spanish government to deny them sanctuary. The report also maintained that Cuba provided safe haven and some degree of support to members of two Colombian insurgent groups, the FARC and ELN. (The State Department's 2002 and 2003 terrorism reports acknowledged, however, that Colombia acquiesced to this arrangement and that Colombia publicly said that it wanted Cuba's continued mediation with the ELN in Cuba.) The 2004 report also noted that more than 70 fugitives from U.S. justice had taken refuge in Cuba. Many of these are accused of committing violent actions in the United States, including Joanne Chesimard, who is wanted for the murder of a New Jersey State Trooper in 1973.

In general, those who support keeping Cuba on the terrorism list argue that there is ample evidence that Cuba supports terrorism. They point to the government's history of supporting terrorist acts and armed insurgencies in Latin America and Africa. They point to the government's continued hosting of members of foreign terrorist organizations and U.S. fugitives from justice. Critics of retaining Cuba on the terrorism list maintain that it is a holdover of the Cold War. They argue that domestic political considerations keep Cuba on the terrorism list and maintain that Cuba's presence on the list diverts U.S. attention from struggles against serious terrorist threats. (For further information, see CRS Report RL3 225 1, *Cuba and the State Sponsors of Terrorism List,* and CRS Report RL32730, *Cuba: Issues for the 109th Congress.)*

U.S. Policy

As in other parts of the world, the United States has assisted Latin American and Caribbean nations over the years in their struggle against terrorist or insurgent groups indigenous to the region. For example, in the 1 980s, the United States supported the government of El Salvador with significant economic and military assistance in its struggle against a leftist guerrilla insurgency. In recent years, the United States has employed various policy tools to combat terrorism in the Latin America and Caribbean region, including sanctions, anti-terrorism assistance and training, law enforcement cooperation, and multilateral cooperation through the OAS. Moreover, given the nexus between terrorism and drug trafficking, one can argue that assistance aimed at combating drug trafficking organizations in the region has also been a means of combating terrorism by cutting off a source of revenue for terrorist organizations. The same argument can be made regarding efforts to combat money laundering in the region.

Although terrorism was not the main focus of U.S. policy toward the region in recent years, attention increased in the aftermath of the 9/11 terrorist attacks on New York and Washington. Anti-terrorism assistance has increased along with bilateral and regional cooperation against terrorism. In 2002, Congress approved the Bush Administration's request to expand the scope of U.S. assistance to Colombia beyond a counternarcotics focus to also include counter-terrorism assistance to the government in its military efforts against drug-financed leftist guerrillas and rightist paramilitaries.

As noted above, the United States has imposed sanctions on three groups in Colombia (ELN, FARC, and AUC) and one group in Peru (SL) designated by the Department of State as Foreign Terrorist Organization (FTOs). Official designation of such groups as FTOs triggers a number of sanctions, including visa restrictions and the blocking of any funds of these groups in U.S. financial institutions. The designation also has the effect of increasing public awareness about these terrorist organizations and the concerns that the United States has about them.

Through the Department of State (Diplomatic Security Office, Office of Antiterrorism Assistance), the United States provides Anti-Terrorism Assistance (ATA) training and equipment to Latin American countries to help improve their capabilities in such areas as airport security management, hostage negotiations, bomb detection and deactivation, and countering terrorism financing. Such training was expanded to Argentina in the aftermath of the two bombings in 1992 and 1994. Assistance was also stepped up in 1997 to Argentina, Brazil, and Paraguay in light of increased U.S. concern over illicit activities in the tri-border area of those countries.

ATA funding is generally provided through the annual foreign operations appropriations measure. For FY2001, $4.7 million in ATA training was provided to Western Hemisphere countries. In FY2002, a total of $27.5 million was provided for the region, with $25 million for an anti-kidnapping program in Colombia (appropriated through an FY2002 supplemental appropriations measure, P.L. 107-206) and $2.5 million for the regular Western Hemisphere program. For FY2003, the Administration's $3.6 million in ATA assistance was provided for the region, with $3.3 million of that for Colombia. For FY2004, $5.3 million in ATA assistance was provided for the region. For FY2005, an estimated $1 1.1 million in ATA is being provided for the region, with $3.9 million for Colombia and $0.5 million for the tri-border area of Argentina, Brazil, and Paraguay. The FY2006 ATA request for Latin America is $9.7 million, again with $3.9 for Colombia and $0.5 million the tri-border area.

The United States also works closely with the governments of the tri-border region — Argentina, Brazil, and Paraguay — through the "3 + 1 regional cooperation mechanism," which serves as a forum for counterterrorism cooperation and prevention among all four countries.

Money laundering in the region has been a major U.S. concern for some 20 years, largely because of its association with drug traffickers, but terrorist organizations may also be involved in money laundering as a means of hiding their financial assets. The United States works through the Financial Action Task Force (FATF), a multilateral anti-money laundering body, to help develop and promote policies to combat money laundering worldwide. According to the Department of State's March 2005 *International Narcotics Control Strategy Report,* 14 nations in the region are jurisdictions of primary concern to the United States because of their vulnerability to money laundering. These are Antigua and Barbuda, Bahamas, Belize, Brazil, Cayman Islands, Colombia, Costa Rica, Dominican Republic, Haiti, Mexico, Panama, Paraguay, Uruguay, and Venezuela.

Increased Regional Cooperation Since 9/11

Latin American nations strongly condemned the September 2001 terrorist attacks on New York and Washington and took action through the OAS and the Rio Treaty to strengthen hemispheric cooperation against terrorism. The OAS, which happened to be meeting in Peru at the time, swiftly condemned the attacks, reiterated the need to strengthen hemispheric cooperation to combat terrorism, and expressed full solidarity with the United States. At a special session on September 19, 2001, OAS members invoked the 1947 Inter-American Treaty of Reciprocal Assistance, also known as the Rio Treaty, which obligates signatories to the treaty to come to one another's defense in case of outside attack. Another resolution approved on September 21, 2001, called on Rio Treaty signatories to "use all legally available measures to pursue, capture, extradite, and punish those individuals" involved in the attacks and to "render additional assistance and support to the United States, as appropriate, to address the September 11 attacks, and also to prevent future terrorist acts."

In another resolution, the OAS called on the Inter-American Committee on Terrorism (CICTE) to identify urgent actions aimed at strengthening inter-American cooperation in order to combat and eliminate terrorism in the hemisphere. The CICTE was reinvigorated in the aftermath of 9/11, and has cooperated on border security mechanisms, controls to prevent funding of terrorist organizations, and law enforcement and counterterrorism intelligence and information. At a January 2003 CICTE meeting in El Salvador, OAS members issued the Declaration of San Salvador, which condemned terrorism and pledged to strengthen hemispheric cooperation through a variety of border, customs, and financial control measures. At the conference, the United States pledged $1 million to the OAS to help the growth of CICTE "as a technical body devoted to increasing counterterrorism expertise in the Americas."[2] At the February 2005 CICTE session held in Trinidad and Tobago, OAS members reaffirmed their commitment to deepen cooperation in the fight against terrorism.

In June 2002, OAS members signed a newly completed Inter-American Convention Against Terrorism. Signing the treaty for the United States, Secretary of State Powell said that the OAS had "produced the first new international treaty since September 11 targeted at improving our ability to combat terrorism."[3] The Convention, among other measures, would improve regional cooperation against terrorism, commit parties to sign and ratify U.N. anti-terrorism instruments and take actions against the financing of terrorism, and deny safe haven to suspected terrorists.

On October 27-28, 2003, the OAS held a Special Conference on Security in Mexico City that focused on identifying new threats, concerns, and challenges facing the hemisphere and agreed on a cooperative approach toward addressing them. Among the threats identified in the adopted Declaration on Security in the Americas were "terrorism, transnational organized crime, the global drug problem, corruption, asset laundering, illicit trafficking in weapons and the connections among these activities."[4]

---

[2] U.S. Department of State, International Information Programs, "U.S. Donates $1 Million to Combat Terrorism in Western Hemisphere," *Washington File,* January 22, 2003.

[3] U.S. Department of State, International Information Programs, "Transcript: Powell Stresses Security at OAS General Assembly," *Washington File,* June 3, 2002.

[4] Organization of American States. Declaration on Security in the Americas. October 28, 2003.

Congressional Action

President Bush submitted the Inter-American Convention Against Terrorism to the Senate on November 12, 2002, for its advice and consent, and the treaty was referred to the Senate Foreign Relations Committee (Treaty Doc. 107-18). The committee held a public hearing on the treaty on June 17, 2004. In the 109th Congress, the committee formally reported the treaty on July 28, 2005 (Senate Exec. Rept. 109-3), and on October 7, 2005, the Senate agreed to the resolution of advice and consent.

The 1 08th Congress called for two reports from the Administration regarding terrorist activities in Latin America. The FY2005 Ronald W. Reagan National Defense Authorization Act (P.L. 108-375) required a report on the activities of Al Qaeda and associated groups in Latin America and the Caribbean (Section 1047) and a report regarding any relationships between foreign governments or organizations and terrorist groups in Colombia (Section 1021). The 1 08th Congress also expressed concern regarding the investigation into the July 1994 AMIA bombing in Buenos Aires. Both houses approved similar resolutions — H.Con.Res. 469 (Ros-Lehtinen) and S.Con.Res. 126 (Coleman) — that, among other provisions, urged Argentina to provide resources to investigate all areas of the AMIA case, encouraged U.S. law enforcement support, and encouraged the establishment of an OAS task force to assist in the investigation.

In: Latin American Issues and Challenges
Editors: L. Naciamento and G. Sousa

ISBN 978-1-60692-349-8

Short Commentary

LINGUISTIC AND CULTURAL CHALLENGES IN THE BILINGUAL COMMUNITY: EMPIRICAL AND APPLIED PERSPECTIVES

Jeanette Altarriba *

Department of Psychology, University at Albany, State University of New York, Albany, New York, USA

Marilyn Dabady Lynk

Center on Health Disparities at Adventist HealthCare, Rockville, MD, USA

The United States population is increasing rapidly with high rates of growth among immigrants from Latin America and other Hispanic regions. Latinos are the fastest growing ethnic minority in the U.S. (U.S. Census Bureau, 2004) and Spanish is the most common language spoken by non-English speakers (U.S. Census Bureau, 2006). According to projections provided by the Pew Hispanic Center, close to 30 percent of the U.S. population will be of Hispanic descent—both foreign and U.S. born—by mid-century (Pew Hispanic Center, 2008). Linguistic skills among Latin Americans will vary in one or both languages by immigrant status, level of acculturation in the U.S., age and generational status, and educational attainment as well (National Research Council, 2006). On the one hand, some of these individuals will have limited English proficiency or none at all (e.g., foreign-born adults). Limited English proficiency and linguistic isolation, particularly of Asian and Latin American communities are major concerns in many social and economic domains including employment, education, and health care which is our current focus. These concerns are warranted because these populations are two of the largest minority groups (with Latinos growing rapidly) in many U.S. cities including New York City, Chicago, Houston, San Antonio, Phoenix, San Diego, and Los Angeles. On the other hand, some Latin Americans will demonstrate some degree of linguistic proficiency in more than one language (e.g.,

* Send Correspondence to: Jeanette Altarriba, Ph.D. Department of Psychology, Social Science 369, University at Albany, State University of New York, 1400 Washington Avenue, Albany, New York 12222. Tel: (518) 442-5004; Fax: (518) 442-4867; Ja087@albany.edu (third character is a zero).

foreign-born youths and second or third generation Latin Americans). Thus, the number of individuals who will consider themselves bilingual, in varying ways, could change over a relatively short period of time within the U.S. This rapid demographic change calls for a concerted effort to better understand shifts in language acquisition and skills, the development of language abilities in bilingual speakers, the ways in which bilinguals store and use their linguistic knowledge, and generally how language influences the degree to which individuals integrate themselves into the larger community.

Cognitively speaking, bilingual speakers possess two sets of lexical entries, some of which are associated across languages and others that are unique within a language (see e.g., Altarriba & Mathis, 1997). From a developmental perspective, it is thought that an emerging bilingual speaker often translates their word knowledge in a new or second language into their first or better known language in order to understand information at a semantic or conceptual level (Kroll & Stewart, 1994). Over time, the object of becoming truly proficient calls for the ability to directly access the meaning of words in one's second language without having to rely on translating through the first. In fact, various research studies have supported the notion that the second language in a bilingual develops as a function of this kind of mediation via the first until, ultimately, an individual can think and react as a proficient speaker of their new language.

While this kind of development seems rather straightforward in bilinguals, and has been supported via data using word priming techniques and other cognitive tasks (see e.g., Altarriba & Basnight-Brown, 2007), the process best describes the learning of concrete words and words with one-to-one translations (e.g., chair-silla (Spanish); table-mesa (Spanish)). Newer research suggests that words that are emotional in nature (e.g., love; fear; coffin; prisoner) may be represented differently in memory, as opposed to concrete words or even abstract words (e.g., liberty; fact). That is, a newer field of bilingual research has emerged wherein wordtype effects are being investigated (e.g., Altarriba & Canary, 2004; Sutton, Altarriba, Basnight-Brown, & Gianico, 2007), and results are indicating that to learn a new language does not imply that different kinds of words are all learned at the same rate and in the same way. Emotion words may be coded differently when compared to other types of words both within languages and between languages. For example, Altarriba and Bauer (2004) found that monolingual English-speaking participants recalled a greater number of emotion words when compared to concrete and abstract words that were controlled in various ways. Emotion words are salient, they capture attention, seem to be remembered better, and influence various cognitive abilities.

Additionally, in emotional contexts, it has been shown that bilinguals may code their emotional, autobiographical memories more deeply and richly in their native language when compared to their second language (see e.g., Altarriba, 2003; Rubin, Schrauf, Gulgoz, & Naka, 2007) underscoring the importance of a clear understanding of code-switching and language-mixing practices. It has been reported that emotion words in a bilingual's first or native language more easily bring to mind a specific context, from memory, than words that are non-emotional. It appears, then, that memories are often "tagged" in the language in which they occurred (Altarriba & Soltano, 1996), but more importantly, emotional memories are very closely tied to the language in which they were originally created and stored. Knowing how these words appear in memory can inform a whole host of situations involving bilingual speakers, from how languages can be used strategically in medical and health settings, to knowing how to better retrieve memories from bilingual eyewitnesses, to providing for a strategy to more effectively elicit emotion when counseling or otherwise interviewing a bilingual speaker. In recent research, for example, Santiago-Rivera, Altarriba, Pol, Gonzalez-Miller, and Cragun (2009) reported that within a mental health context, therapists and their clients would switch languages in the context of therapy in very strategic and useful ways. For example, when patients are asked to discuss a previous event, perhaps one that was salient in terms of their emotional well-being, it was reported that non-emotional contexts could be easily discussed in the first language, while highly emotional events were sometimes discussed only in the second language, in order to provide distance from the event. Thus, the switching from the native to the second language served a distancing function, particularly when the event being described was negative or threatening. In other situations, the patient or client used the second language to discuss an event when they did not know the corresponding first-language term or when the event was more neutral, in terms of its emotional content.

Furthermore, word storage and word retrieval can also be a function of dialect and cultural background and not merely a function of the languages themselves. Culture and cultural norms and beliefs often dictate the actions and behaviors of a particular ethnic group, and often, can dictate the ways in which languages are used (Altarriba, Basnight, & Canary, 2003). Culture, a shared set of beliefs, goals, and ideals, can often provide the guidelines, explicit or implicit, for how individuals are to view themselves and others in the world. The notion of culture also implies shared ideas, communication styles, and attitudes. It sets up a worldview or framework within which to operate with those inside of the group, as well as how to deal with those outside of the group. Language and culture are intertwined, and in the bilingual community, various cultural mores and standards are often transmitted through the use of language. For instance, both verbal and nonverbal communication of respect and interest in making a personal connection are helpful during medical encounters with Latino patients and their families (Matthews-Juarez & Weinberg, 2006). Such cultural knowledge and skills among health providers can help facilitate the expression of health beliefs, practices, and concerns of Latin American patients and the delivery of patient-centered care.

The bilingual, Hispanic community that has evolved over time within the U.S. is quite diverse in many senses of the word. Within this community, individuals may hail from numerous Latin American, Caribbean, South or Central American countries, as well as from other Spanish-speaking countries abroad (e.g., Spain). Though individuals consider that they are homogenous with regards to language, the opposite is in fact true—vocabulary and language usage varies greatly across these different cultural and dialectical groups. Thus, one issue that faces bilingual communities today is the idea that all of these varied linguistic and cultural features must be finessed and considered within the context of the development of forms of communication and the dissemination of various social, psychological, and health services, across bilingual communities. For example, the same kinds of communication that may work in one Spanish-speaking neighborhood may not work in another, predominantly Spanish-speaking neighborhood (see e.g., Royer & Carlo, 1993).

One of the challenges in working with members of a bilingual, multilingual, and multicultural community is achieving effective cross-cultural communication in health care settings. Cultural and health beliefs may affect how Latin Americans or Latinos/Hispanics[1] interact with the U.S. health care system and utilize health care services. Latin American individuals—whether bilingual or limited English proficient—have their own cultural beliefs about health, illness, and medicine (Matthews-Juarez & Weinberg, 2006). These beliefs may influence responses to illness, health care decision-making, use of nontraditional treatments, and sources of support. For example, some Latin American immigrants or limited English proficient individuals may avoid Western medicine and the U.S. health care system completely, turning instead to alternative medicines and treatment or *curandéros* (traditional healers) in their communities for their health care needs.

Another challenge in health care is the notion that biases (both conscious and unconscious) persist among health care providers and those providing a variety of services that can influence the ways in which a population's needs are addressed. In fact, evidence suggests that providers' unconscious biases may contribute to racial/ethnic disparities in the use of medical procedures such as thrombolysis for myocardial infarction (Green et al., 2007). Biases and perceptions about socioeconomic status, educational attainment, immigration status, language proficiency, and health literacy of Latin Americans and other minority populations may affect provider attitudes, behavior, and quality of care to patients. For example, there is ample literature to suggest that within some contexts, African-American patients were attributed a greater degree of pathology than their White counterparts (see e.g., Neighbors, Jackson, Campbell, & Williams, 1989). African-Americans with depressive symptomatology tended to be misdiagnosed with schizophrenias. In another study, White therapists rated Chinese clients as more depressed, more inhibited, less socially poised, and having lower capacity for interpersonal relationships than did Chinese therapists (Li-Repac, 1980). In that same study, Chinese therapists rated White clients as more severely disturbed than did White therapists. Sue and Zane (1987) indicated that the ethnicity and language skills of the health services provider may be a less relevant focus than a provider's ability to establish credibility or to respond according to cultural expectations. Thus, an emphasis has recently been placed on the development of culturally sensitive approaches to working with diverse populations.

The U.S. Department of Health and Human Services Office of Minority Health has issued standards to health care organizations on culturally and linguistically appropriate services. Health care organizations (federally funded) are required to provide language services to limited English proficient patients including access to bilingual staff and trained interpreters (U.S. Department of Health and Human Services, 2001). These standards are guidelines that health providers can use as well to make their practices more culturally sensitive and linguistically accessible. The American Psychological Association also has endorsed a series of measures and procedures to raise awareness among training facilities and institutions of their own cultural biases and ways in which to avoid transmitting those biases to the workplace and particularly to settings in which people are receiving care and services. Once a client or patient perceives a level of cultural understanding and awareness from a service provider, various positive outcomes typically occur—perceived credibility of the provider, the development of a stronger alliance between the service provider and the client,

[1] In the U.S. health care literature, the terms "Latino" and "Hispanic" are commonly used to describe people from Spanish-speaking countries. Therefore, when discussing challenges in health care, we use the terms "Latino", "Latin American", and "Hispanic" interchangeably.

the promotion of trust, greater utilization of services, adherence to recommended treatment, the development of a bond or the creation of a greater sense of commonality, familiarity, and trust.

At an applied level, proficiency in both English and Spanish likely means greater ability to bridge cultural and linguistic gaps in order to better navigate the U.S. health care system. Many Latin American immigrants, however, have limited or no English proficiency upon entering the U.S. and often face challenges in accessing and obtaining quality health care services. As a result, they disproportionately have poorer health status and outcomes due to socioeconomic and immigrant status, miscommunication in patient-provider interactions, and health disparities in access to care (Institute of Medicine, 2003). For example, Hispanics are less likely to have a primary care provider, more likely to be uninsured, and more likely to face language barriers (National Research Council, 2006; U.S. Department of Health and Human Services, 2007). Hispanics in general also are more likely to suffer from heart disease, cancer, accidents, stroke, and diabetes (Centers for Disease Control and Prevention, 2008). However, the prevalence of disease and incidence rates varies across Hispanic subgroups. For instance, while Hispanics in general have lower infant mortality rates as compared with non-Hispanic whites, the rate is higher for Puerto Ricans who are also more likely to suffer from asthma, chronic obstructive pulmonary disease, HIV/AIDS, obesity, suicide, and liver disease (Centers for Disease Control and Prevention, 2008; U.S. Department of Health and Human Services, 2007).

Shifts in cultural and linguistic diversity are challenging for health care organizations and providers of care who seek to understand and meet the needs of bilingual speakers within their communities. Yet these demographic trends also drive the need for better cultural competence among physicians, nurses, and other health care professionals as well as improved access to language services and quality care (e.g., trained interpreters, bilingual physicians, etc.). Cultural competence is having the knowledge, skills, and ability to provide care that acknowledges and respects the cultural and health beliefs and practices of diverse patients. To become culturally competent, health care providers and organizations first need to be aware of the diversity within the Latin American community. Data detailing the race, ethnicity, language preference, and country of origin for residents in local communities should be collected by health care organizations. Factors such as nationality, generational status, level of acculturation, and language profiles can have major implications on health care service delivery. Therefore, having complete and accurate patient demographic data is essential to improve the quality of health care and services to the Latin American population. Second, it is necessary that organizations offer and that providers know how to access language services for members of the community such as translated materials, trained interpreters and bilingual staff. Limited English proficient patients face significant barriers—linguistic isolation, lack of access, uninsured rates, immigrant status, mistrust of providers, bias and discrimination, and health disparities (Center on Health Disparities, 2007; Institute of Medicine, 2003). Accessible health information, resources, and services as well as culturally competent staff are critical to the provision of culturally and linguistically appropriate health care.

Given that learning a second language is complex and emotion words are coded more saliently and deeply in one's native tongue (see above), it might follow that recalling details of a medical emergency or trauma, say, would be easier in one's native language. Yet another challenge would be conveying those details to a health provider and receiving the appropriate treatment. These challenges can have implications for those with limited mastery of English who have difficulty accessing and understanding health information or describing their symptoms to a health provider. Words that look or sound similar between languages can be confusing and be misinterpreted in health settings. A doctor who writes a prescription instructing her patient to take pills "once" a day risks that the note might be erroneously translated to *once,* or eleven, in Spanish. In one example, non-Spanish speaking paramedics misinterpreted a young man's symptoms because his companion used the term *intoxicado* to describe his explanation of feeling nauseated. Medical terminology is often very technical; both doctors and patients may not fully recognize challenges with health literacy or communicate lack of understanding during medical encounters. Thus, poor communication and interpretation can have potentially dangerous consequences.

Language barriers and poor health literacy in particular can lead to adverse health consequences such as miscomprehension, misdiagnosis, poor medical care, and inappropriate medical treatment (e.g., prescribing the wrong medication). Ensuring access to language services such as bilingual physicians or trained interpreters can lower these risks and help reduce medical errors, avoid unnecessary and costly treatments, and improve patient safety. Furthermore, improving health literacy among Latin American immigrants can improve patient-provider communication during medical encounters. In a recent study, a researcher conducted focus group interviews with low-literacy immigrants from various countries including Central and South America and found that they had difficulty describing their symptoms during medical visits and understanding how to take prescribed medications (Kimbrough, 2007). They cited the importance of face-to-face communication, trained interpreters, written health materials and instructions, and provider understanding of cultural notions of respect and trust to improve communication between patients and providers. Such approaches to ensure understanding can help improve health literacy among patients and, ultimately, eliminate barriers to access and health disparities.

Cultural awareness and competence, knowledge of demographics and health disparities, and effective cross-cultural communication are critically important for the provision of quality health care and services. Above all, patient-provider communication can significantly affect patient outcomes such as satisfaction, adherence to treatment, access to care, and utilization of services (Institute of Medicine, 2003). Cross-cultural communication may be enhanced when the health care provider and the patient speak the same language because it can reduce the risk of miscomprehension and limits the use of an interpreter (Agency for Healthcare Research and Quality, 2006; Wilson et al., 2005), although one must be cautious of cultural and linguistic variations among Latin Americans, as well. Nevertheless, bilingual physicians, trained interpreters, and culturally competent health care providers and organizations are key players in eliminating health disparities among Latin American patients and delivering culturally and linguistically appropriate quality care to patients and their families.

REFERENCES

Agency for Healthcare Research and Quality. (2006). *National healthcare disparities report.* U.S. Department of Health and Human Services. (AHRQ Publication No. 07-0012). Rockville, MD: AHRQ Publications Clearinghouse.

Altarriba, J. (2003). Does *cariño* equal "liking"? A theoretical approach to conceptual nonequivalence between languages. *International Journal of Bilingualism, 7,* 305-322.

Altarriba, J., & Basnight-Brown, D. M. (2007). Methodological considerations in performing semantic and translation priming experiments across languages. *Behavior Research Methods, 39,* 1-18.

Altarriba, J., & Bauer, L. M. (2004). The distinctiveness of emotion concepts: A comparison between emotion, abstract, and concrete words. *American Journal of Psychology, 117,* 389-410.

Altarriba, J., & Canary, T. M. (2004). Affective priming: The automatic activation of arousal. *Journal of Multilingual and Multicultural Development, 25,* 248-265.

Altarriba, J., & Mathis, K. M. (1997). Conceptual and lexical development in second language acquisition. *Journal of Memory and Language, 36,* 550-568.

Altarriba, J., Basnight, D. M., & Canary, T. M. (2003). Emotion representation and perception across cultures. In W. J. Lonner, D. L. Dinnel, S. A. Hayes, & D. N. Sattler (Eds.), *Online readings in psychology and culture.* Bellingham, WA: Western Washington University, Department of Psychology. Center for Cross-Cultural Research Web site: http://www.ac.wwu.edu/~culture/readings.htm

Altarriba, J., & Soltano, E. G. (1996). Repetition blindness and bilingual memory: Token individuation for translation equivalents. *Memory & Cognition, 24,* 700-711.

Center on Health Disparities (2007). *Partnering toward a healthier future: Eliminating health disparities in Frederick, Montgomery, and Prince George's Counties in Maryland.* 2007 Progress Report. Available at: http://www.adventisthealthcare.com/AHC/health-disparities/research/2007-progress-report.aspx. Accessed February 18, 2009.

Centers for Disease Control and Prevention (2008). *Health of the Hispanic/Latino population (various years).* Available at http://www.cdc.gov/nchs/fastats/hispanic_health.htm. Accessed February 18, 2009.

Green, A. R., et al. (2007). Implicit bias among physicians and its prediction of thrombolysis decisions for black and white patients. *Journal of General Internal Medicine, 22(9),* 1231-1238.

Institute of Medicine (2003). Unequal treatment: Confronting racial and ethnic disparities in healthcare. B.D. Smedley, A.Y. Stith, & A. R. Nelson (Eds.), *Committee on understanding and eliminating racial and ethnic disparities in health care.* Washington, DC: The National Academies Press.

Kimbrough, J. B. (2007). Health literacy as a contributor to immigrant health disparities. *Journal of Health Disparities Research and Practice, 1(2),* 93-106.

Kroll, J. F., & Stewart, E. (1994). Category interference in translation and picture naming: Evidence for asymmetric connections between bilingual memory representations. *Journal of Memory and Language, 33,* 149-174.

Li-Repac, D. (1980). Cultural influences on clinical perception: A comparison between Caucasian and Chinese-American therapists. *Journal of Cross-Cultural Psychology, 11,* 327-342.

Matthews-Juarez, P., & A. D. Weinberg (2006). *Cultural competence in cancer care: A health care professional's passport.* Intercultural Cancer Center. Baylor College of Medicine.

National Research Council (2006). Multiple origins, uncertain destinies: Hispanics and the American future. Panel on Hispanics in the United States. M. Tienda and F. Mitchell

(Eds.), *Committee on Population, Division of Behavioral and Social Sciences and Education.* Washington, DC: The National Academies Press.

Neighbors, H. W., Jackson, J. S., Campbell, L., & Williams, D. (1989). The influence of racial factors on psychiatric diagnosis: A review and suggestions for research. *Community Mental Health Journal, 25,* 301-311.

Pew Hispanic Center (2008). *U.S. population projections: 2005–2050.* Available at http://pewhispanic.org/reports/report.php?ReportID=85. Accessed February 18, 2009.

Royer, J. M., & Carlo, M. S. (1993). Assessing language comprehension skills in cross-cultural settings. In J. Altarriba (Ed.), *Cognition and culture: A cross-cultural approach to cognitive psychology* (pp. 157-175). Amsterdam: Elsevier Science Publishers.

Rubin, D. C., Schrauf, R. W., Gulgoz, S., & Naka, M. (2007). Cross-cultural variability of component processes in autobiographical remembering: Japan, Turkey, and the USA. *Memory, 15,* 536-547.

Santiago-Rivera, A., Altarriba, J., Poll, N., Gonzalez, N., & Cragun, C. (in press, 2009). Therapists' views on working with bilingual Spanish-English speaking clients: A qualitative investigation. *Professional Psychology: Research and Practice.*

Sue, S., & Zane, N. (1987). The role of culture and cultural techniques in psychotherapy: A critique and reformulation. *American Psychologist, 42,* 37-45.

Sutton, T. M., Altarriba, J., Gianico, J. L., & Basnight Brown, D. M. (2007). The automatic access of emotion: Emotional Stroop effects in Spanish-English bilingual speakers. *Cognition and Emotion, 21,* 1077-1090.

U.S. Census Bureau (2004). *U.S. interim projections by age, sex, race, and Hispanic origin: 2000-2050.* Available at http://www.census.gov/ipc/www/usinterimproj/. Accessed February 18, 2009.

U.S. Census Bureau (2006). Population and housing narrative profile: 2006. *2006 American community survey.* Available at http://factfinder.census.gov/servlet/NPTable?_bm=y&-geo_id=01000US&-qr_name=ACS_2006_EST_G00_NP01&-ds_name=&-redoLog=false. Accessed February 18, 2009.

U.S. Department of Health and Human Services (2001). *National standards on culturally and linguistically appropriate services.* Available at http://www.omhrc.gov/templates/browse.aspx?lvl=2&lvlid=15. Accessed February 18, 2009.

U.S. Department of Health and Human Services (2007). *Hispanic/Latino profile.* Available at http://www.omhrc.gov/templates/browse.aspx?lvl=2&lvlID=54. Accessed February 18, 2009.

Wilson, E., et al. (2005). Effects of limited English proficiency and physician language on health care comprehension. *Journal of General Internal Medicine, 20(9),* 800–806.

INDEX

C

D

E

F

G

H

I

J

K

N

O

P

Q

R

S

Y

Z